A PERFECT DAY *for a* WALK *by the* WATER

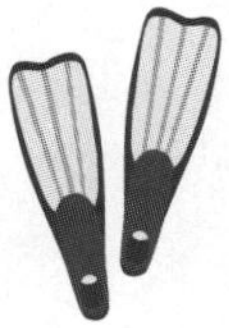

A PERFECT DAY *for a* WALK *by the* WATER

Exploring Vancouver's Shores

BILL ARNOTT

ARSENAL PULP PRESS
VANCOUVER

ARSENAL PULP PRESS
Suite 202 – 211 East Georgia St.
Vancouver, BC V6A 1Z6
Canada
arsenalpulp.com

The publisher gratefully acknowledges the support of the Canada Council for the Arts and the British Columbia Arts Council for its publishing program and the Government of Canada and the Government of British Columbia (through the Book Publishing Tax Credit Program) for its publishing activities.

BRITISH COLUMBIA | BRITISH COLUMBIA ARTS COUNCIL An agency of the Province of British Columbia | Canada Council for the Arts Conseil des arts du Canada | Canada

Arsenal Pulp Press acknowledges the xʷməθkʷəy̓əm (Musqueam), Sḵwx̱wú7mesh (Squamish), and səlilwətaɬ (Tsleil-Waututh) Nations, custodians of the traditional, ancestral, and unceded territories where our office is located. We pay respect to their histories, traditions, and continuous living cultures and commit to accountability, respectful relations, and friendship.

Arsenal Pulp Press is committed to reducing the consumption of non-renewable resources in the making of our books wherever possible. We make every effort to use materials that support a sustainable future. This book is printed on paper made with 100 percent sustainable recycled fibre content.

Cover and text design by Jazmin Welch
Edited by Catharine Chen
Proofread by JC Cham
Indexed by Catharine Chen

Printed and bound in Canada

Library and Archives Canada Cataloguing in Publication:
Title: A perfect day for a walk by the water : exploring Vancouver's shores / Bill Arnott.
Names: Arnott, Bill, 1967- author
Description: Includes bibliographical references and index.
Identifiers: Canadiana (print) 20250158159 | Canadiana (ebook) 20250158167 |
ISBN 9781834050201 (softcover) | ISBN 9781834050218 (EPUB)
Subjects: LCSH: Coasts—Recreational use—British Columbia—Vancouver—Guidebooks. |
LCSH: Outdoor recreation—British Columbia—Vancouver—Guidebooks. |
LCSH: Walking—British Columbia—Vancouver—Guidebooks. | LCGFT: Guidebooks.
Classification: LCC GV191.46.B7 A76 2025 | DDC 333.7809711/33—dc23

For the explorer in all of us

It was hard to say where the water ended and land began.

—RACHEL CARSON, *UNDER THE SEA-WIND*

CONTENTS

AUTHOR'S NOTE

DISCOVERING, SHAPING, AND SHARING these *Perfect Day* walks has often felt like a dream. Walking to work, a stroll from my home, some days simply licking a finger, holding it up to determine the wind, smelling for rain, and then heading out. My companion: you, reader and friend, even if we haven't yet met. The beauty of ink put on paper, shared thought and experience. Add to this a few maps and photos, some new and some old, and we're able to walk this whole thing together, multimedia in real time.

Each of these walks, those solely on land and these microexcursions borne by the water, feels like an ongoing geocache. The treasure, mind you, is never buried nor hidden, but still easily missed. Overlooked in our busy lives, masked by different priorities. I get it. I often behave the same way. Yet, hopefully, these small journeys, most of which take minimal effort, money, or time, will offer disproportionate rewards. A reminder that Vancouver, with all its shortcomings and grandeur, remains an inherently magical place. Like anywhere, and everywhere, given an open mind and a sense of wonder.

That's my hope, my incentive, with these walks. For each wandering spirit, every lover of nature and modest adventure, whether you're a local or visiting, this is for you. And for me too. As I say, it's all shared. Same as the space where this city now sits, the land of the Musqueam, Squamish, and Tsleil-Waututh Nations, the xʷməθkʷəy̓əm, Sḵwx̱wú7mesh, and səlílwətaɬ.

These walks around Greater Vancouver range in distance from a few city blocks to a couple of half-marathon treks and take place over the better part of three seasons. Previous *Perfect Day* walks have occurred in autumn, winter, and spring, while these water endeavours begin in the summer and continue through fall and winter. I feel they dovetail nicely, capturing the better part of each season and all of a year.

Last time, on foot, we witnessed a couple of snow days, rare in Vancouver but a joy to experience—if you don't need to get somewhere quickly. But for these beach-based walks, the snow kept to the mountains. The city, however, experienced colossal seaside weather, with the wind one day reaching 100 kilometres an hour, dropping trees, killing power, and sinking vessels. Frightening, but not tragic, as the wrecked boats were unoccupied, so far as I know.

While most of these walks hug the shore, I also spend time *on* the water and *in* it as well. Obviously these additional jaunts aren't walking as such but rather an extension of those strolls. Sailing, rowing, paddling, diving, swimming, even riding ferries and the SeaBus have enabled me to go deeper, I believe, with respect to exploring the water, along with taking a virtual plunge into maps and map-making, charts to capture the city and the ocean—all of which I find quite romantic. Like the notion of a life lived at sea. Never quite as beatific as it is in one's mind, that allure of horizons, the thrum of waves on a hull. Then again, on occasion, it is.

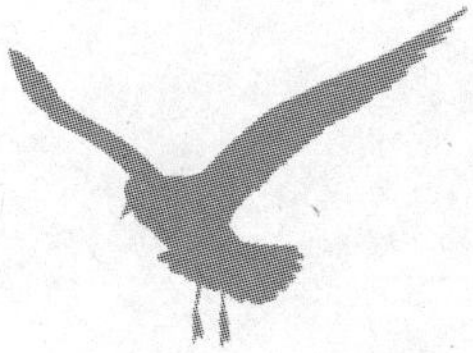

Soft susurration
As sea melds surf with the shore
New journeys begin

VANCOUVER ON THE MAP

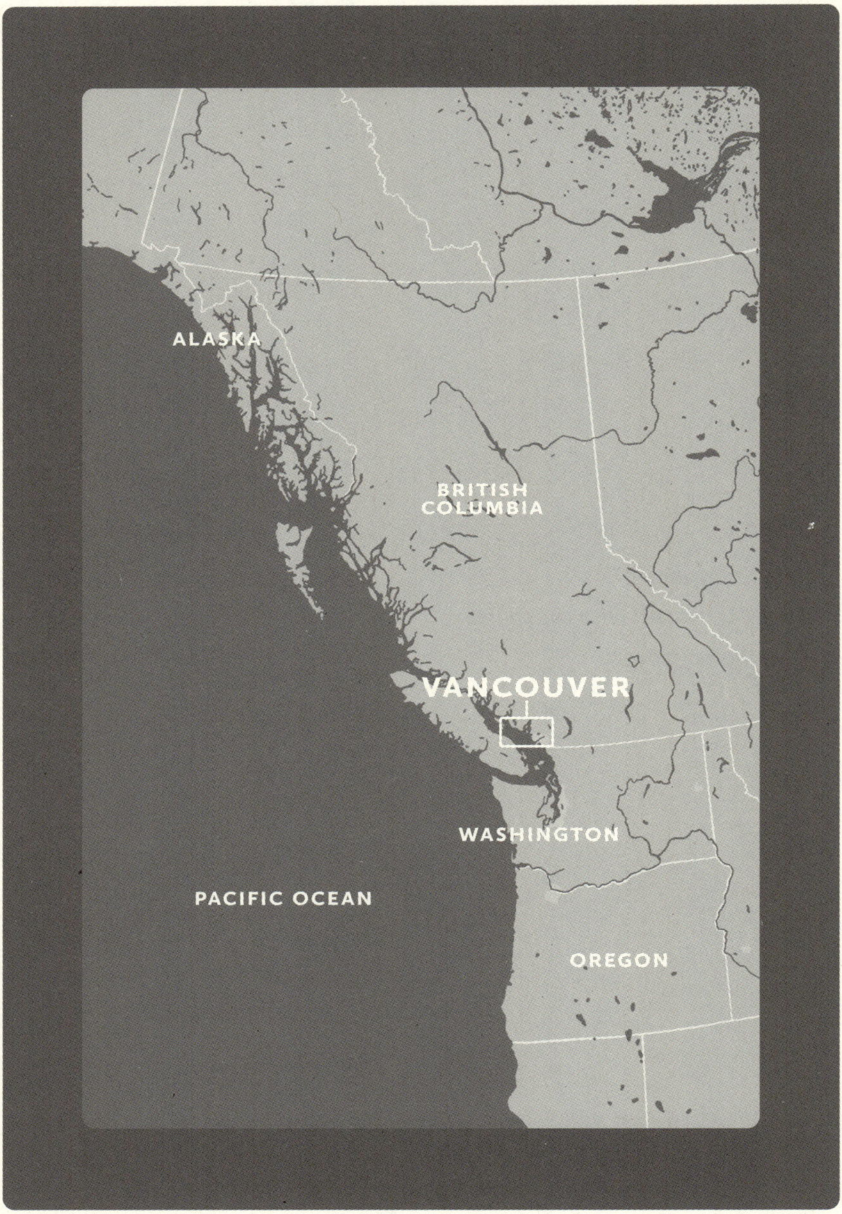

VANCOUVER SHORES AT A GLANCE

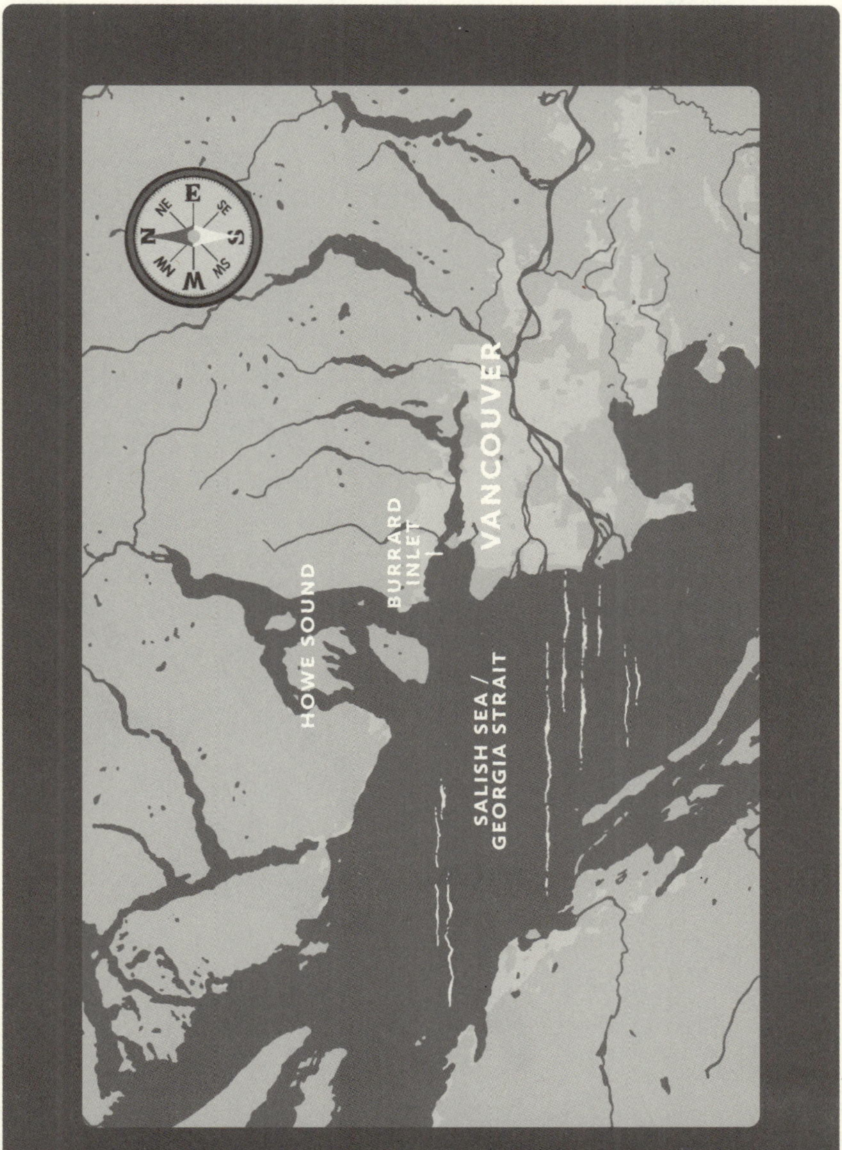

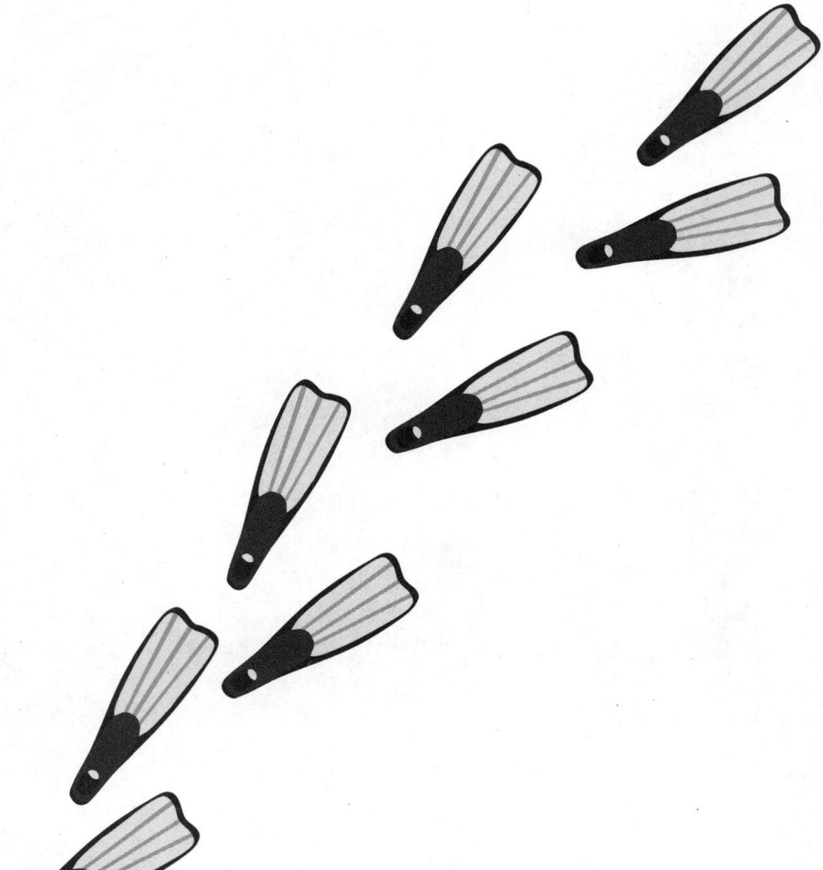

Introduction

LAND'S EDGE

AT THE EDGE of the shoreline, the beach, and the land, I wriggle my toes in the sea. Feel the tug of the tide, a siren song lure. A call, I suspect, to where we began: water, cool and embracing, a connection of saline, a dissolving of time. I think of what may be my favourite book, *Land's Edge* by Tim Winton. The title alone offers a leap into watery blue, a pursuit of horizons.

And yet where I am—a sand beach with pebbles and barnacled rock on the west side of Vancouver—is, in truth, no edge at all. This living shore, accumulating, eroding, is of course nothing more than a gradual descent in the land. One iteration of earth, angled acutely where it mingles with undulating saltwater. Today these two bands, water and earth, are diluted in apt tones, the beach a speckle of amber and grey with the bight of the bay in rough tourmaline lines. Beyond that, a deepening indigo.

I consider the cycle. A drop of sea thrown in spindrift, caught on a breeze, joins a cumulous fluff in chill air before strafing to stratus. Moving in wind from the sea, blowing landward, it reaches the peaks of a long coastal range, becomes heavy, condenses, breaks free and scrims through the cold as it freezes, a snowflake unlike any other. It falls to a crusting of snow, the cusp of glaciation, where it sits for a very long time. Until things start to warm. The crystalline structure collapses, a trickle of fresh water, a gradual stream, now a creek that flows into a river. A sifting of silt melds the water with land on an oceanward trek, the salt pull of the moon, as the water returns in a muddle of algae and sea. That's what I'm looking at now.

Where gulls tack a low sky, a heron high-steps the shallows, and kelp adds a tang to the air. Behind me, past the lip of the tide, a tousle of hemlocks are piercing the sky. It brings a smile as I recall a local business named for that pine, an operation that printed paper-based maps, some of which I helped to create. What fascinated me about that whole process, the artisanal science of map-making, was its illusory nature, a hint of clairvoyance turning notions, perceptions, into something concrete.

The dreaminess I associate with this facet of geography came to mind when I drew up some charts, rudimentary cartography, to accompany another book. I was fiddling with coastline and colour, something to share with designers, when I momentarily lost visual perspective. Looking at what I'd created, it was no longer obvious which side of the map-line was water or land. The addition of familiar tones, however—shades of blue for water, green and khaki for land—gave it commonly used points of reference. *Ah, yes, that must be terra firma, while that's a river, a lake, or the sea.* I thought of this moment when I gazed at a map on a museum wall, a depiction of islands and ocean drawn by a seafaring people for whom *water* was the primary element, channels for exploration and trade. Land, on the other hand, was the extraneous part, where one might replenish or rebuild a vessel before returning to frequented waterways. By shifting not only colour but also perspective, an inversion occurred. What previously appeared as dry land became water, and vice versa. Perception determined reality, or in this case what was a landmass as home base and what was *out there* as the beyond of the sea.

Which brings us to this latest excursion, experienced and gleaned by the water, exploring Vancouver once more, now from that inverse perspective. In *A Perfect Day for a Walk*, I explore the city on foot, walking its neighbourhoods; examining history and cultures, flora and fauna, street art, and nature in the heart of Vancouver while visiting with Indigenous locals, international settlers, and travellers. That experience—a half year of walking—revealed more than I'd imagined. The result: a renewed look at Vancouver for residents and visitors alike.

Now I'm tackling the city once more, a revamped point of view. In the same manner that map-making determines perspective, rather than looking out from within, a land-linked observance, this endeavour is more visually external, viewing Vancouver from its coastline and shores. As I've noted before, this is a place that I love, because and in spite of its makeup, beauty and grit, mountains and sea. The urban core and its suburbs now a pincushion of craning high-rises with a meander of saltwater shore grasping the sprawl like a kraken, possessive and proud, squeezing this bustling metropolis.

In that rambling traverse of Vancouver, what started those neighbourhood strolls was the city motto, "By sea land and air we prosper."[1] Again I consider that tagline. A previous generation trying to sum up a city, economically at least, in a handful of words. The fact that "by sea" starts it off says it all. This is a water-based centre. From a settler perspective, one founded on resource and trade, and that meant our waterways. Still does, to a large degree. From the ports of Burrard Inlet to the Fraser River's splayed mouths, not to mention the roadways and rail line termini that feed these shipping lane hubs.

Much like the motto implies, this is a prosperous centre, a conglomerate of abundance, yet replete with lack too. Like so many cities, thriving, striving, surviving, a mosaic of culture and hope. To reintroduce this locale, Vancouver is one of the country's most diverse cities, with English *not* being the first language of half the population. Most residents are what the Government of Canada labels "visible minorities." At first I found this notion ludicrous, the majority deemed a minority. Then I rethought it. Maybe it simply conveys that no one cultural group is in a majority—a fact that I like, knowing the city is truly varied, what I'd call proper community. Meanwhile, this sprawl of humanity continues to rank as one of the world's most livable cities, as well as one of the most expensive.

When you research the city, plumbing archives or asking around, what you find tends to loop. Descriptors emphasize scenic views, mild climate, unparalleled beauty, with beaches and mountains and living outdoors. An online thread poses the question "Is Vancouver a good or bad city?" One reply states, "Yes it is." Which may be a perfect summation. The next contribution, however, says more: "It's a lovely city, one of the world's most beautiful, provided you can afford to enjoy it." Which I see as the crux of the matter in myriad puzzles and queries concerning Vancouver.

I've lived in this city for four decades. It's my home, here on Musqueam, Squamish, and Tsleil-Waututh land. And while I've resided in a dozen different Vancouver neighbourhoods, I find the city forever feels new. Beyond fresh construction, there remains a perpetual renewal, a reinvention, creating a sense of discovery every time I step out the front door, making me a tourist, an explorer where I live and work. Exploration, however, unveils further questions: What am I seeing? Why is it this way? And what will it be like tomorrow? Things that drive me to further examine this city, wanting to better comprehend its "sea land and air," its water-fringed landscape, its beauty and challenges. And while I *did* have queries answered as I walked through the city, observing, researching, and meeting with experts, I uncovered a great many more. Questions that touch on the water, these shifting and nebulous boundaries of sandy beach, shoreline rock, industrial sites, parkland, and fenced private property lines. So I'm doing it again, examining our city with that map-based inversion, turning it all inside out. Or, depending on which map we use, outside in.

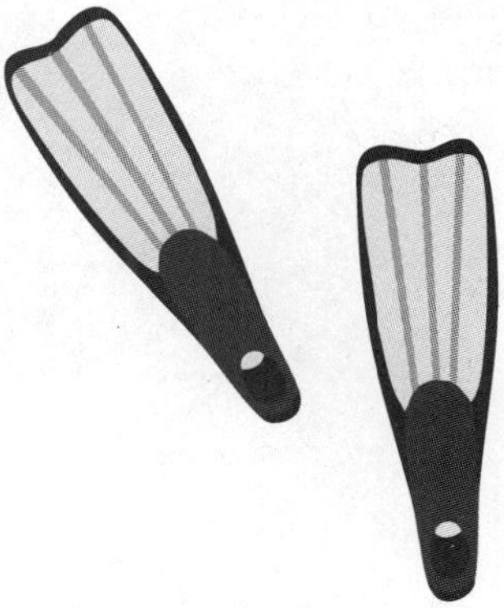

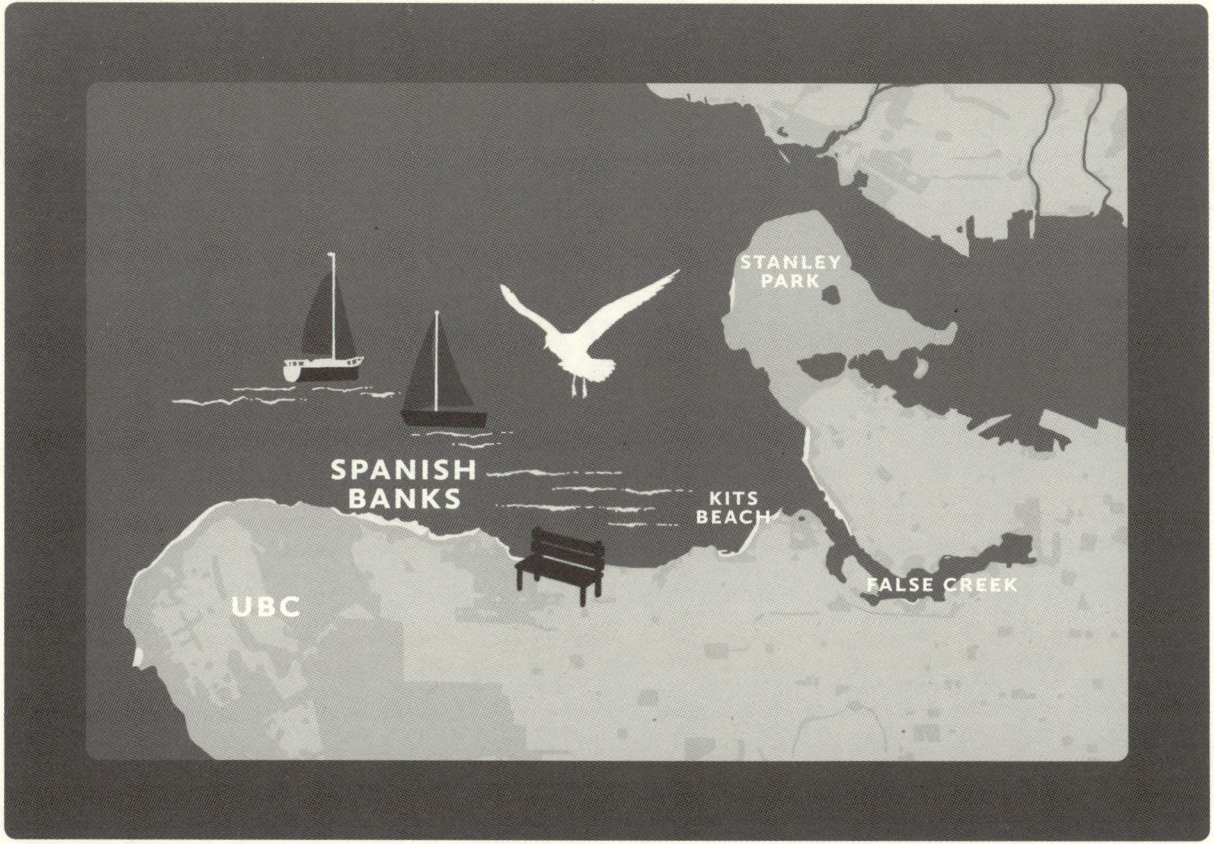
STANLEY PARK
SPANISH BANKS
KITS BEACH
FALSE CREEK
UBC

VANCOUVER'S WEST SIDE

Spanish Banks

MAP-MAKING AND DISCOVERY

I COULD, RATHER tidily, start my search here. For it was right around here, where I stand with my feet in the sea that in 1792 Captain George Vancouver anchored his ships, the union-jacked HMS *Discovery* and HMS *Chatham*, to meet his contemporaries, Dionisio Alcalá Galiano and Cayetano Valdés y Flores Bazán, on their Spanish-flagged ship, the *Mexicana*. The precise locale of that meeting is unclear, but I like to believe it was this spot. Both nation's crews had explored present-day Vancouver Island, their objective being Nootka Sound, a critical centre for trade.

The story goes that the Spaniards welcomed Vancouver aboard the *Mexicana* for supper. No doubt George found the food rather spicy. But as Vancouver planned to chart what is now English Bay, his hosts shared their findings, having already mapped out the harbour. How did he feel at that moment? Disappointed? Frustrated? Relieved? Regardless, the maps were precise, delineating the shoaled shore where a glance along present-day Spanish Banks, Locarno, and Jericho Beaches, beyond Kitsilano to the mouth of False Creek, reveals the area's glaring economic potential. As with Sydney and Falmouth or the Gulf of Saint Lawrence, it's impossible not to envision the waterway teeming with vessels and commerce.

Unsurprisingly, given the terrain, my first stop to begin these walks through the city was the water by the Vancouver Maritime Museum, where the *Ben Franklin* submersible rests on scuffed lawn at the base of Elsje Point. Each time I see the deepwater craft I think of escape, of joining Captain Nemo's *Nautilus* crew to look at these shores through a periscope before retiring to the library, maybe to feast on fresh tuna and turtle. That Jules Verne character has it all figured out: a true life at sea, with carefully charted routes just like the maritime map of those seafaring nations, all determined and derived by the water, land nothing more than distraction. Nemo's knowledge and passion for the sea is infectious, despite his being—what's the correct term?—a nutjob. Clearly Verne was fond of this complex character, as Nemo appears in a few of his works. I've even watched Disney's 1954 movie *20,000 Leagues Under the Sea*, convincing myself it was research. It stars Kirk Douglas as Ned Land and James Mason as Nemo, two actors you can't help but impersonate. But in this version (spoiler alert), Mason's Nemo is shot—for overacting, I presume.

By passing the Maritime Museum heading east at the mouth of False Creek, on the south side, you cross Vanier Park, its peninsularity catching west winds that give the point a harried, dishevelled look. The promontory holds a steel sculpture, the outline of a square with a pried-open base, an installation that resembles another city-bound walker striding next to the water. Constructed in 1980 by Alan Chung Hung, the piece, *Gate to the Northwest Passage*, commemorates that summer Vancouver arrived only to find the place already mapped. I imagine those charcoal-sketched charts on a table inside the *Mexicana*, marked with Spanish place names Vancouver was already planning to change as they sat down to supper.

With a search on my phone, I can see what the City of Vancouver now makes of this westerly shore, or at least how it's described, as one of our most beloved beaches, a place for sunbathing, swimming, skimboarding, and views.

A glance at an atlas of Salish locales indicates this stretch of beach, Spanish Banks, was properly or originally called lỷál̓mexw, "good land," or K̲wek̲w7úpaỷ, "a place of crabapple trees."[2] Looking around at the moment, however, I see no sign of trees bearing apples. Maple and blackberry, yes, but no apple. Leaving us to wonder what it was like when those Spanish and English ships met, whether foraged pome fruit was served with the meal.

From the shore where the tide is now rising, sweeping east in a ripple, I can almost discern what the Coast Salish knew as P'ékwcha or Slhxí7elsh, terms used for "floating," when a whale's back breaks through the surface, an orca perhaps, set to breach or take flight.[3] Looking north across Burrard Inlet, I see the south end of Howe Sound, with Bowen Island a treed mound at the mouth of the fjord. Nestled between Bowen and the westerly tip of West Vancouver is the low lump of Passage Island, what the Salish knew as Smelhmelhél̓ch, meaning "forever enveloped in waves."[4] In other words, a small piece of planet, not quite water nor entirely land but a combination of both. Which may be the perfect descriptor of a transitory Vancouver coastline and what's drawing me forward in the near tidal pull of this new exploration. Only now it occurs to me maybe I *can* find that gap, the blurred space between, and live a short while in the manner of Captain Nemo—*under* this body of water.

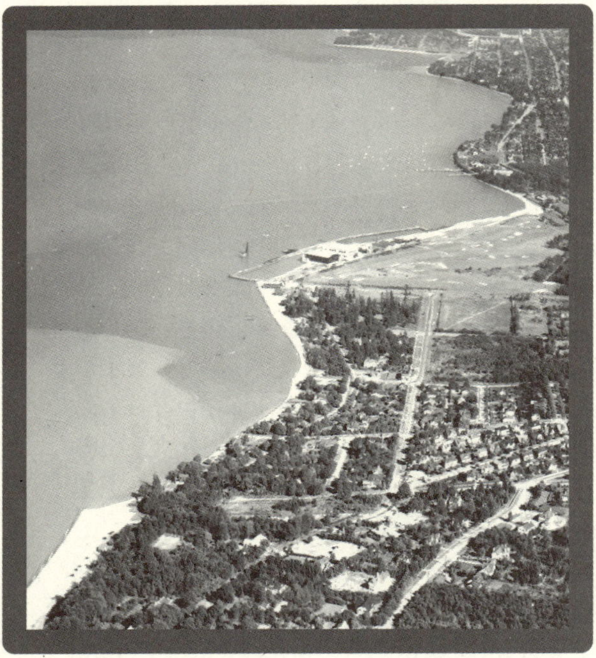

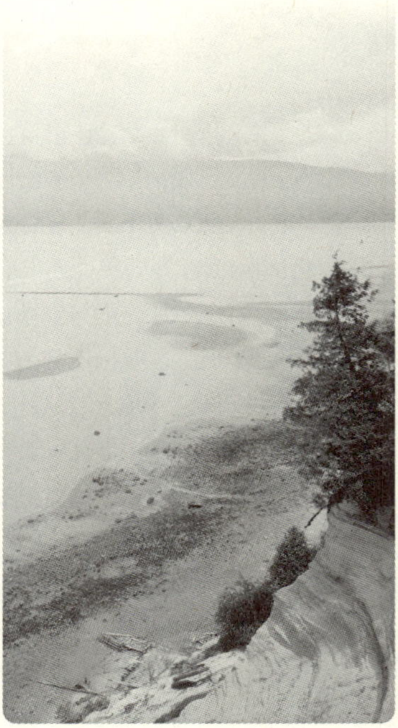

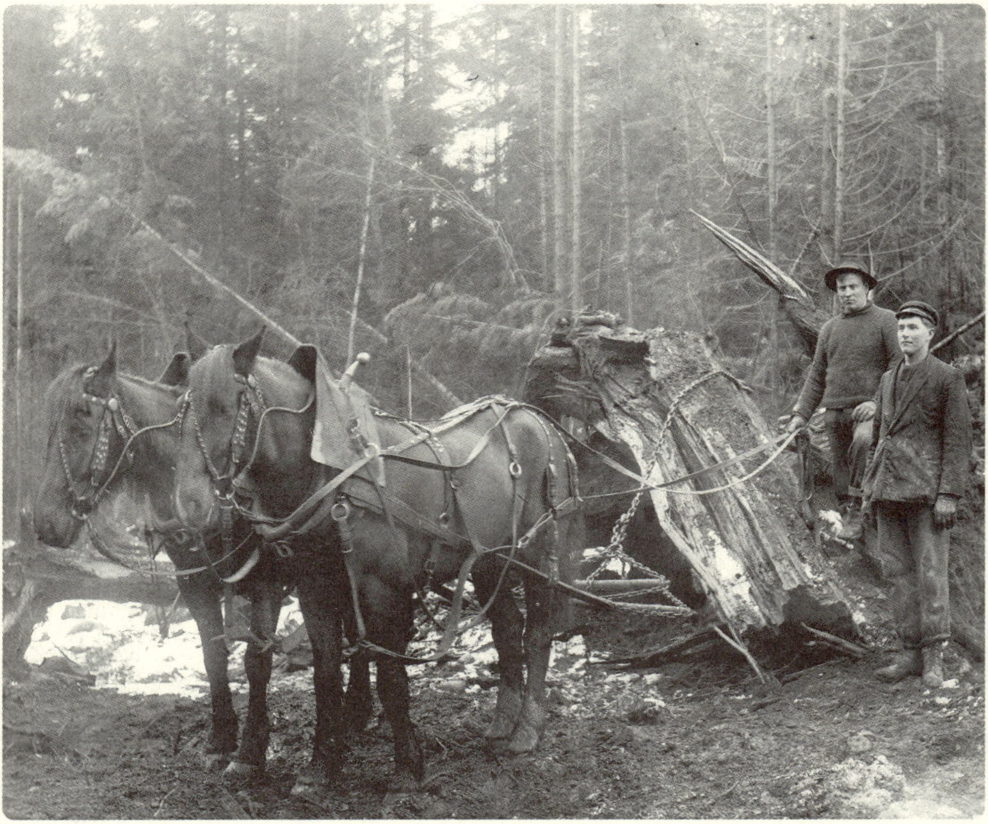

CLOCKWISE FROM TOP LEFT: Spanish Banks, looking east, 1937; Spanish Banks looking north, where Narváez anchored in 1791, circa 1920s; clearing Spanish Banks, 1911.

Point Grey, Locarno, and Jericho

LOOKING NORTH, LOOKING EAST

I HEAD EAST from the Salish "good land" across West Point Grey toward Kitsilano, named for Squamish Chief August Jack Khatsahlano. The City of Vancouver website describes where I am as one of Vancouver's oldest neighbourhoods, best known for Spanish Banks and Jericho Beach, ideal for sunset views of English Bay and beyond. "The local Musqueam people lived here in the ancient village of Ee'yullmough ... Spaniard Jose Narvaez and his crew rediscovered it in 1791 and named it Langara Point."[5]

So it was José Narváez, apparently, who arrived here ahead of his contemporaries. No wonder those Spanish maps were so good. I can imagine Captain George letting out a long sigh, his silver medal turning to bronze.

According to the City of Vancouver, the neighbourhood where I am, West Point Grey, the Salish "good land" that Narváez named Langara Point, has its western edge along Spanish Banks Creek, which flows north to the inlet. Farther west is the expanse of the University of British Columbia (UBC) and the University Endowment Lands, with its forested footpaths and trails. The neighbourhood's eastern border is the north–south line of Alma Street with a kink at the Dunbar Diversion. In the middle is Jericho Beach Park, described by the lighthearted website Vancouver's Best Places as one of the city's most beautiful seaside locations: "The beach at Jericho is always busy in the summer, but especially in mid-July when it hosts Vancouver's popular Folk Music Festival."[6]

Two tidy links connect this locale to my prior explorations on foot. First, there's the area's south-lying boundary of West 16th Avenue, this being the former demarcation of city township and Canadian Pacific Railway (CPR) lands, which I used, more or less, for my walking border as well. It was also where my nana and gramps had their home: West 16th at Arbutus. The joining line, in its way, represents for me another version of Vancouver's land's edge. Second is the reference to the Vancouver Folk Music Festival, which urban planner Lorenz von Fersen helped to create, another part of a rich city narrative, one of music and art, collaboration, and celebration of place. As a cultural strategist, Lorenz provided me with a wealth of socio-historical nuggets to serve as virtual guides. One in particular, about examining a city to reveal its tales from the past, resonates: "It's important to remember, it's not history we share, but stories."

Exactly what I see, what I read, what I hear, as I walk on these beaches. And it was Lorenz, in his city work and volunteer efforts, who helped lay the trails I'd eventually navigate by way of art installations and stories on signs and in granite, effectively steering my *Perfect Day* walks.

Cinching that storyline thread over water, this chunk of shoreline is home to the Jericho Sailing Centre and the Jericho Beach Kayak Centre, the sandy expanse now a jostle of vessels and masts. It was here that I learned how to sail. Prior to this, somewhat foolishly, I joined a sailing adventure, plying the North Atlantic in the wake of famous explorers. That expedition, I'd been told, was appropriate for novices. Which I was, in the extreme. Part of a crew of seven with a crusty old skipper, we managed to sail a nineteenth-century replica pilot cutter from the UK's Carrick Roads to the Isles of Scilly and back, outrunning an increasing gale as it grew to a hurricane. "Survival suits on, secure lifelines!" is the shout I recall, yelled by our captain through a slap of sea spume as our heavy teak mast snapped in two.[7] We set out from Falmouth, same as Captain Vancouver, and the small ship we sailed was a modestly updated version of the craft that accompanied Vancouver's vessels through the same South England shipping lane.

Later, I decided to actually learn all those rope loops and twists I had bungled while plunging through hissing high combers. Even the peaked whitecaps I see on English Bay at the moment—in twelve-knot winds—seem comparatively calm and inviting. So I made my way here to the Sailing Centre and spent a week relearning all that I thought I knew along with their nautical terms. Things that already had perfectly good names, but for reasons unknown, sailors of yore felt a need to confound us landlubbers by renaming *everything*.

In addition to fiddling with knots—bowline, clove hitch, reef, square, and cleat—we learned enough of a lexicon to round out our rudimentary knowledge—tacking, gybing, ease, trim, and luff—before immersing ourselves in the witchcraft of transmuting air into power, something I still find astounding, alchemy akin to those lines sketched on paper realigning the world into maps.

The magic of flying the sea's surface was one thing, dinghies and sloops with a mainsail and jib, but one of the best memories from that time was the raptor I saw, a barred owl, keeping watch from a larch like a wizard's familiar, eyeing me as I trod to the boatshed.

Setting up each craft also required its own learning. Balancing a six-metre mast like a wobbly caber, hauling and installing a tiller and centreboard, not to mention the sheets and the lines. But the most striking visual was when I sailed across the heart of English Bay to a tanker sitting at anchor. From the water's surface, the 100,000-ton goliath in red and black felt like the largest thing I'd ever seen, an unending loom of neck-craning steel spitting water from bilges, corrosion speckling its hull. As I navigated the beast, circling it like an island, I felt I'd been cast in *The Truman Show*, where the character realizes his entire life has been contained in a bubble simulating the world. When he tries to escape, in a craft like the one I was sailing, he realizes that his world abuts a continuous, impenetrable wall. No plummet from the lip of the planet, no "here be dragons." Just a soft barrier he strikes with a *boing*! Forcing him to turn back, set sails anew, and re-evaluate his place in the cosmos.

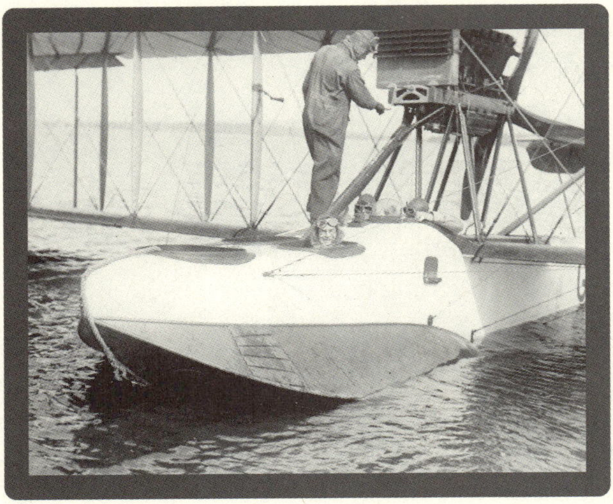

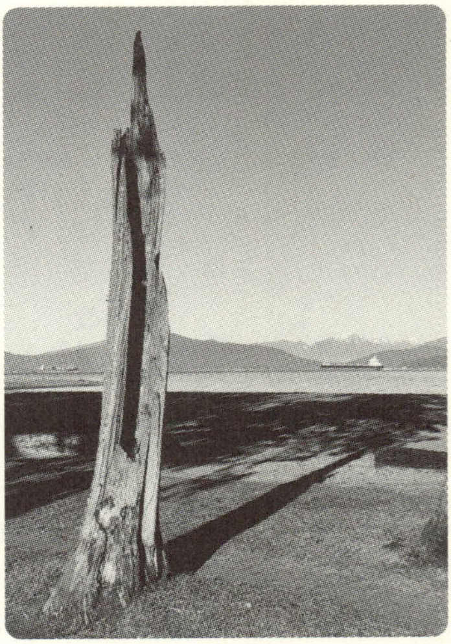

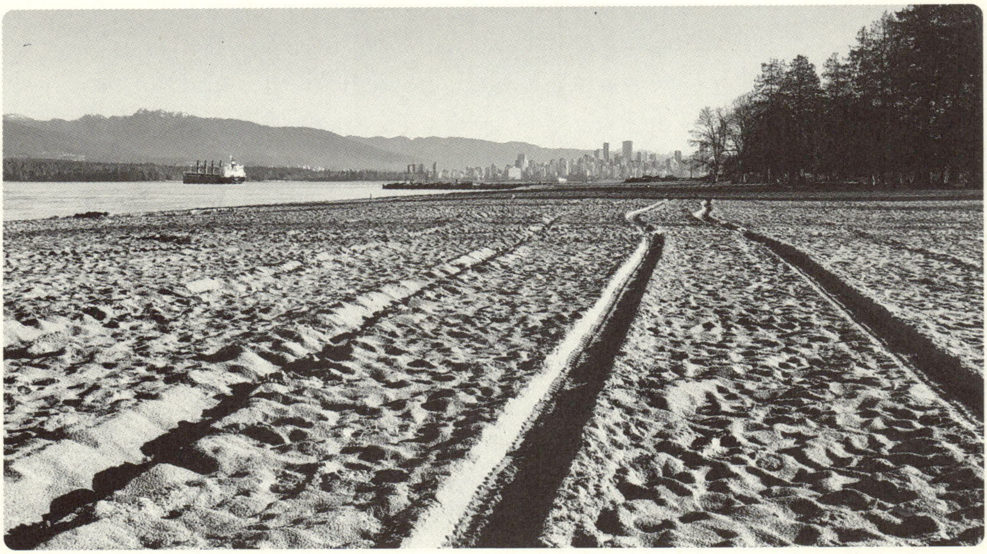

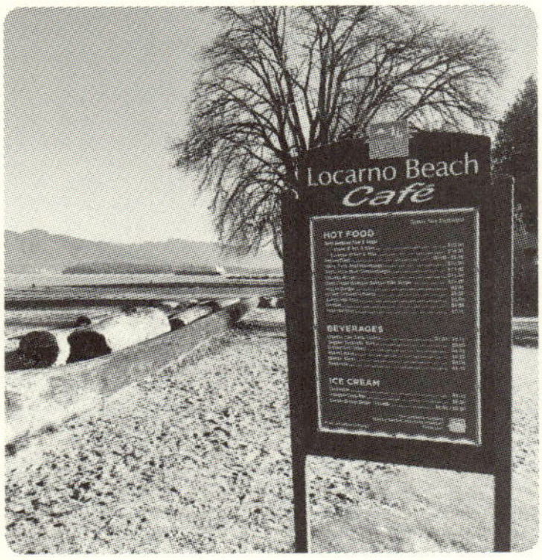

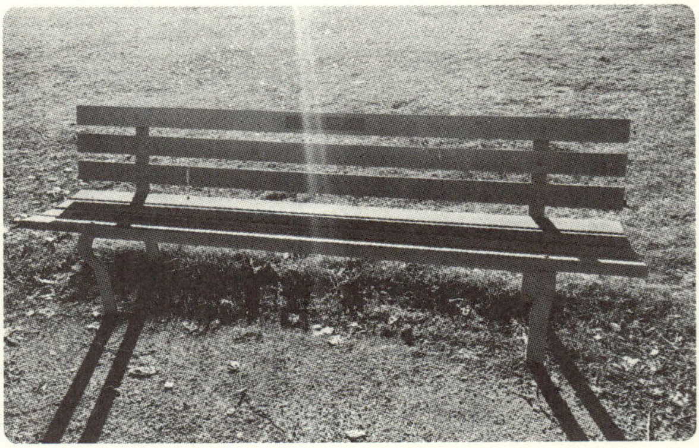

CLOCKWISE FROM TOP LEFT: a seaplane at Jericho Beach, 1926; Jericho Beach, looking west, with tankers beyond; Jericho Beach, looking east; a commemorative bench at Jericho Beach; food options at Locarno Beach.

Around UBC

SHAPING THE SHORE

ANOTHER BRIDGE BETWEEN the beach and the sea appears here in the form of commemorative benches, a serpentine of wood beams with steel noting those who've passed on. Planks now silvered with weather, plaques patinaed, all with a dusting of spindrift. Much like a natural cemetery, where loved ones are left to the land. No coffins or flowers or headstones, just a place of burial and remembrance, with a sea view as well. Taking a few silent minutes, I note a few plaques and their words.

> Brothers, sailors, adventurers. This beach shaped our lives.
>
> Look around. Feel the wind, smell the air. Listen to birds and watch the sky.
>
> In loving memory of our mom. Happiest in the sun, near the sand and the sea.

Each bereaved family adding moments to a map of the shore, as though shared in a sonnet, its meter the tempo of waves. Now, approaching high tide, this littoral space is erasing its trails, the footsteps or tracks a hunter might think of as "foil." I can make out residual indents of soles and feet as they deviate from marked trails, the preferred shortcuts or desire lines we follow. Not always what's bordered or paved, but the improvised paths that we *choose*. In the footfalls, perhaps, of those who first walked the land.

Bringing to mind the songlines of Aboriginal Australians, when a route walked not only writes its own narrative but shapes the very land into being. The pulse of the tide on the shore where I am adds that cadence of storytelling and rhyme, of tracks mapped in real time. Looking back, I still see the scratch of my footsteps, Morse dashes and dots, their message fading to sea.

A rock of white granite commemorates Charles Borden, "the grandfather of BC archaeology."[8] Borden may be best known for re-excavating the ancient Musqueam settlement at one of the mouths of the Fraser River, another southern border to this watery city. The dig took place at what's called the Marpole Midden (also known as the Great Fraser Midden), the former Musqueam village of c̓əsnaʔəm.

A short distance behind me, up a beachside embankment, is UBC's Museum of Anthropology (MOA), a dizzying collection of overlapping disciplines, the anthropological study of sociocultural history along with its archaeological artifacts. The same scattered pieces Borden and others pursued to reassemble past puzzles.

Each time I enter this museum, the MOA, I experience a momentary leap between place and time with the larger-than-life sculpture of *The Raven and the First Men*, commissioned in 1973. The piece is yellow cedar, four tons of it, kilned, laminated, and sculpted into one piece of cultural art, its dimensions over twelve cubic metres. The carving was done by a team: George Norris, Guujaaw (Gary Edenshaw), George Rammell, Bill Reid, Jim Hart, and Reg Davidson, a group spanning different First Nations. The result: the Haida story of creation retold in three dimensions.

A facet of this art that I love is that it "began as a miniature boxwood carving inspired by the works of 19th-century Haida carver Charles Edenshaw."[9] Imagine a small, perfect piece that fits in the palm of your hand, re-envisioned as something enormous. As though that first legend you witnessed, the original carving, wasn't tiny at all but glimpsed from a distance, like a ship from afar. When the story is shared, it draws closer and grows. From abstraction, it takes form, becoming intimate and intensely personal as it nears.

That's what I see and feel when I approach the carving, an Indigenous story of beginnings, or, more accurately, *the* beginning: the Haida legend of Raven and the First Men.

> According to Haida legend, the Raven found himself alone one day on Rose Spit beach, on Haida Gwaii. Suddenly, he saw an extraordinary clamshell at his feet, and protruding from it were a number of small creatures. The Raven coaxed them to leave the shell to join him in his wonderful world. Some were hesitant at first, but eventually, overcome by curiosity, they emerged from the partly open clamshell to become the first Haida.[10]

I've since learned many versions of similar stories. In some cultures, the First Peoples, who also emerge on a beach, are carved from driftwood or shaped out of clay. Invariably there's a greater entity who grants these fresh creatures life, a new animation as humans take shape, populating the planet. And while biblical scholars might long to place an Eden-like garden on a map of the world (often Botswana or Basrah), only this Haida story of creation, as far as I know, pinpoints a location with certainty: a shore much like this one on a northerly coast.

Rose Spit sits at the top end of Haida Gwaii, the northern point of Naikoon Provincial Park, a sharp spit of land resembling a compass finding true north. Something about the shoreline, the wash of the sea, gives the promontory the look of a crooking finger, beckoning you to come closer. *Let me tell you a secret.*

When I finally went there, I felt a jolt of belonging. Maybe it's one of those mystical spots with an energy vortex, like desert mesas you find in Sonora. Or it could be the inaudible hum of the Pacific Ring of Fire, a burble of sea-muted magma waiting to reform the land. Whatever it was, it felt palpable, and I relished standing in a spot that was new to me but felt utterly familiar.

Even here, on a Vancouver shore, I feel a residual glimmer of that liminal spot to the north, a place called "the end of the world." What spiritualists might call a "thin place," where earthliness shifts to the ethereal. A hint of that same connectivity, I believe, adheres to these beaches as well.

Along a trail leaving the water, I meander uphill on a path to further explore seaside stories in the same manner as scientific explorers. Another hybrid endeavour, akin to Smelhmelhéỉch, the ocean-washed island, only in this case with a swirling of disciplines—anthropology and archaeology—here on the UBC campus.

I'm meeting with Ashley Samsone, who works with department heads and professors, her focus being ancient studies and archaeological work, which includes anthropology. A recipient of the Outstanding Leader Award for Faculty Achievements, she's been active in local research and, fascinatingly, digs around Transylvania. Fighting the urge to ask about vampires, I frame our visit by asking Ashley how a coastline influences people and place, what I see as a leap between Old World and New, thinking of those earliest ships that first mapped the shore we now see from her high office window.

"Well, you can't look at a coast on its own," she explains. "Like countries. We can't simply isolate regions or people. Each area's a collection. Especially in colonized places. There's always a much bigger picture as traditions shift and blend over time. That goes for people, culture, and art."

Rather ideally, centring our view of English Bay and Howe Sound is Smelhmelhéỉch, Passage Island, which I point out, sharing the Salish place name.

"There's a perfect example," Ashley says. "We speak of Coast Salish language. Land acknowledgments too, the fact this is Musqueam, Squamish, and Tsleil-Waututh land. Cultural lines aren't distinct—back to that blending of tradition. Another great example is fishing, where traditional methods shift and adapt over time. Land plays a part. Think of our mountains, the deepwater there." She indicates the North Shore, today in shades of blue-green. "Fishing there requires a different approach to where we are here, where the shore's flat and the water is shallow."

I nod, considering boats and nets that I've seen.

"I was on the East Coast, in Nova Scotia," Ashley continues, "where Indigenous Mi'kmaw, like others, adapted to their surroundings in ingenious ways. When fishing deepwater, for example, they use sea foliage—seaweed and kelp—to cover the bottoms of their boats to fool deepwater predators, often sharks, into thinking the water is shallow. Bigger fish will keep away to avoid beaching themselves. So, unwanted fish stay away while the fish that *are* wanted remain and then can be harvested."

I think of *The Old Man and the Sea*. If only Santiago had known that trick, his marlin might've made it to market.

"We see parallels around here," Ashley adds. "The Pacific Northwest and the Arctic. Coastal geography has its own climate. With travel, new methods get shared and passed on. Art is another example. Here, check this out." Swivelling her monitor, she pulls up a photo of a decorative vase painted with the image of a multi-armed cephalopod.

"This is terracotta. Cypriot. Now, look at the octopus design. This shows its significance in that cultural area. In this case, Mediterranean, but we see similar influences here. Zoomorphic, we'd call that, when animals might be revered. Like an ibis or a hawk in ancient Egypt."

Bringing to mind ravens or thunderbirds, art bridging the space between people and gods, plugging gaps where belief becomes faith, in this case much of it stemming from water, or at least within sight of the sea. Being here, I consider Charles Borden and that hunk of white granite reminiscent of installations around town where bits of land are reinvented as art. And I ask Ashley about this, specifically the Great Fraser Midden and Borden's digs in the area.

"Well, to be honest, that name rarely came up, even during my studies of archaeology history. We didn't touch much on him. Sure, he was a professor here for a long time." She grins. "The grandfather of BC archaeology."

Of course, now, I hear it. Patriarchy. Appropriation of land. And I say as much.

Ashley gives a partial tilt of the head, considered. "I grew up in Ontario, and I've travelled for work and for pleasure. But I've never seen people so affiliated with their neighbourhoods as I do around here. Kits, Mount Pleasant, East Van. People *associate* with where they live and grew up, so it seems, here more than anyplace else. Very neighbourhood-specific within the overall city."

Which I hadn't considered and likely took for granted. Although I recall public events in which folks from East Van waved that fact like a flag. At times with apology, occasionally with aggression, but mostly with pride.

"Even while I've been here," Ashley says—she's been here for a decade—"Kits, for example, I see becoming more affluent. Each neighbourhood has its own history. Sure, there's a blending again, like cultures everywhere. But even in that, there's still a sense of region. It's interesting." She laughs. "Getting to work here on campus, I don't know a lot of places where you have to go through a forest to get to work. Some days it feels like wayfaring!"

A perfect descriptor. Plotting a course through the city, its neighbourhood gridwork and mishmash of shores. With thanks and a last look at the water, I leave Ashley to her work meshing the past with the now.

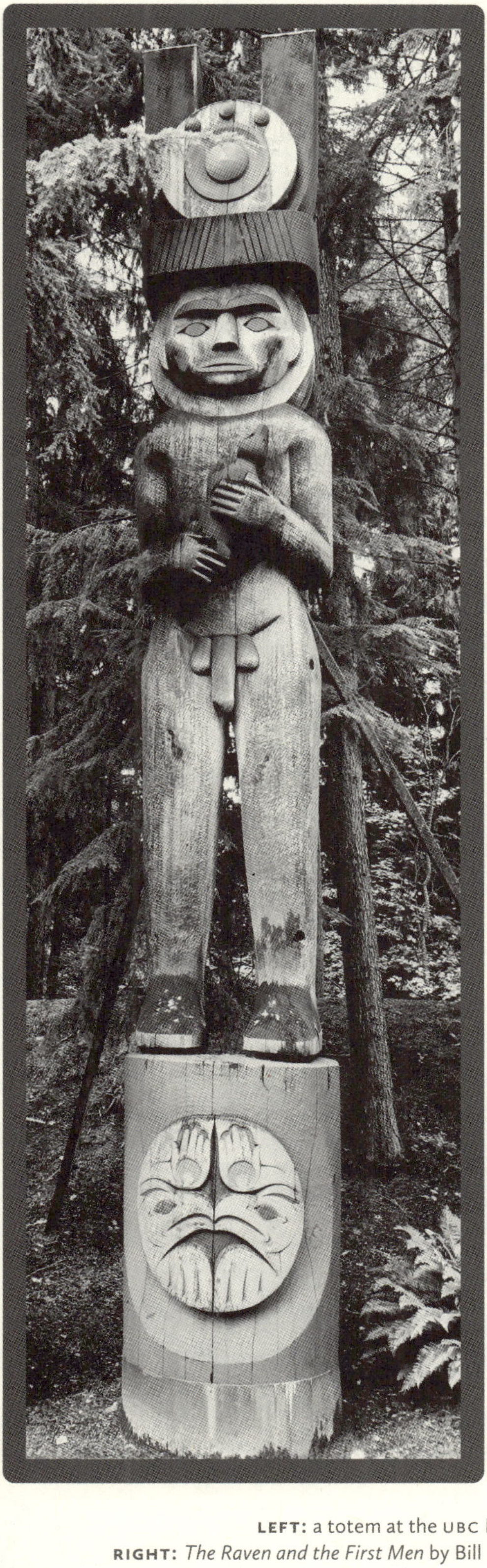

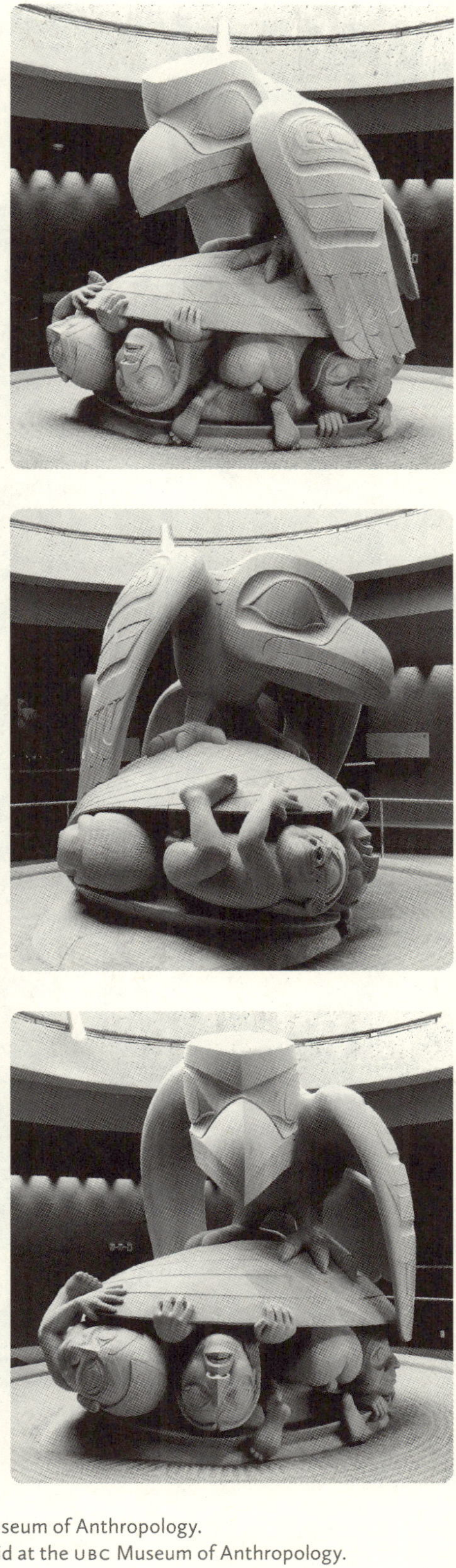

LEFT: a totem at the UBC Museum of Anthropology.
RIGHT: *The Raven and the First Men* by Bill Reid at the UBC Museum of Anthropology.

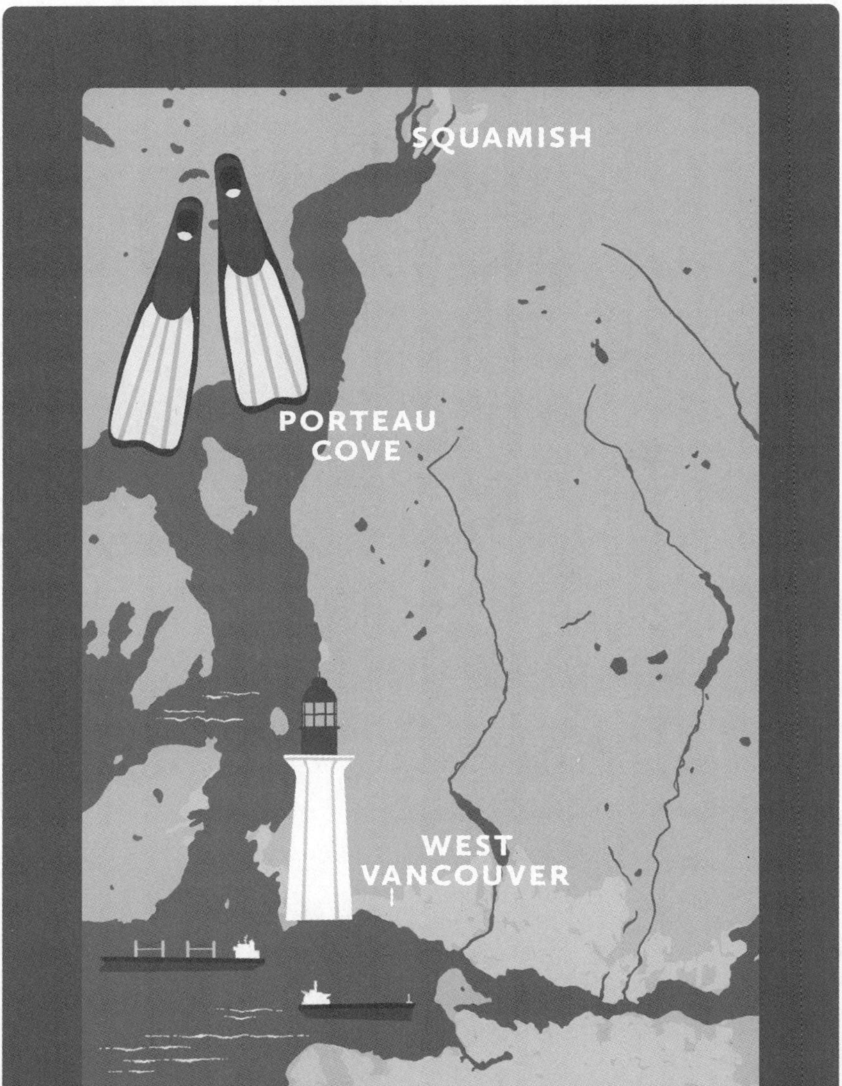
SQUAMISH
PORTEAU
COVE
WEST
VANCOUVER

TOWARD HOWE SOUND

West Side to West Van

SCUBA DEPTHS

FROM UBC IT'S a seven-kilometre stroll, west to east, along Spanish Banks, Locarno, and Jericho to get to Kits Beach, all of this fronting English Bay and Burrard Inlet. When I pull up an aerial map, the neighbourhood of Kitsilano resembles a nearly uniform rectangle. Alma Street is the western border, Burrard Street its east side. West 16th Avenue serves as its southern boundary, saltwater forms its north edge, and Vanier Park adds a northeasterly bulge, creating the mouth of False Creek.

Leaving the sidewalk, I follow a path of tamped mud and soil, skirting the water where blackberry strangles the shore. From here I veer south to a scuba shop offering classes in diving. Maybe *this* can offer a portal to that elusive submersible world.

Two instructors and four other students are here to teach and to learn the basics of scuba diving in a classroom, to start. The shop feels like a nautical general store, everything smelling of rubber and plastic with an essence of sea salt, sunscreen, and sand. I sign up and join the class. Then ask Koa, one of the instructors, what he thinks of the water here in Vancouver.

"Well, it's not for everyone, but I love it. It can be cold, and dark, and visibility varies. But it's awesome. We take it easy, start in the pool, never the ocean. Take it slow, make it safe, so everyone can enjoy it. The open water, though, is excellent."

Not that I needed convincing, just another take on what's in store.

After learning a few terms and scribbling a quiz, we're ready for the water. But not open water, not yet. With a vanload of equipment, we're hauled to the UBC pool, where we suit up, check our gear, and leap in. Parents and babies are splashing around while others do laps with sponges strapped to their hands. It's all very loud, smells of chlorine, and in no way resembles my imaginings of a life undersea. But like George Vancouver, I realize it's a means to an end, and the more I give in to the experience, the more I realize this is actually fun.

Our first test reminds me of ocean-washed Passage Island, a transition from air to water. We begin by adjusting our weight belts and tanks, then head to the deep end of the pool. The objective is to sink to the bottom, turn off our air, remove our masks, and practise the concentrated and relaxed process of fiddling, realigning, and reapplying our gear with eyes open while holding our breath in deepwater. The test is mostly mental in nature. We in fact have plenty of oxygen in our bloodstream and lungs to work away at this for a while, but the mind does its thing, convincing us that we're drowning, nature's way of telling us to get air and get it now!

The five of us perform this test one at a time. A chance for our instructors to get a sense of what we're each capable of. Our little group is comprised of four fit men in their thirties, and me. The first in our group begins as instructed; he sinks to the bottom, cuts his air, takes off his mask, then does his best to put it all back together down there. But within a few moments the panic sets in—as it's supposed to—and he launches himself up from the pool floor, shooting to the surface with a sputter and a cough, unable to complete the task as required. Even in the din of this busy public space, it now seems silent. Something has frayed, and no words are spoken. Each of us feels for our classmate, our new friend. We're also aware that we're testing for future dive buddies. Who do you want to have with you down there when things go wrong? Cool-headed competence becomes a life-saving necessity. If this were a round of *Survivor* we'd have no choice but to vote this man off. But of course, this is why we're in class, practising under guidance, in a pool.

What happens next is an interesting and unsurprising glimpse into human nature: fear, self-reliance, and pride. The rest of our little group does well at the test (sink, cut air, remove gear, reassemble, return to the surface). I can say with certainty that we four do it, and do it well, *because* our one poor companion was unable to. Something about having witnessed that, feeling what it was like, and not wanting to "fail" made us all that much better. I can't help but wonder what might have happened if that first person had been successful. I just suspect that the rest of our group owes our immediate shift into confidence to that first-timer's bolt to the surface.

The next time through reinforces the group dynamic—in this case, accumulated, collective competence. Our first-timer wills himself to succeed at the task, mind over matter. A bit of fumbling, but he does it, cementing our group from now on.

Two full days of drills in the pool, and we're ready for the ocean. We're taken once more in the van with our tanks and shrink wraps of neoprene, from Kits through downtown to the Stanley Park Causeway over Lions Gate Bridge and Burrard Inlet's First Narrows, where the water today, far below, is a similar tone to the bridge, mottled green tinged with cornflower blue. On the north side of the bridge we veer west and follow the ogee curves of Marine Drive to Lighthouse Park, which is described by the City of West Vancouver as a nationally significant natural park.

> The park is a biologically rich and unique resource and is an example of a remaining old growth coastal forest in the Lower Mainland. The lighthouse and light station grounds at Point Atkinson are a national historic site and one of the most photographed and recognizable landmarks in the entire Lower Mainland.[11]

Sure enough, the proud lighthouse is here, red and white, posing at the head of the bay. To the left, Lions Gate Bridge cuts a likeness of California's Golden Gate, a pair of frames to the cruise ships that track the West Coast. A far cry from those first map-making vessels, with navigation now done largely by satellite.

The day is ideal, sunny and cool. Our van parks, and we unload in a rubber-squeaking chorus to lug our kit down a gravelly trail to the shore. Around us are arbutus and evergreens, with a few maples starting to blush as though someone's just shared an off-colour joke.

We reinspect our gear: BCD, the buoyancy control device, a jacket worn for diving that can be inflated or deflated as needed; mask, fins, snorkel, and weights; regulator and tank; compressor and depth gauge (check, check, check, and check). Finally, we enter the ocean, where I can study this coast from beneath the saltwater. That inverse view of the city some might consider an immram, a sea journey into another world.

At first our little group stays loosely gathered, but then we disperse, each drawn to discover an individual new world. Perspective shifts as rocks, shells, and plants magnify underwater. There's a sense of bodily flight, or, more accurately, weightless suspension. I do somersaults, my tank bubbles trailing in lava lamp shapes. Then dive to eighteen metres, the limit of our certification tickets.

I see shellfish, something that might be a perch, and a monstrous lingcod, a single fish that could feed our whole group. I do mental math. *If that fish appears one-third larger than it is according to what we've been taught, that makes it ... um ... never mind, it's just huge.* I swim with the lingcod, technically a greenling, as it stirs seabed gravel with its pectoral fins. Maybe nesting, as some species do. These predators live out their lives, often twenty-five years, in a very small area. I could probably come back in a decade and find it right where it is now, still stirring pebbles and gobbling other fish. I can't help imagining how I'd prepare it. A few fillets sautéed, a whole side on the grill, maybe some baked in the oven. Good thing I haven't encountered a merman. On that North Atlantic sailing excursion, I read a grim poem of a merchant seaman facing starvation and hauling a merman aboard. The flesh, claims the sailor, is delicious.

Later, finishing the day at home on the sofa, I'm sorting through photos, one of which shows me after the dive, a gleam of sun on my wetsuit and tank. For supper, there's no lingcod or merman on hand, so I've settled for a tin of sardines. I put away my dive certificate, still crisply new, and imagine I'm now part of an exclusive undersea club.

Stepping outside, I savour the sunset, a proper nautical one in deep crimson. *Red sky at night, sailors' delight.* Above the fiery wash is a last bit of blue where three swifts slice the evening, birds I've not seen here before, their boomerang wings rowing the sky. High over that in a whisked stratus smear, a lone cloud resembles a feather, a mariner quilling a chart. It could be flat art or a woodcut design. But the image is somehow deeper, more than I'm able to comprehend. And I go to bed with a sense that my map has been singed at one edge, leaving me to wonder what lies ahead.

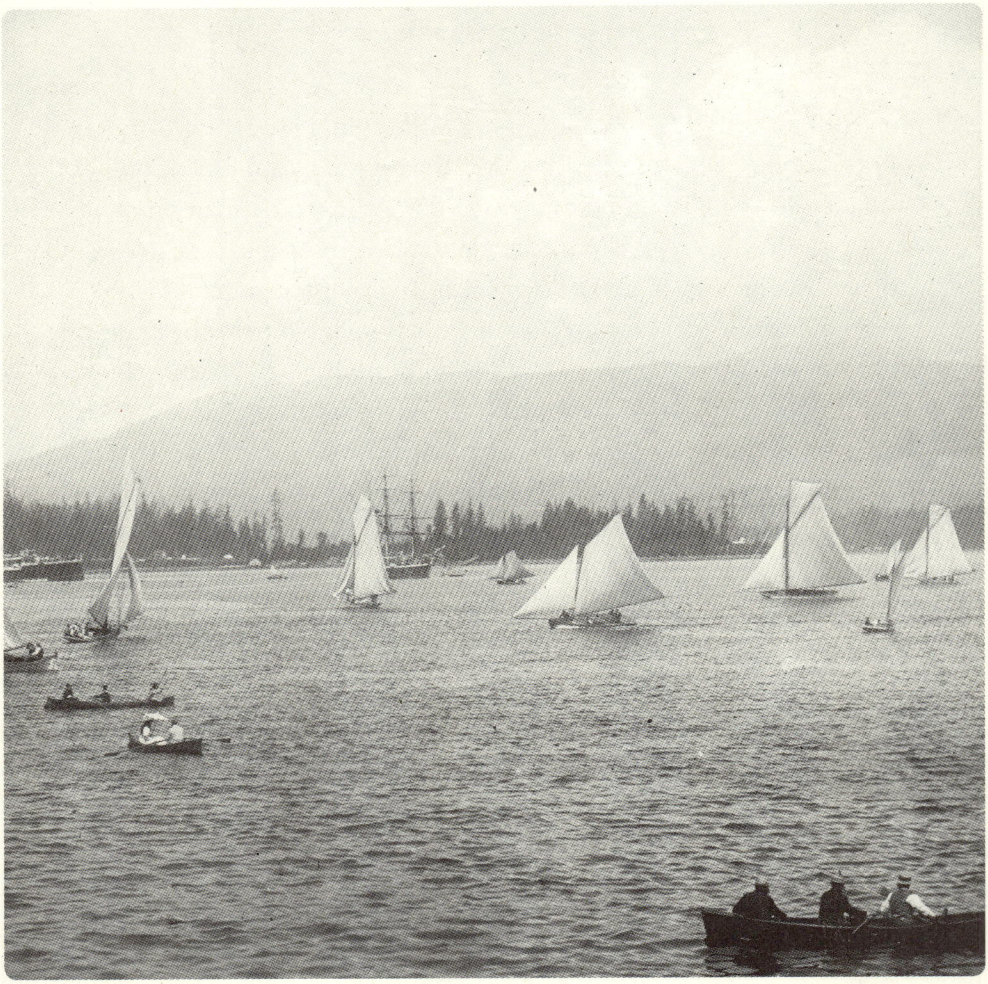

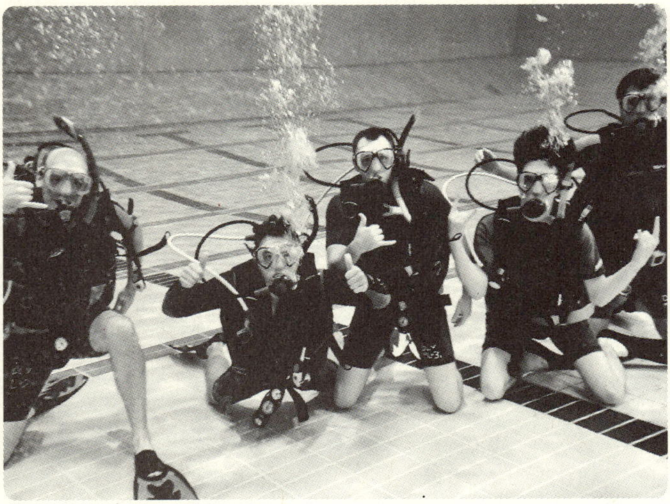

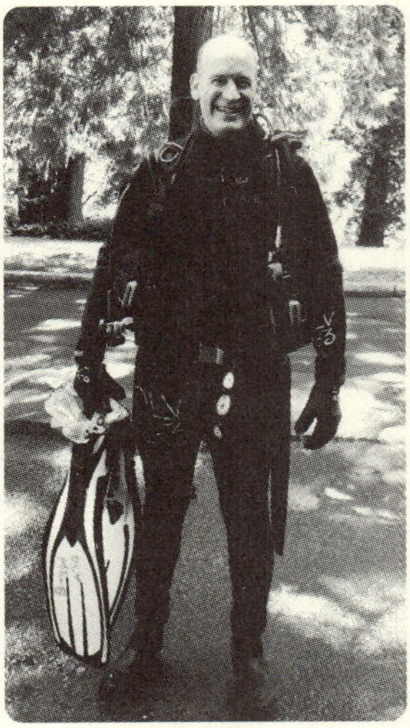

CLOCKWISE FROM TOP: Burrard Inlet Regatta, 1890; scuba diving at Lighthouse Park in West Van; a scuba class in the UBC pool, with Bill on the left.

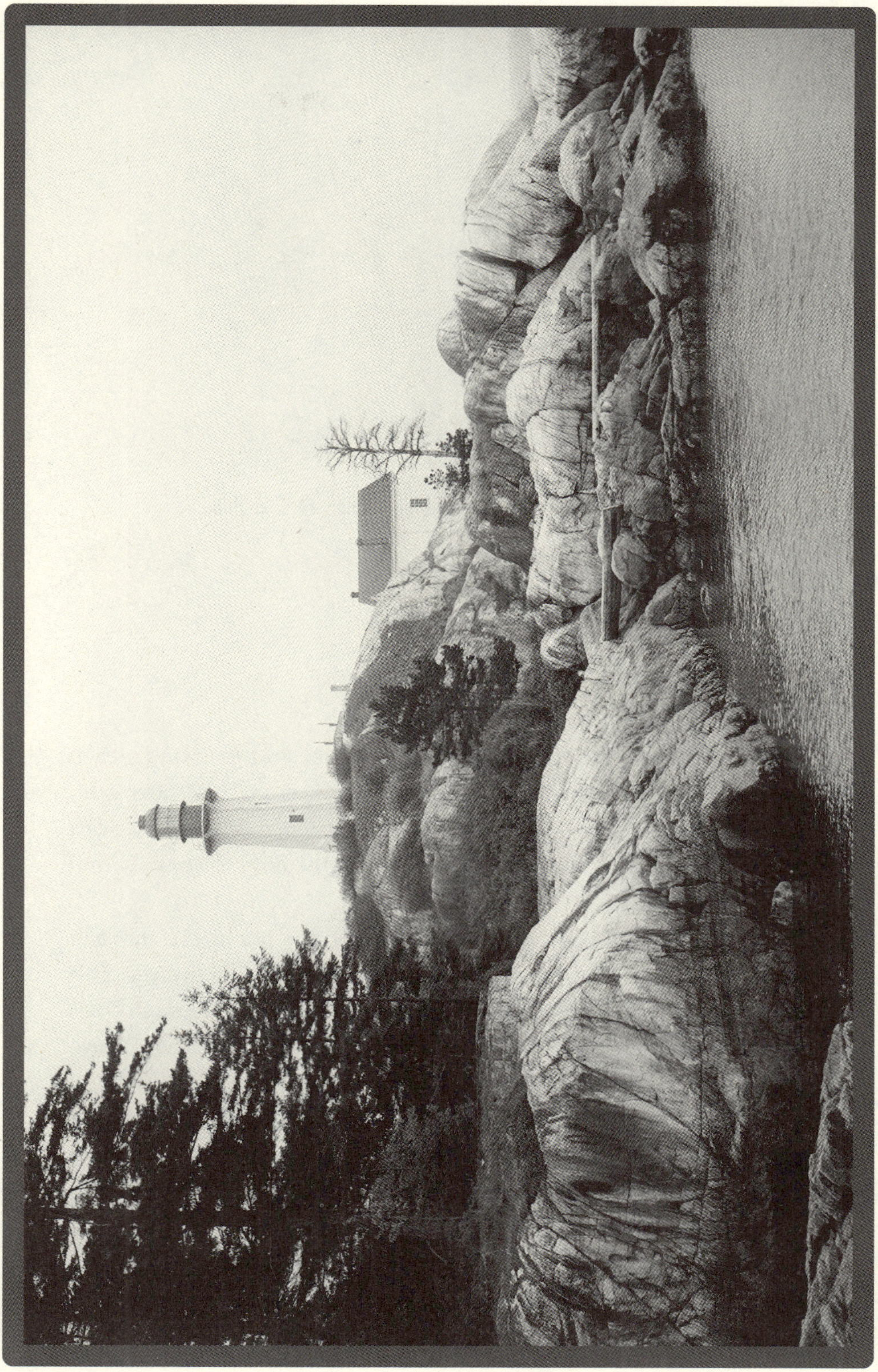

Lighthouse Park, circa 1940s.

Howe Sound

SHIPWRECKS AND REEFS

A NEW DAY, and with it, new water, as our scuba group reassembles to make one more dive, enabling me to further examine this underwater perspective. Specifically, we're venturing past the north and the west of Vancouver, beyond Burrard Inlet, to where the fjord of Howe Sound meets the Salish Sea.

Back in the van filled with gear, we retrace our route through downtown to West Van. But today we keep driving on Highway 99 past Horseshoe Bay, heading north along Howe Sound with its rail lines aimed at Squamish and Whistler, finally stopping at Porteau Cove Provincial Park.

This stretch of road, the Sea to Sky Highway, was initially considered impossible to construct, much like the train line that snakes along with it. In 1953, the committee responsible for oversight, financing, and construction of this rail and road stated it couldn't be done. Rock cliffs on the shore ascending to mountains were, to say the least, an engineering conundrum. "When construction began on the two-lane Squamish Seaview Highway from Horseshoe Bay to Squamish in February 1955, workers claimed it was the most difficult road ever built in British Columbia."[12]

Now we take it for granted, apart from the unending views it provides. But what brings me here with my rubber-wrapped friends is another waterscape, for directly offshore are a number of reefs with shipwrecks put here for the purpose of creating a play space for scuba divers. BC Parks provides a description:

> Here at Porteau Cove Provincial Park, a series of reefs and sunken shipwrecks have enhanced the growth of marine life and the opportunities for recreational diving.
>
> The artificial reef network has been constructed from chains of tires, hollow concrete piles, concrete blocks, and steel H-beams. Over 100 species including octopuses, plumose anemones, lingcod, and several types of shrimp flourish in this important habitat.

Making this a kind of waterlogged wrecking yard, one that fosters a healthy environment and provides ideal diving for all levels of experience.

After parking the van, we gather our gear and head to the water. Unlike our scramble down the forested slope of Lighthouse Park, this is essentially sea level. Set back from the beach are those impossible railway tracks following the inlet beyond Squamish to Whistler. Although the steel lines are silent right now, a strong wind gives a diesel-like roar with a blustery view of the fjord.

Sun shines through the breeze, striking whitecaps in diamond-like glints. The surface could pass for a sastrugi range, windswept ice fields mistaken for waves on long polar excursions. It's a day made for sailing, not diving.

A frown from Holly, our driver, fellow diver, and instructor. "Might affect visibility," she says, "stir up the water." A shrug. "Let's give it a go."

Yesterday's dive offered shelter in a cove by the lighthouse. Today, however, despite breakwater spears of rough boulders, the chop is discouraging. Rotten weather for snorkels, but with luck we'll be fine using tanks down below. We take extra time with our BCD vests, adjusting the mix of flotation and weight. Eventually finding a buoyancy balance, we return to our undersea world.

It's a bit murky below, as strong currents blur sightlines, and it takes more effort to stay put. Strands of kelp gently sway their interpretive dance, jellyfish are doing the sidestroke, and starfish in purple are spread-eagled on undersea rock. A sea cucumber lies flopped on the reef while plants I don't know reach from the seabed like oversized fungi: chanterelles, maitake, enoki. Now I want mushrooms to pair with that cod.

Moments pass, then that weightless sensation returns, similar to the feeling at Rose Spit, a connecting with infinity. Which may simply be how it feels when immersed in a miniscule part of the water that covers the planet: expansion far beyond one's own body.

Next I drift over what may be the show's diva, the largest of the three shipwrecks. Beyond a shallow reef and a corroded old jungle gym sits the steel hull of the *Granthall*, a twenty-eight-metre, steel-hulled CPR tugboat built in 1928. Now crusted in sea growth, the vessel triggers a whole other plunge, this one emotive and sensory, as though I'm approaching the *Ben Franklin* or the *Nautilus*, an outsider from above looking in.

A small hatch remains open, and a ladder descends within. Every surface is coated in new life, waving plants, growing shells. The ship has been sunk right-side up, its hull nestled in pebbles and stone. Plants move with the current: There's a sponge and a cluster of something like cauliflower or brains. I descend and peer into the ship, where I hear a low, haunting moan. Then realize that it's me, saying something like "ahhh" or "oohhh," but that's how it sounds through my regulator mouthpiece, dampened by ears filled with water.

Imagining the interior as a deepwater craft, I can parse out the nebulous image that's now part of the reef, both growing and frozen in time. And I understand, I believe, Jules Verne's mental meander taking shape in those visions of Nemo.

I find a good current and drift while I size up the vessel. Peering in portholes, I imagine settings for supper, private berths, and a rumbling engine. It feels like Atlantis: life from the surface, submerged. Bringing to mind legends of drowned societies. Much like tales of creation, many cultures share epic flood lore about when the Earth was covered in water, most often in a purging followed by a coming together of humans and deities, or at least godlike intermediaries. More blending of timeline, place, and belief.

There's a story I've read, apparently true but rarely shared, like those mysteries hidden in military files, of a former president aboard Air Force One, flying over Anatolia's Mount Ararat. The commander-in-chief was certain he saw the remains of a wooden ship near the summit, at around four thousand metres. A few aging locals confirm that a wreck is up there, an ark, they believe, built to ship wildlife in twos, but no one dares to announce it, knowing it would draw unwanted attention and sully the sacred locale. Consistent with all myth, I like knowing it's out there, neither verified nor disproven, slowly growing like seaweed and coral.

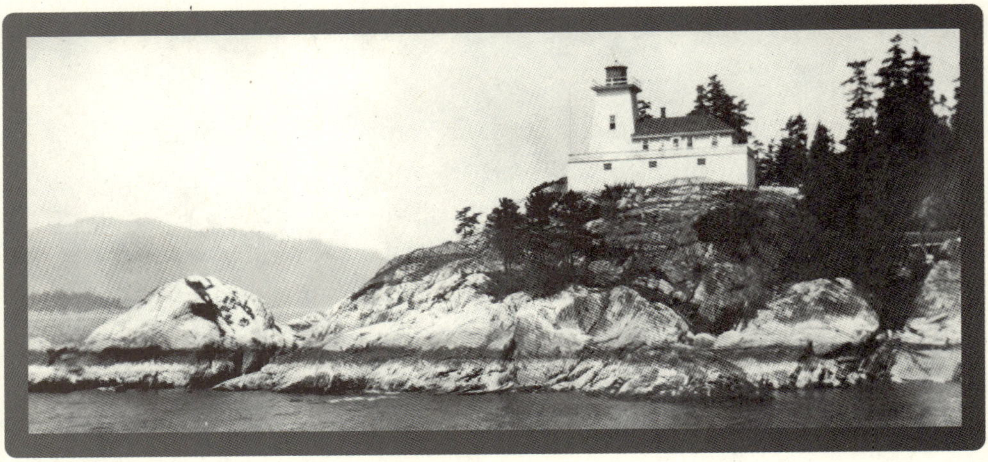

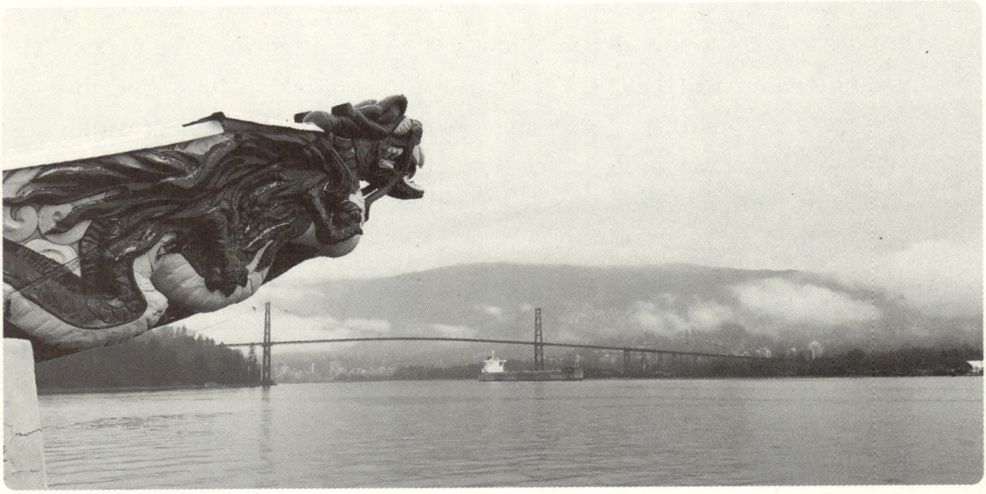

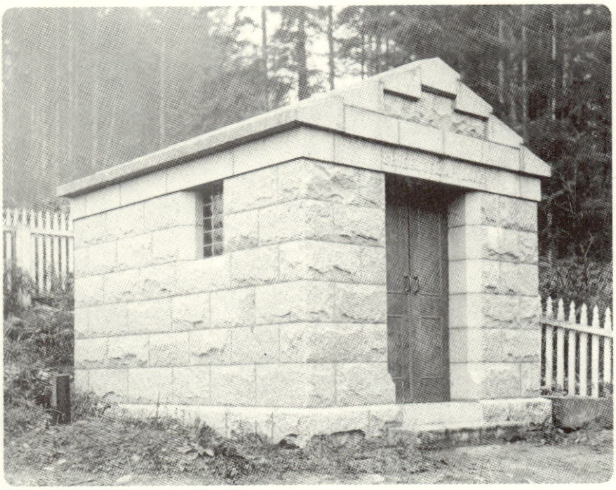

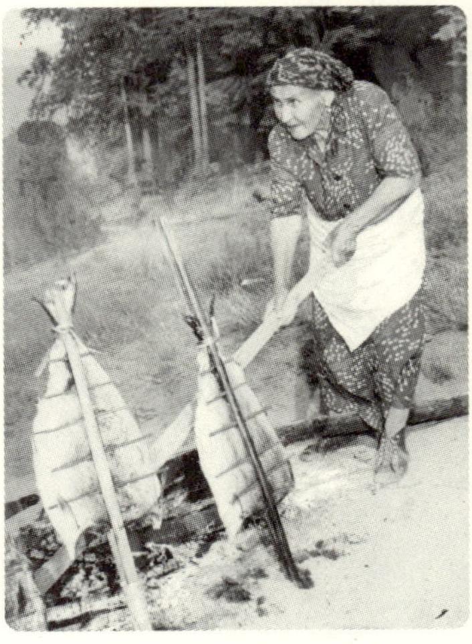

CLOCKWISE FROM TOP: Point Atkinson, Lighthouse Park, circa 1905; the SS *Empress of Japan's* figurehead, looking toward Lions Gate Bridge and West Van; Annie George (neé Harry) cooking salmon over a fire at Burrard Inlet No. 3 Reserve near Squamish, 1940; Chief Joe Capilano's mausoleum in West Van, 1920.

Toward Squamish

THROUGHWAYS AND AUGUST JACK KHATSAHLANO

HERE AT THE EAST EDGE of Howe Sound, if I kept heading north, I'd reach the present-day community of Squamish, which I learn "had its beginning during the construction of the Pacific Great Eastern Railway in the 1910s. It was the first southern terminus of that railway (now a part of [CNR])."[13] Another water-based throughway, rail meeting river and sea, with access to forests, mining, and fish. The inlet, speckled with isles, also offers a glimpse of tectonic and volcanic activity with a subsequent shifting of sea. Between here and the mouth of the fjord lie the sharply cragged islands of Anvil and Gambier, Bowyer and Bowen, and the waterlogged hybrid of Passage, with Cypress Mountain just to the east.

I could simply take to the water again and follow the fjord south as it yawns into sea, past Lions Bay to the Horseshoe Bay ferries, through Whytecliff Park toward the granite-cliffed corner of Lighthouse Park point. The Squamish name for the promontory is Sk'íw̓itsut, meaning "go around." Which is what we do, heading back, our van weaving with the road at one edge of Sḵwx̱wú7mesh Úxwumixw, the Squamish Nation, situated here for eight thousand years. A cultural region covering present-day Whistler, Squamish, Howe Sound, West and North Vancouver, and the tributary waterways surrounding English Bay and Burrard Inlet.

On a previous trip from that sunken ship beach I *did* carry on farther north to where the Squamish River feeds the top of the fjord. I was part of a group tackling whitewater with paddles in a RHIB, a rigid-hulled inflatable boat, effectively a big bouncy dinghy. It was a team-building event, forcing co-workers to spend time with each other and providing us an opportunity to feel uncomfortable in a group outside of the office. To heighten discomfort, we all were in swimsuits. And apart from the gang at the dive shop or possibly those lifeguards on *Baywatch*, I've never known a work environment where business attire includes Speedos.

In spite of this, we got to the river, freshwater heading toward salt, launched our raft, and navigated a series of increasing rapids—Class II, Class III, and Class IV—a chance to get saturated and, in theory, become better acquainted with each other. Which we did in a way, as our group got drunk at day's end, doing our best to forget the uncomfortable outing. *Then* it was fun. I should mention that the people involved were quite nice. A forced outing, however, is something I prefer to avoid. But we witnessed spectacular scenery, this being a crossroads of provincial parks: Shannon Falls, Alice Lake, and Brackendale Eagles. Beyond were the peaks of Mount Tantalus, Serratus Mountain, and Mount Garibaldi, an area famous for mountain climbing and the bald eagles that gather to scour the Squamish River for salmon.

As we jostled and bounced through the froth in our raft, mentally updating our resumes, I learned a bit more about water. Waves, in particular, which have their own language, a liquid form of topography. Each crest of wave and water peak has a moniker: whaleback and roller, stramash and clutter. Later I learned from commercial fishermen there are more colourful names too: humper, dirty bastard, and one even worse they wouldn't tell me. All I know is that water in motion has as many moods and personalities as people.

At the moment, heading back from our dive, Howe Sound and the inlet appear mostly happy, still in sun, a few lumps on the aquamarine. The van even has its own shimmy, reminiscent of that day on the raft.

And with memories of Squamish, I consider August Jack Khatsahlano, the Squamish Chief who may well have served as a guide when I entered the scuba shop in the neighbourhood bearing his name.

Born in 1877, August Jack was a trapper, canoe builder, logger, and guide. One of the last traditional shamans, he's believed to have been the very last of the Squamish to perform adulthood rituals, coming-of-age ceremonies including a vision quest, trekking these very mountains to meditate and connect with the spirits.[14]

August Jack was born at Snauq, the village at the mouth of False Creek in present-day Kitsilano. For my *Perfect Day* walks, this was among my first stops, beneath and beside Burrard Bridge, now part of Seṅáḵw, "the largest First Nations economic development project in Canadian history," a construction initiative for multi-use towers and several thousand new homes.[15] The Seṅáḵw website explains that this name, a version of "Snauq," translates to "the place inside the head of False Creek."[16] Much like the "good land" to the west, map-making by way of linguistics.

If an archaeologist were to dig where August Jack had made a home, they'd reveal a vertical timeline much like the mountain-edged shores of Howe Sound. Only there, among traces of middens, they'd find clay over sandstone and shale, then eventually granite, the metamorphic rock of former volcanoes.

Seṅáḵw began a series of encounters, personal and online, with many of the city's Places That Matter sites, curated by the Vancouver Heritage Foundation, which for me became archival breadcrumbs. Through the Foundation, I sourced a quote from Musqueam First Nation historians:

> The area now known as Burrard Inlet is host to numerous Musqueam villages, camps, and transformer sites.
>
> Burrard Inlet was also part of our core hunting and fishing area. Our families stayed here while hunting elk and waterfowl. Səṅaʔqʷ (Seṅáḵw) was also important for harvesting and processing salmon, sturgeon, and smelt that frequented False Creek and its many streams, many of which have been lost to urbanization and development.[17]

A plentiful place, this was effectively a water-based larder where August Jack grew up on a diet of shellfish, fish, fowl, and game. His parents were Owhaywat and Khay-Tulk of Chaythoos, anglicized to Sally and Supple Jack. But Supple Jack passed away on the day August Jack was born. August Jack lived at Snauq until the unceded land, then a reservation, was purchased and assumed by the government in 1913, at which point August Jack and other False Creek Squamish people were forcibly relocated to Howe Sound, near what's now the modern city of Squamish.

August Jack married Swanamia (anglicized to Mary Anne), and together they had five children: Emma, Celestine, Wilfred, Irene, and Louise. As a family they lived within sight of the river and sea for the rest of August Jack's life, until he passed away in 1967 at the age of ninety-one.

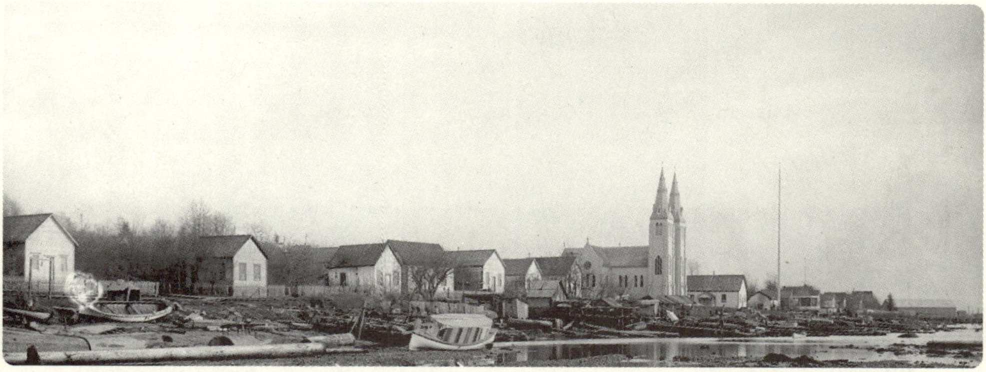

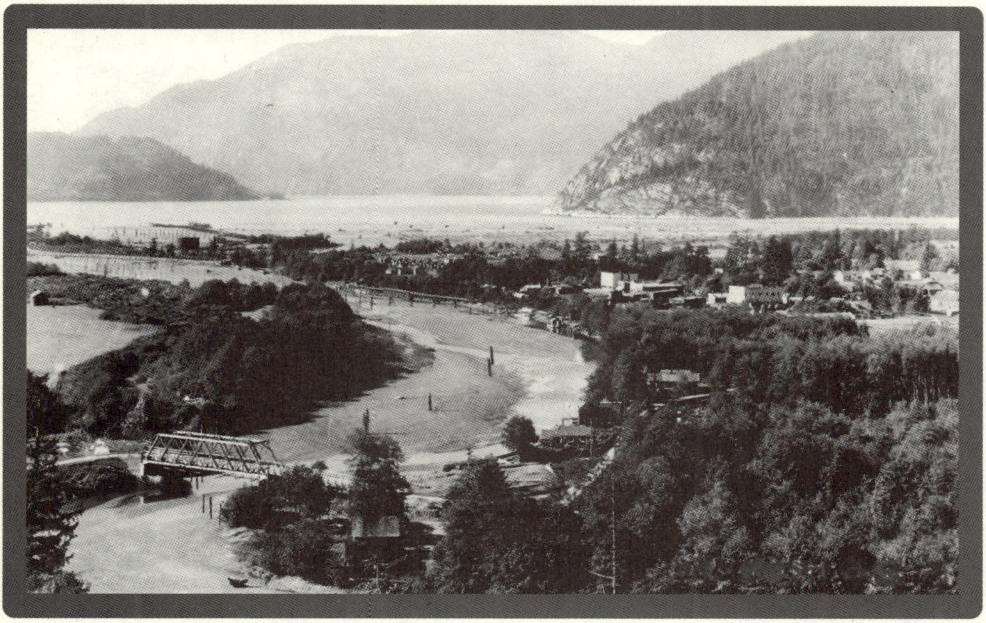

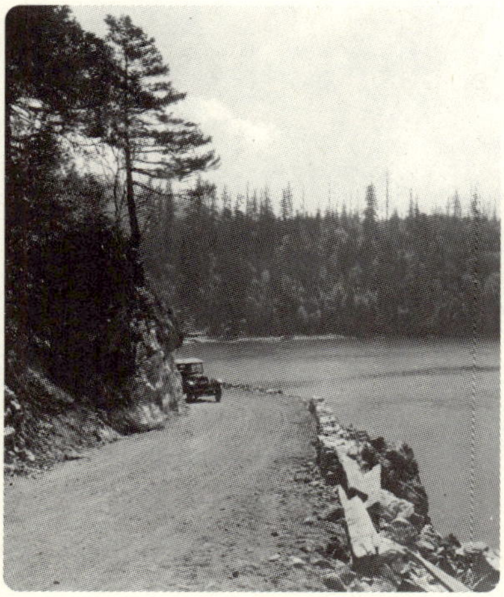

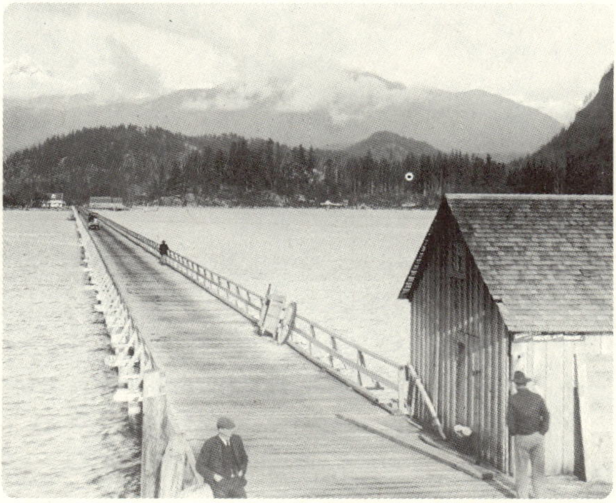

CLOCKWISE FROM TOP: Squamish village Eslhá7an (Ustlawn) on Indian Mission Reserve No. 1 in North Van, 1908; Squamish, circa 1920s; Squamish Government Wharf, circa 1920s; Old Squamish Highway, circa 1920s.

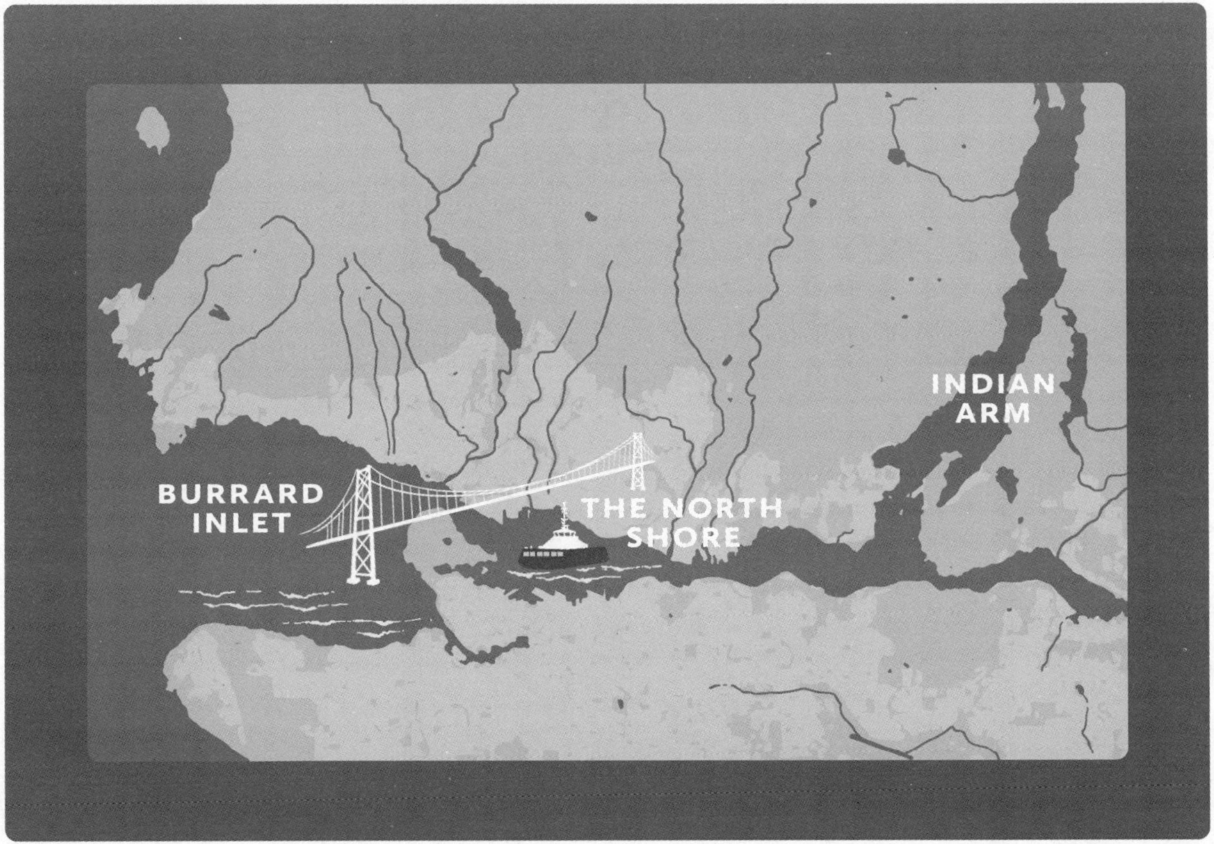
INDIAN ARM
BURRARD INLET
THE NORTH SHORE

BURRARD INLET *and* NORTH SHORE

The North Shore

SPIRIT TRAIL AND CHIEF CAPILANO

RATHER THAN DRIVE THROUGH DOWNTOWN, our van takes a leisurely route, bypassing Lions Gate Bridge to bisect West and North Van, communities divided by the north–south flow of the Capilano River. Known collectively as the North Shore, the area offers a south-facing sweep of Burrard Inlet. This stretch of terrain with its broad inlet view was known by the Squamish as Tl'alhemá7elkw, or "saltwater."[18] And apart from forested hills and the river we've crossed, saltwater is all I can see.

On a map, these regions are a bit of a jumble. The municipality of West Van covers a large forest swath, including Cypress Mountain and Cypress Provincial Park, while the District of North Van expands even farther, a vast range of mountains and trees encompassing Lynn Canyon, Lynn Valley, and Mount Seymour Park. The City of North Vancouver, however, is a compact yet densely populated pocket with the inlet on its south side, where West and North Van municipalities become bookends that not only frame what they hold but cover it too.

Our van takes a curve to give an aerie-like view, a macro perspective where industrial ports line the inlet. On the north are shipping terminals with the steelmaking components of potash and coal, the forestry products of lumber, logs, wood pulp, and paper, and grain terminals handling durum, canola, barley, wheat, flax, and rye. Across the water, on the south side of the inlet, the cranes at the Port of Vancouver do their slow waltz with freighters. Containers in kaleidoscope colours are stacked into towers for shipping. I can almost feel the sway of those vessels at sea, bashing through stramashes and clutters. Another reminder of the motto "By sea land and air we prosper" and a quote by Tom Zoellner: "If you want to understand the soul of a city, look at the economic reasons for its founding."[19] Which at the moment are all on display: transport and farming, logging and steel, the same resources that brought those first ships to this harbour, their map-making a by-product of commerce.

Having crossed the Capilano, stories unfold in my mind of the Chief whose name is now part of the river: Chief Joe Capilano, grandfather to Mary See-em-ia, another guide on my walks through Vancouver's downtown and West End. It was Mary and her husbands, Eihu and Joe Nahanee, both Native Hawaiians, who ranched the land on what's now Coal Harbour, fronting present-day Stanley Park. Their marriages strengthened a growing trans-Pacific community, adding key facets to the ethnic makeup of Vancouver's port workers, as well as its shores.

With the river shrinking behind us, I consider the story of Chief Joe, birthname s7ápelek̲, born in 1854 on the Squamish Nation territory. According to the Canadian Encyclopedia, his influence stemmed not only from vision and intellect but also keen leadership skills: "As the chosen successor to Chief Láwa Capilano, Joe s7ápelek̲ became better known as Chief Joe Capilano or Hyas Joe, and spent the rest of his life advocating for Canada's recognition of Indigenous rights."[20]

With a bit more searching, I find a photo of Joe standing with pride and certainty, looking not quite at the camera but a point just beyond. The year is 1900. It strikes me as prescient, Joe having knowledge of what's ahead. He wears a fur hat, maybe beaver, with a buckskin jersey and soft leather boots. He's physically fit and clean shaven apart from a dark, full moustache. A blanket is drawn tight around his shoulders. It looks like heavy spun wool trimmed in tassels with a bright border, a geometric design in triangle shapes and what might be a thunderbird pattern.[21]

The garment resembles star blankets I've seen, often as art installations. Statements of culture and place, these traditional Indigenous quilts are woven with a radiating pattern, the star, representing not only a rising celestial body associated with morning but also the eye of the Creator. The item commemorates the recipient, offering physical coverage as well as spiritual shelter. In other words, its wearer remains protected, connected, and safe. Joe's blanket was likely a gift, part of a celebration acknowledging admiration, honour, and respect.

Late in the 1870s, Joe and his wife, Mạry Agnes Líx̲welut from Howe Sound, along with their growing family of ten children, relocated from Squamish to the north shore of Burrard Inlet, where our van is now passing. By 1880 they'd moved to what was called the Mission Indian Reserve near Moodyville, a southeast section of what's presently North Van.

Joe gave up hunting and fishing to work at the Moodyville Sawmill, the largest business around, where he became foreman at the docks by the base of the slope. The job helped finance a trip that he made, sailing to England to meet with King Edward VII to discuss First Nations land claims. At this time, in 1906, Squamish longshoremen established the first union, Local 526 of the Industrial Workers of the World. Its membership was Indigenous locals and English and European settlers, as well as Native Hawaiians, including family and in-laws of Joe.

The bustling centre once located here is another snap of this place at that time, when life revolved around lumber and logs and the port on the shore of the inlet. Despite its economic size and importance, the Moodyville Sawmill not only closed but virtually disappeared early in the twentieth century, leaving barely a trace of its presence and surrounding settlement in this pocket of forest, a community ghost in the trees. From the Museum and Archives of North Vancouver I find these details:

> The lost sawmill community of Moodyville was the first significant non-Native settlement on Burrard Inlet, now the harbour of Vancouver ... It soon became one of the biggest exporters in the new province

> of British Columbia, and the community achieved many firsts in the region, including the first wedding, school and electric lights. By the early 1890s, however, voracious logging and a worldwide depression had depleted its trees and fortunes. The mill closed in 1901 and the City of North Vancouver gradually absorbed the site. Curiously, almost no physical traces have survived—no buildings or landmarks, and only a few artifacts and photographs remain.[22]

Forcing us to imagine what it was like, going from something to nothing in a very short time. Maybe *that's* what Joe glimpsed past the lens of the camera: the crest of a long rolling wave.

Last time I was here, not jammed in a van but on foot, I lived a short distance away. Two places in fact, in North Van. For a stint, I lived near the water on Lonsdale Avenue, roughly the centre of town, and then I lived slightly north, at the base of the hills in Lynn Valley. From both of those places, I'd walk through the haunt of the Moodyville woods, now a park overlooking the tracks and the port. Consistent with an essence of lingering past, the North Shore Spirit Trail became a companion.

The multi-use path, a blend of paved greenway with stretches of sand, dirt, and rock, links the Districts of North and West Vancouver, the City of North Vancouver, and the Squamish and Tsleil-Waututh First Nations that mirror the weave of Burrard Inlet's North Shore.

Hiking and trekking the Spirit Trail is how I experienced much of this section of shore, tracing the land through its industry, houses, and forest, over asphalt and tree roots and earth. By the former site of the mill, a suspension bridge crosses a gully and passes a bald eagle's nest. It's another mystical place, not quite a closet to Narnia, but not entirely unlike it, either. I'd see crows, and then ravens, as though the same birds that flew with my *Perfect Day* walks had magically grown, shifting from mid-size to large. And in the same way I've followed mosaics, murals, and outdoor exhibits, the Spirit Trail shares its own art, subtly snaking through forest as it follows the inlet, in this case paying homage to those corvids, an echo of footsteps in time.

In a pocket of tall pines you can find a series of rocks—grey granite, some round, others flat and flush with the ground. Every few metres, a stone is engraved with an image or brief story pertaining to crows; it's a work called *Site Memories: Murmuring Crows* by Ingrid Koivukangas. One image shows a corvid in flight, another emerging from under a cedar. It's easy to miss, the art a subtle extension of land. I note a few lines etched on a rock: "Murmuring crows create connections from the past to the present, from the world of site memories to the present day." Near one end of the path, another stone reads, "Many cultures believe the crow sees the past, present and future all at once."

Seeing the past, present, and future simultaneously is a concept I've read of, finding this overlap of logic and myth in multiple sources. It boils down to alternate ways we can view the world, specifically how time is interpreted. It may seem that notions of past, present, and future are obvious, and yet, not all perspectives are the same. According to ancient Greeks, for example, the future approaches from behind, part of the reason we can't clearly see it until it's upon us. Therefore, what we see and experience, as it's laid out before us, is the past—literally what happens, what happened, *before*. Leaving only that moment when something occurs: the present, where we stand in this riverlike passage of time.

Diving deeper into this premise, the present becomes nearly imperceptible, as the moment we become aware of an occurrence, it's already happened. The present, as a stop-motion moment, is incalculable, like splitting an item in half. It can go on forever, until all that's left is null space, nothing more than a notion.

Comparing the flow of time to a river, however, is tidy. Ribbons and roadways are easy notions to grasp. We tend to be linear creatures. Boundaries are comfy, familiar. Ensconcement, like comprehension, equates to understanding, and with that comes peace of mind. But time isn't necessarily organized, not always that stringent. Minutes and hours were created largely for commerce, and also for mapping. Time equals distance. And with it comes the influence of political motives and power.

Alternately, present moments are all that we tangibly have. That's where the infinite lies, with the future and past being mere concepts. Despite the cliché, we all experience moments when time seems to stand still. When perception and intuition supersede fundamentals.

This leaves time not as a construct or principle but rather a concept. And concepts are fluid. Less like a creek and more like the sea, the ebb and flow of the tide, circularity paired with the turn of planets. More in tune with the pulse of the earth. Which is much closer to the concept of time that many cultures have historically embraced, knowing that no one particular moment is coming nor gone, but instead, all occurrences are concurrent—the past, present, and future all happening now—and in fact, that infinite present is all we can possibly know.

This is the fluid, ever-present world view mythically linked to the corvid. Another neat melding of logic and myth. How, when, or why this came to be is beyond me. Instead I simply accept it. Varying views of this nature can be found throughout time and in many Indigenous cultures, those traditionally linked to the land and to the ebb-flow of seasons and migrations, and with them, that circular bending of time—the free, fluid flow that links each facet of time to the present. Despite its conflicting with contemporary Western thinking, I find this makes sense.

So what's science, what's myth? Where's the line between fact and illusory? Hard to say. All I know is that this stretch of watery trail, weaving through ghost-pockets of urban and Indigenous terrain, with its echo of time-blurring birds, evokes the extrasensory, instilling a sense of limitlessness I can't help but immerse myself in.

Many modern researchers too embrace tangential facets of a time-bending notion with the concept of manifestation as it relates to scientific observation, when the process, comprised of the observer, the observing, and the observed, effectively dissolves as the very act of observance solidifies things into being; that "thing" simply isn't there until you observe it, until you focus your attention on it. A kind of omniscient wayfinding or map-making, with time as a wave, the same undulation I see in crinkles now rippling the inlet.

Each time I stroll the Spirit Trail, east or west doesn't matter; its blend of forest, streetscape, and shore also conjures a sense that I'm walking shared songlines. The same delineation a cartographer might cinch to show steepness, when topography lines tighten and then overlap to depict a high place. Or a thin place, perhaps, encroaching on enlightenment. In its way, another virtual vision quest.

The throughway we're on hasn't changed but has gained a new name; no longer Highway 99, it's become Highway 1, the Trans-Canada. Still in the van, our direction shifts with the road, southeast to due south, as we cross Burrard Inlet again, this time at the Second Narrows on the Ironworkers Memorial Bridge.

In an old engineering text, I find a terse but complete overview of the events that occurred when the previous bridge, partially built, crumpled into the narrows, killing nineteen people.

> On June 17, 1958, as a crane stretched from the north side of the new bridge to join the two chords of the unfinished arch, several spans collapsed. Seventy-nine workers plunged 30 metres (100 ft) into the water. Eighteen were killed either instantly or shortly thereafter, possibly drowned by their heavy tool belts. A diver searching for bodies drowned later, bringing the total fatalities for the collapse to 19. In a subsequent Royal Commission inquiry, the bridge collapse was attributed to miscalculation by bridge engineers.[23]

Beyond tragic, and entirely due to human error. A lower rail-crossing bridge is still here and still active, for trains crossing the water to service the ports. This higher span, catering to commuters, now shuttles 130,000 vehicles daily over this easterly throat of the channel, double the volume that crosses the First Narrows on Lions Gate Bridge. Both spans, it would seem, are now stretched well beyond their capacity.[24]

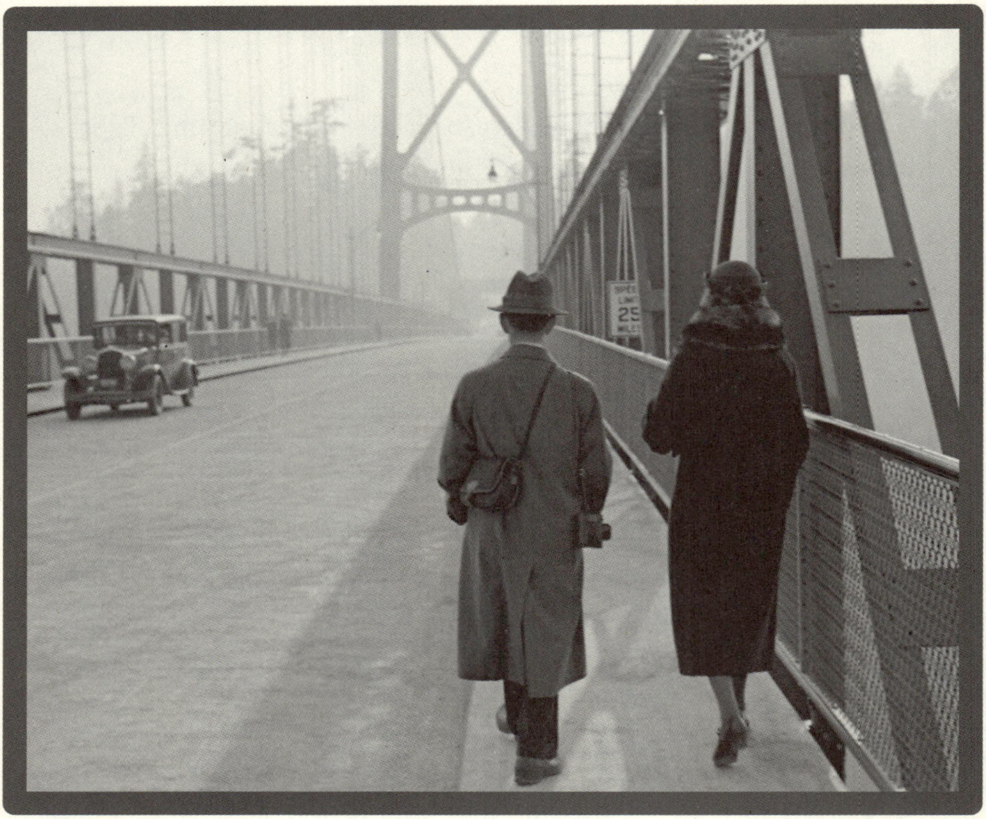

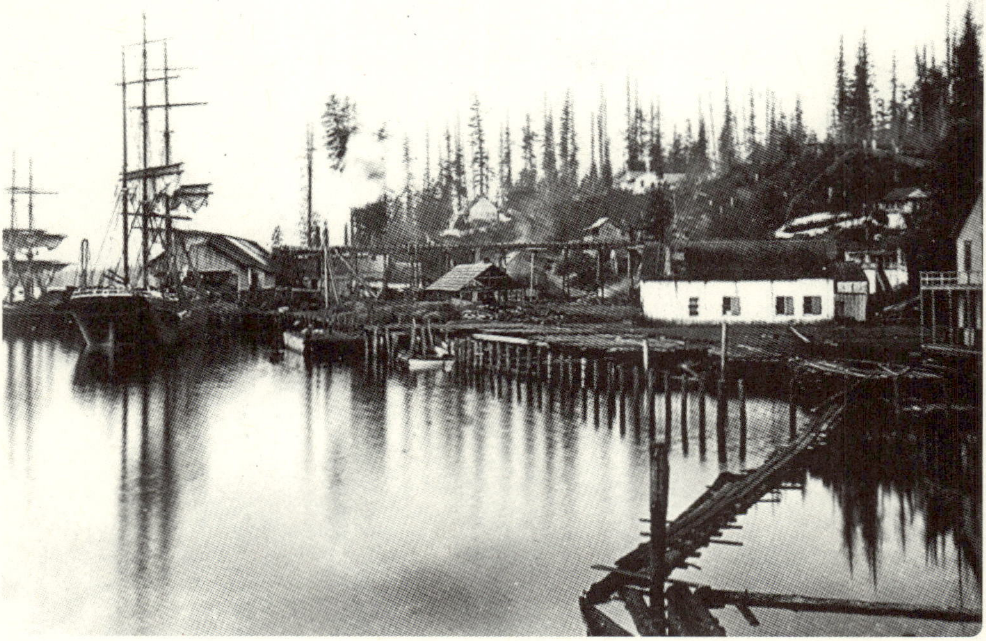

TOP: crossing Lions Gate Bridge on foot, 1939.
BOTTOM: Moodyville Sawmill, 1882–90.

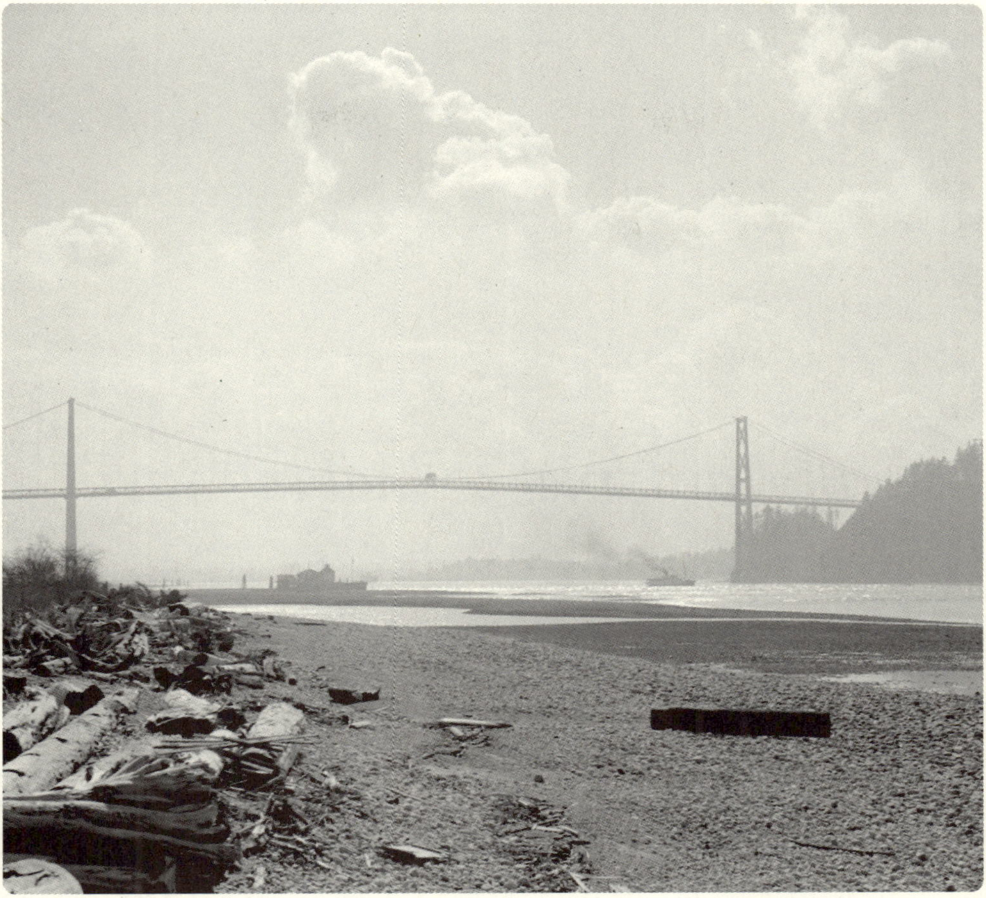

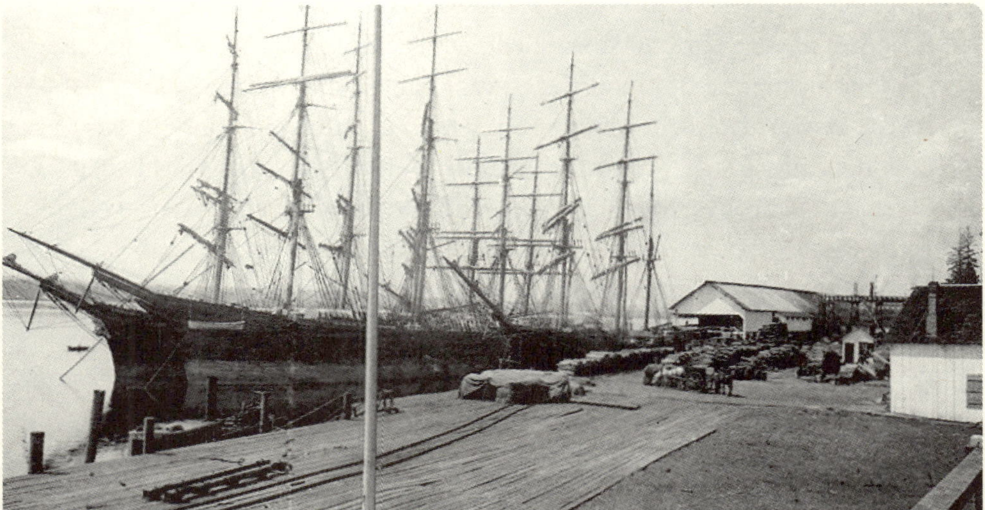

TOP: Ambleside, looking east toward a new Lions Gate Bridge, 1939.
BOTTOM: ships loading lumber at Moodyville, 1888–89.

Burrard Inlet to Indian Arm

END OF THE LINE, FOR A TIME

DUE EAST IS PORT MOODY, one end of the inlet and, for a time, the culmination of the first transnational rail line. It was the summer of 1886 when CPR Engine 371, diesel black with a coating of dust, pulled into the port, the first scheduled "Pacific Express" and inaugural transcontinental train journey. A year later, a slightly newer locomotive, Engine 374, which is now on display in Yaletown's Roundhouse Community Centre, continued west from Port Moody on freshly laid track to Vancouver, hauling 150 excited and overdressed passengers to the wood-planked terminal at the edge of Coal Harbour.

Where that engine arrived to disgorge its passengers was Kanaka Ranch, the farmland of Mary See-em-ia, Eihu, and Joe Nahanee. *Kanaka* was a term used by Polynesians to define themselves, and the Kanakas who were here at the time were predominantly Native Hawaiians.

Mary's land, however, was expropriated by the CPR, consistent with countless land seizures spearheaded by government and industry. Despite the fact that the land was the established homestead of Mary and her family, the CPR forced them out with threats of violence.

Articulate and passionate, Mary took up her fight with rail officials and government, but agents responded by burning her farmhouse and barn. Fearing for the safety of those around them, Mary, Eihu, and Joe moved their family across the water to the north side of Burrard Inlet, where they re-established themselves on the same shore as Mary's grandfather, Chief Joe Capilano.

Our van exits the highway, an off-ramp curving west, as the Trans-Canada bends eastward to meet with the rail again, as the ribbons of concrete and steel make their arduous way to the next ocean over. Craning back in my seat, I can make out Deep Cove and the last north-probing arm of Burrard Inlet, still known as Indian Arm, BC's most southerly fjord.

The proper name for the channel is səl̓ilw̓ət, which translates to "People of the Inlet" in the hən̓q̓əmin̓əm̓ language and applies to all of Burrard Inlet. This body of water, these shores, are the place from which the səlilwətaɬ (Tsleil-Waututh) name is derived.[25]

Up until that first iteration of Moodyville vanished, the Tsleil-Waututh used Burrard Inlet and the fjord of səl̓ilw̓ət in the same manner as the roadway our van is now on. Cedar canoes were the main form of transport. Food staples were salmon and herring, waterfowl and clams, maintaining the same sustainable balance Mary fostered on the grassland and beach at Kanaka. Tides paced the day, determining when harvests shifted from gathering to hunting, scouring shoreline or paddling deepwater. Like elsewhere on the inlet, the səl̓ilw̓ət watershed served as throughway, food storage, and home all in one. Trails criss-crossed the region, both water and land, with each route a line of communication. Defence from marauders was paramount too. According to the Bill Reid Centre,

> Oral histories, supported by the archaeological record, tell of the existence of lookout stations and large defensive structures that fenced in villages and would have been instrumental in protecting the səlilwətaʔɬ from external raiders.[26]

On a map, this arm of the inlet, səl̓ilw̓ət or Indian Arm, resembles a smaller version of Howe Sound, a fjord of granite sloping to sea. I can stand on a beach here facing any direction and feel that I could be almost anywhere. Anywhere, that is, in the Pacific Northwest, each view revealing quintessential terrain of the region: evergreen coast with salal, frequent fog, and plenty of rain.

These outlooks, these views, were the starting point of many personal water-bound journeys. Some in a kayak launched from Deep Cove, where a view from the sky, a satellite image, makes the watery arm reminiscent of an inverse Rose Spit, shifting land into water, its top end like a north-pointing finger. Another place of creation, but rather than clams on the sand filled with people, the shores remain rugged, sharp seascapes of timber and rock with their tight topographical lines.

To the south is the T-junction of Burrard Inlet on its way to Port Moody, where tankers can be found at the base of Burnaby Mountain. Paddling away from Deep Cove, you pass the peninsular point of Belcarra and the small islands named Hamber, Boulder, and Grey Rocks. To the north, you find Cosy Cove and Jug Island. Beyond that, Raccoon Island and Twin Islands.

The west side of the arm does, however, offer pockets of shore with creek outflows and places to dock or relaunch, what a paddler might call "put-in points." And apart from one embarrassing flip in the shallows, I was taught well by a kayak instructor named Robyn who trained me in the stroke basics—forward and backward, sweep, draw, and pry—and, perhaps most important, how to look cool while doing them. A highlight of this was learning to spin a paddle around your neck and shoulders in a nifty baton-twirl move that gives the impression of competence, irrespective of actual capability. It reminded me of culinary school, when we learned to spin pans and toss knives long before we really knew how to use them. But again, we liked to believe that we looked awfully good.

Other trips up that stretch of səl̓ilw̓ət took me powering north in a motorboat. An hour or two, based on tides and our speed, to a series of camps near Thwaytes Landing Regional Park, waterfront stretching between the bases of Mount Seymour, Mount Elsay, and Mount Bishop, with Croker Island and Say Nuth Khaw Yum Provincial Park.

It's hard to believe that you're still more or less at the edge of Vancouver, if measured via raven or crow. But the travel time needed—transport and transfers on buses or the SeaBus, then car, boat, and foot—make it feel like a proper excursion, an expedition "beyond." On those travels, I worked with youth groups. Not team building, as such, but transitional treks akin to those alternate vision quests. Sessions were referred to as "leadership training" for young adults, bringing to mind the early days of Chief Joe encouraging those who might one day offer guidance to others.

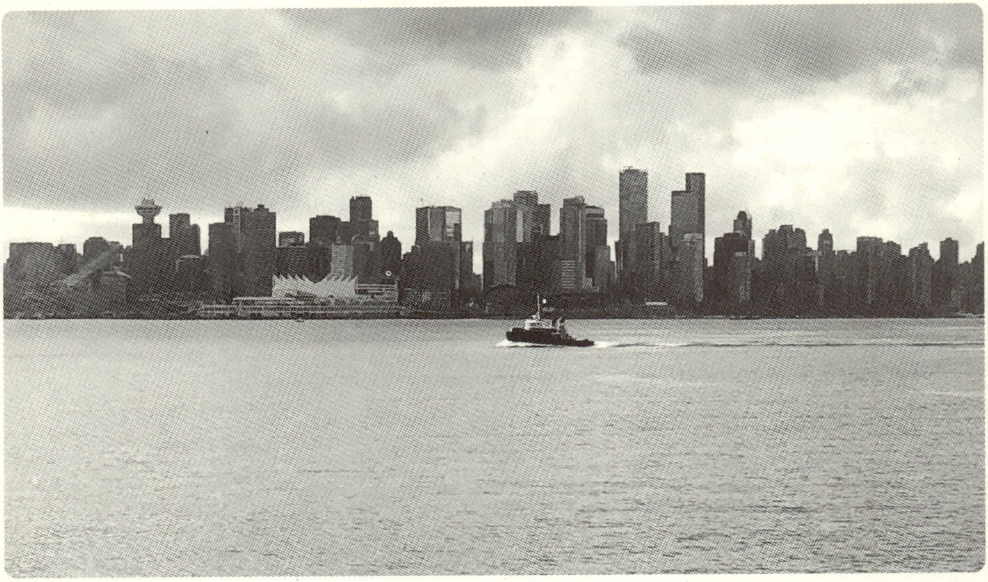

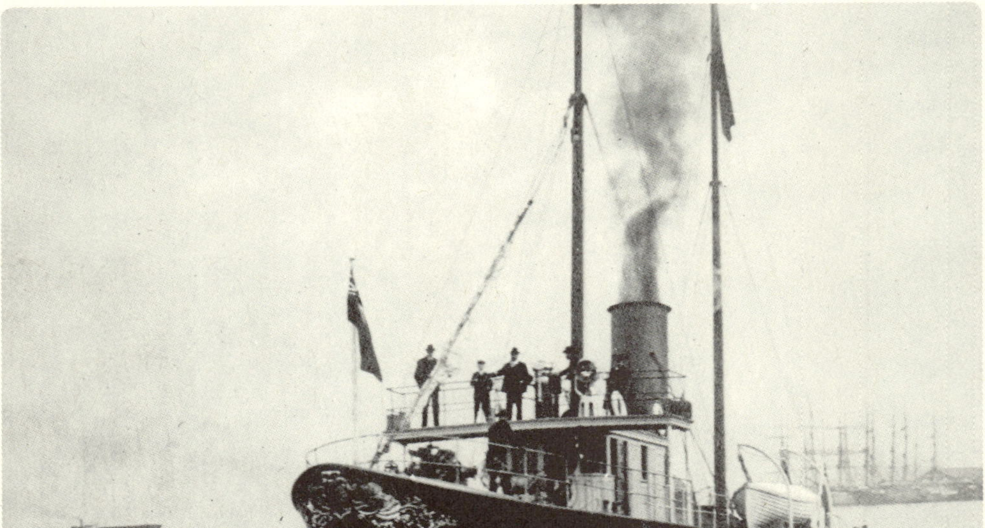

TOP: a tugboat bearing east through Burrard Inlet.
BOTTOM: the *Kestrel* in Burrard Inlet, 1899.

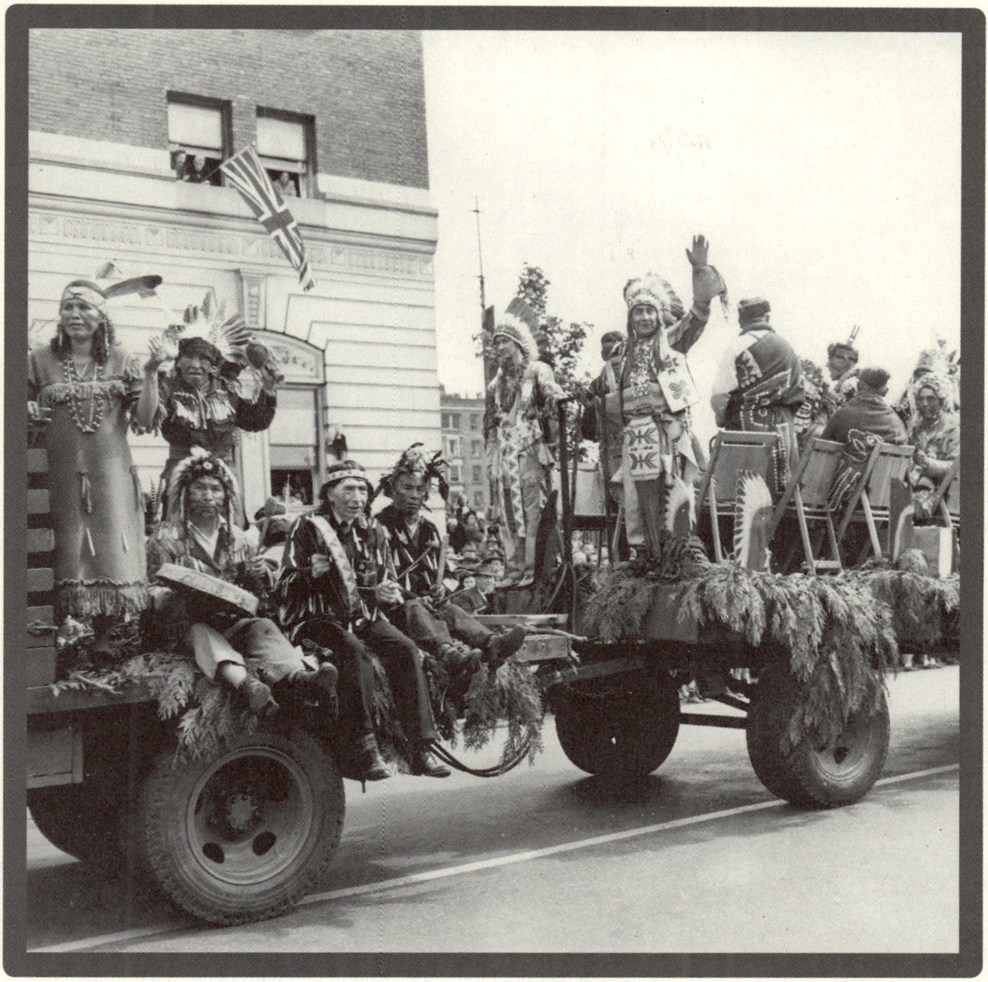

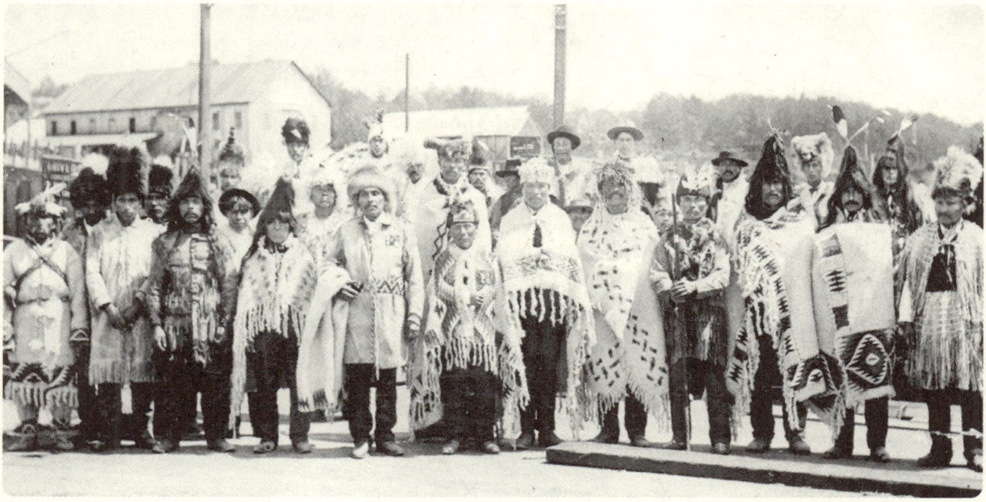

TOP: August Jack Khatsahlano, seated in centre, 1946.
BOTTOM: Chief Joe Capilano with Elders at the North Van ferry dock, 1906.

Waterside Healing

THE STORY OF MR. MANN, THE BROKEN CAT

NO SCUBA DIVING or kayaking today, but I'm still near the water, where I see a little travel trailer, striped orange and brown, parked with a shiny white pickup. As a lover of small camping trailers, I strike up a conversation with its owner, Craig, who seems happy to chat about his pristine, tiny home on two wheels. Six, if we're counting the truck.

Craig shares his story. Retired in his forties, he took to the gym, with occasional day labour and odd jobs. Fitness and training, however, were his passions, until a debilitating spinal condition ended all that. An unusual compounding of deterioration and injury relegated Craig to an excruciating combination of prescription narcotics, bedrest, and a shuffling gait that, as he puts it, made him "look like a drunk."

A series of specialists explained that if he were to be operated on, regardless of who did it or how, he would assuredly be left a quadriplegic. All he could do was wait and hopefully heal. After two years Craig gave up the pain pills, although he still staggered and swayed as his spine did its best to send signals, to communicate with his brain. Then, one day eight years later, Craig awoke without any pain.

"Not only could I walk, and walk straight, but I felt I could run!"

At which point he redrew his life, reconfiguring his experience. A radically different outcome to that story of the sailor trapped in a bubble. Suddenly, remarkably, the walls of Craig's cosmos dissolved, freeing him to go anywhere and to do as he pleased. So he took to the road, a modern-day nomad.

"I'm a bachelor," he explains. "Always have been. So it was just me. And I was parked one day, staying put for a while, when I saw this cat, a big ginger, get hit by a car. Didn't quite kill him but destroyed his tail. Mangled it pretty good. And I scooped up the cat—no collar, no home as far as I could tell—and took him to the vet. Vet said he had to cut off the tail. And I looked at the cat and said, 'No, don't do that.' Then I took the cat with me, called him Mr. Mann."

"Two *n*'s?" I ask.

"Of course," Craig says, as if it's a stupid question, which it is.

"Anyway, two years later, I'm watching TV. Mr. Mann's on the floor between me and the set, and I see the tip of his tail give a twitch. Just a little flick. And I knew he was healed, like me."

All I can do is nod, having no real point of reference and yet understanding it all.

The inside of the trailer, by the way, is just what you'd want it to be: cozy and perfect for a traveller and a four-legged companion. Healing bodies embracing a new world.

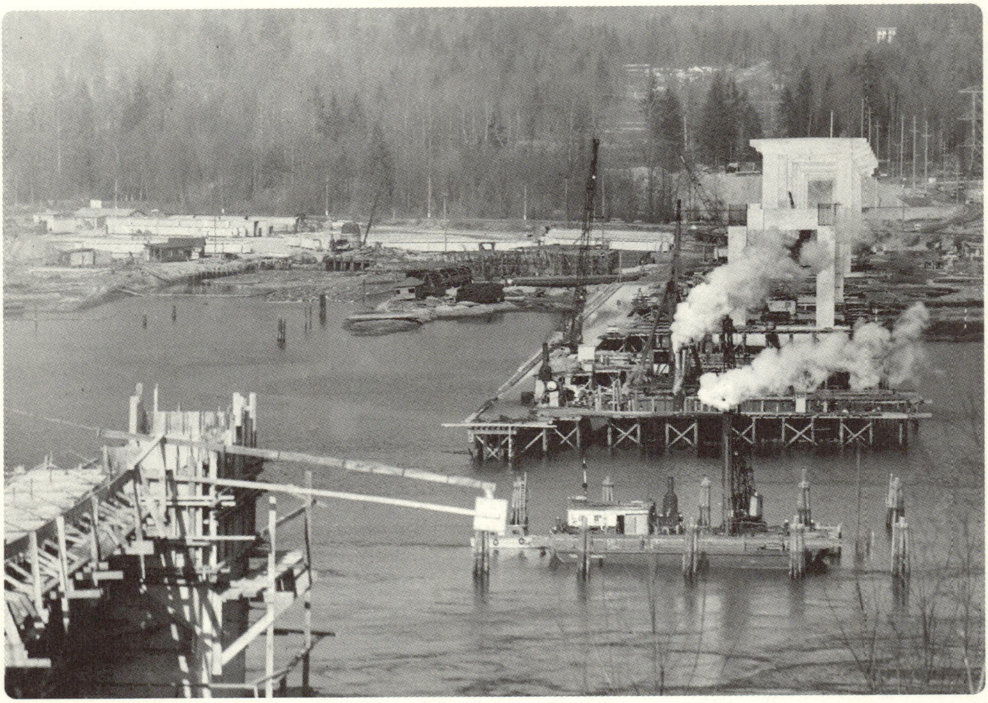

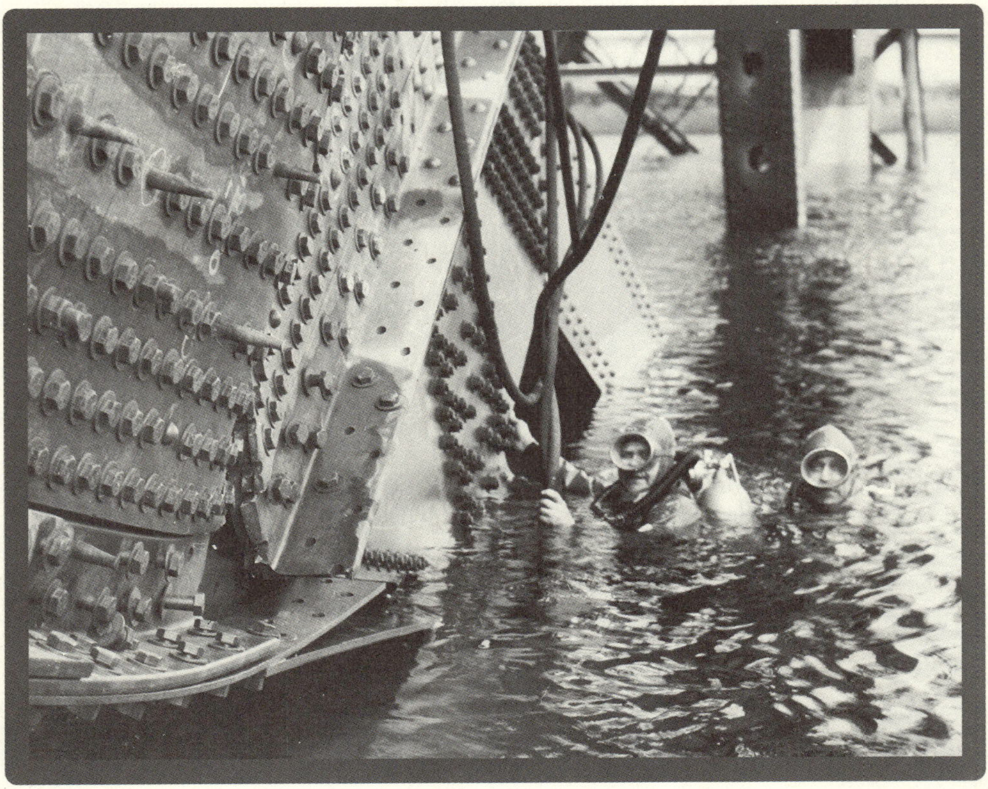

TOP: Second Narrows Bridge construction, 1956.
BOTTOM: rescue divers at the Second Narrows Bridge collapse, 1958.

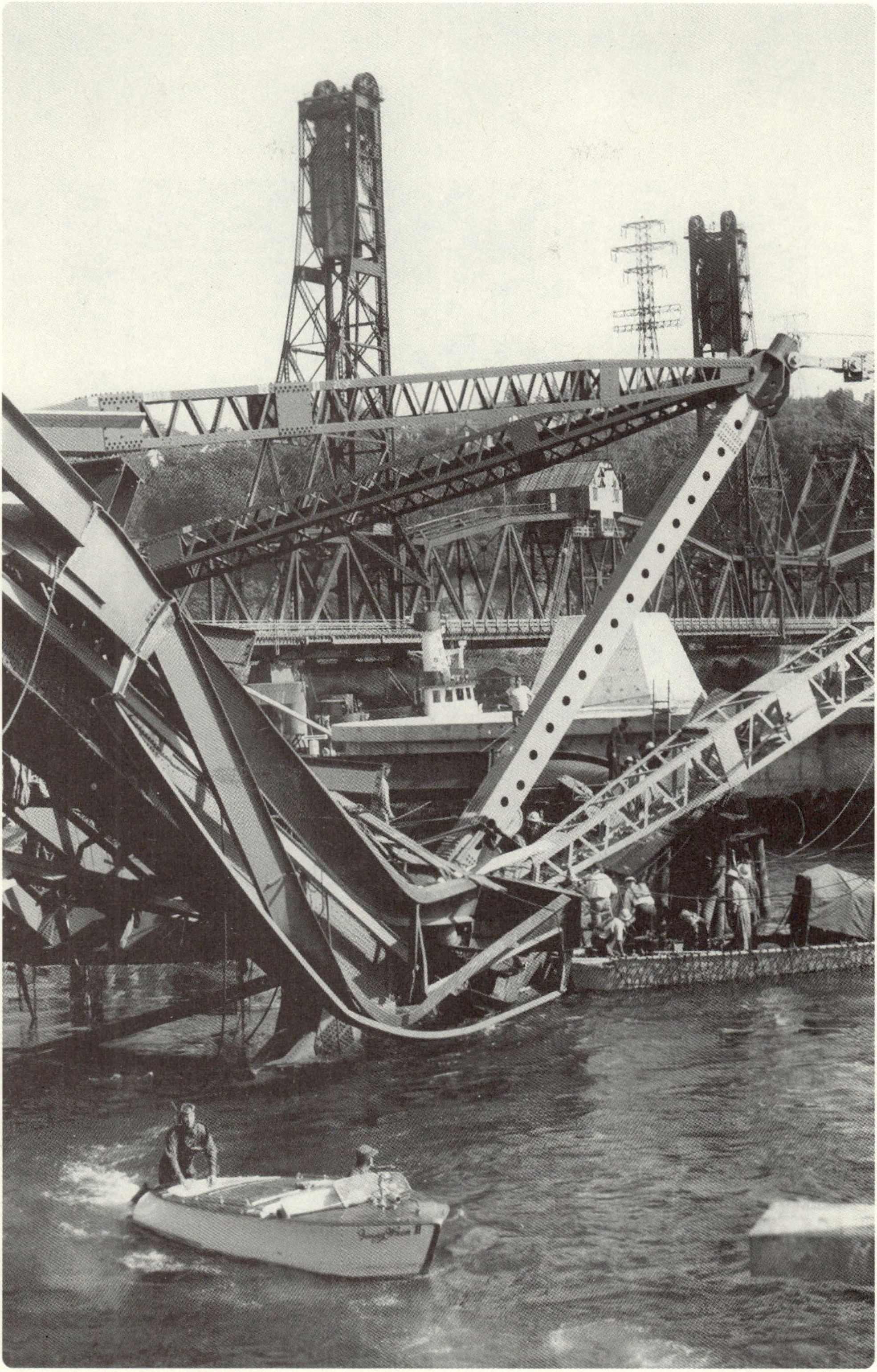

Second Narrows Bridge wreckage and rescue attempt, 1958.

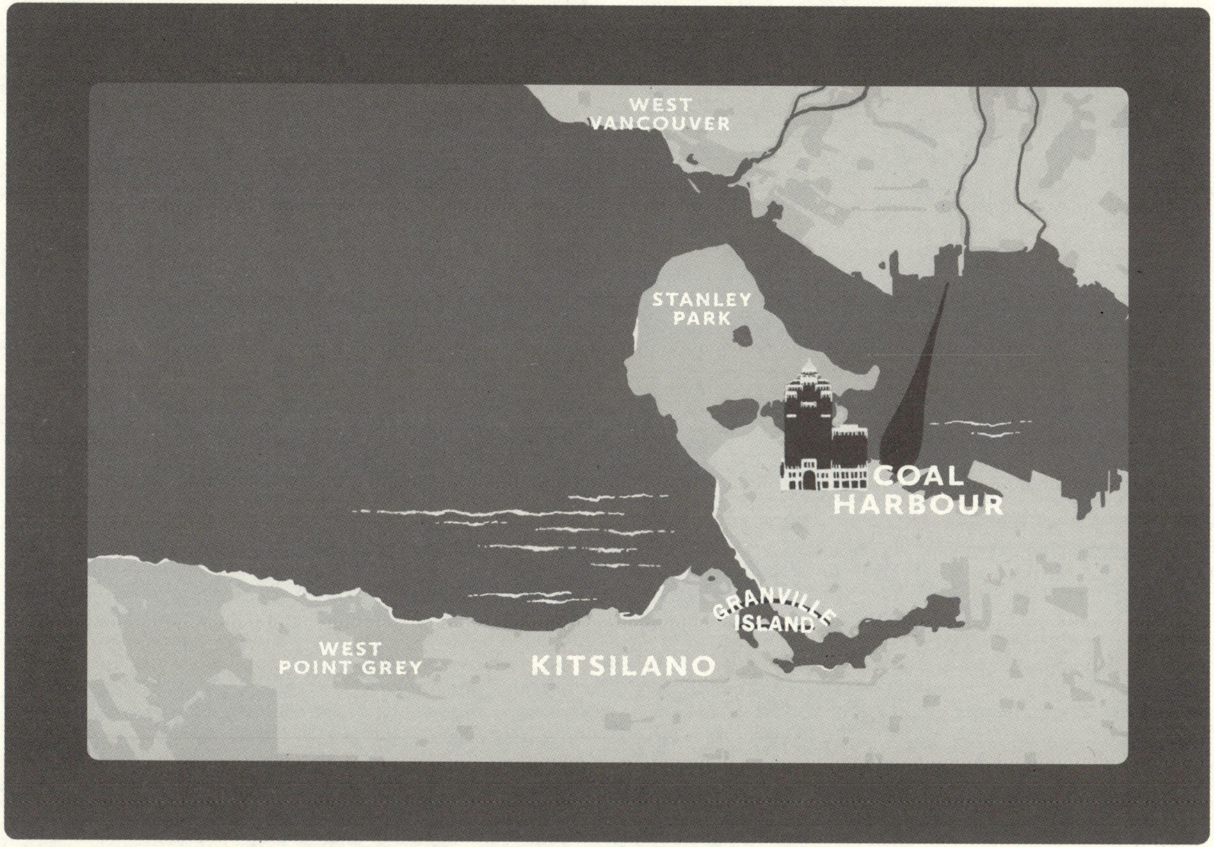

WEST VANCOUVER
STANLEY PARK
COAL HARBOUR
GRANVILLE ISLAND
WEST POINT GREY
KITSILANO

COAL HARBOUR *and* GRANVILLE ISLAND

Kits to Coal Harbour

SNAUQ AND KANAKA

PICKING UP WHERE I last left the shore prior to those days underwater, I'm at the south end of Burrard Bridge, the east edge of Kits, to resume my walk at Seńák̲w, August Jack's home of Snauq. False Creek Ferries are mincing the inlet under the rapid flight of some cormorants. For a sense of the place, a refresher, I revisit the City of Vancouver's neighbourhood summary, which names Kits Beach as one of the "top 10 best city beaches in the world." The article continues with a glance to the past:

> At the turn of the century, the area from Burrard to Alma Streets was a dense, wildlife-filled forest, in spite of earlier logging. A salmon canning factory at the foot of Macdonald Street was once unable to cope with the "hundreds of thousands of salmon" caught in 1900.[27]

Stopping here, where waterfowl bob, I spot buffleheads, mallards, wood ducks, and a glaucous-winged gull doing nonchalant aerobatics, no doubt planning a heist on the others. Then a kingfisher plunges, strikes the water, and emerges with a fingerling. There's a glint as the bird lands, fish in beak, to brain its prey mercilessly against a rock. *Wham! Wham! Wham!* The little fry is assuredly dead, probably from the first crushing blow. *Wham! Wham! Wham!* Now it strikes me as comical. *Wham! Wham! Wham!* Okay, now it's unsettling. *Wham! Wham! Wham!* And now it's disturbing. *Wham! Wham! Wham!* There's no sign of it stopping, and I feel like I've stumbled into a Scorsese film, so I take my leave, done with nature for now.

The image lingers, so I shift to recollection of fish collectively. Sure, I've done my share of skull bashing while fishing, but nothing as horrific as *that*. I hope the kingfisher enjoys its meal of fish paste. Then I consider that historical stat of commercial salmon pulled from this water: hundreds of thousands of fish, more than the cannery could handle. A stark contrast to the sustainable harvests practised by Seṅák̲w's first residents.

Which brings to mind a visual from when I walked around Stanley Park, south to north and under the Lions Gate Bridge. Salmon that day were leaping in numbers, a "rise," we might call it when fishing. Flashes of silver like musclebound gems. Splashes rang like wet slaps, and I longed for a fly rod and gear. But I had to satisfy myself with memories of being aboard a boat that launched from Coal Harbour, a twenty-five-foot Bayliner Trophy that I chartered for a day, its moorage at the network of piers near the Vancouver Rowing Club, former Kanaka Ranch land. My skipper was Jon, and the two of us burbled our way to the inlet, toward the same spot where those salmon were leaping.

From Coal Harbour Marina, we steered the boat north and east, curling past Deadman's Island and the HMCS *Discovery* Naval Reserve. One story in particular resonates around this small isle, a geological toe to what's now Stanley Park. With nearly 360 degrees of accessible shore and yet still attached to the mainland, this islet was prime real estate for gathering seafood. I've read that this tidal pocket of land was a conflict point among Indigenous locals. And at some point, before Joe Capilano was Chief, rival bands fought frequently here. In 1862, when Joe was a child, settler John Morton traipsed the island's perimeter with an eye to harvesting its softwood. What he found, however, was a place of interment. Not in the ground, but high overhead. Cedar mortuary boxes had been placed in the uppermost evergreen boughs, coffins suspended between branches. In lieu of flowers, a dusting of needles and cones. Morton felt it was ghoulish, macabre, an upending of what he believed "proper" burial should be.

Details are sketchy, but records indicate Morton spoke with Joe's father, or possibly his grandfather, a previous Chief Capilano, who relayed the story of a battle that took place in this spot. There was mention of "northern" and "southern" tribes, and a skirmish in which people were kidnapped. Raids of this kind weren't uncommon, at times to find slaves, at other times to find spouses. Haida warriors, for example, were known to paddle this coast, marauding and hunting. Other Indigenous Peoples who lived farther south also came here, along the same routes now used by ferries and cruise lines. The story goes on to describe a hostage exchange, women and children for young "foreign" warriors. But the swap was a ruse, and once women and children were safely returned, locals slaughtered the warriors, sending a clear, violent message.[28]

Parts of the story, however, don't ring true. Particularly with respect to those bodies suspended in coffins. Who were these fallen people? Foreign warriors? Raiders? Yes, at times a corpse might be "strung up" to indicate the deceased was a "villain"—thieves hung from the Tower of London, for example, or heads stuck on pikes. No different than drug cartels using grisly tactics to keep others in line. But I can't fathom the fabrication of burial boxes to inter mortal foes. Certainly, honorary rites might sometimes be used for the funeral of an enemy. But on such a scale, I'm not sure I buy it. When I went to "the end of the world," to Haida Gwaii, which may have been where those warriors came from, I saw mortuary poles with boxes, the same cedar construction, high in oceanside pines, there to show honour, respect. And in no way could I imagine that same ceremony and effort orchestrated for anything else.

I also consider celebrations I've joined—Indigenous mask dances with storytelling and song—some here in the city, others on Salish Sea islands. Those legends, shared through drum beat and the *clack* of raven-beak masks, don't often conclude. Rarely is there a "happily ever after" or even "the end." Life doesn't play out that way. Every ending starts a new saga, and conclusions are, of course, continuity. No doubt this story too, with its "deadman burials" raised to the sky, has different versions based on the storyteller or who's hearing the tale, leaving us with only a sense of what may or may not have happened.

Continuing east from Burrard Bridge toward Granville Island, I can't shake thoughts of fishing and fish. When Jon and I trolled the First Narrows under Lions Gate Bridge, we were, in effect, fishing the outflow of the Capilano River, where freshwater meets salt. Through the summer and fall, small fishing boats are common, anglers hoping to catch river-bound salmon.

The first fish I hooked on that day was a "jack," a salmon not yet four years old. An adolescent, you could say, still thriving in saltwater, not yet ready to return to its birthplace. It was a healthy fish, maybe two kilos, and as I put it back in the water, it gave a good slap of its tail to douse me rather indignantly before vanishing into emerald water. I liked its attitude, a surly teen with a swagger, and thought of those vision quest treks, coming of age, and new leadership. Maybe I was overthinking it, feeling romantic at sea. Regardless, it was a good visual, a nice feeling too. Grasping something alive, a near hitch in time, putting nature on hold for a moment, then letting it go. In that I found a true sense of sport, my own version of sustainable management.

More time elapsed before I hooked a proper-sized fish, a six-kilo chinook. A whack of the priest, one clean blow with a club, and I had my catch for the day. Back in Coal Harbour we tied off Jon's boat, and I filleted my salmon at a table built onto the dock. Jon gave me a nudge and jutted his chin to the water to indicate we had company. A harbour seal surfaced, looked directly at us, and winked. *No, that can't be*, I thought. But as the seal bobbed there, staring, I realized it had only one eye, the permanent wink of a friendly, inquisitive selkie.

It occurred to me that "Wink" knew exactly what I was doing and was hoping for handouts. I didn't stop to think about it, and what I did is a no-no, feeding the wildlife. But I tossed the seal the neatly skinned remnants—salmon head, tail, and skeleton—which struck the water with a *plaap*, then floated with surprisingly lifelike movement. The seal, however, didn't simply snatch the free meal but instead circled and dove to take the carcass from beneath, simulating the hunt, lunging to the surface and chomping the skeletal fish from below. And with a violent, bone-snapping shake, Wink crunched through the head, spraying salmon-meat flecks and offering another unfiltered look at a circle of life.

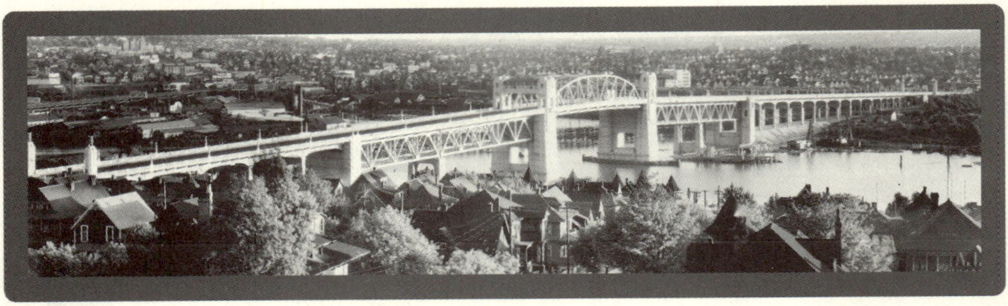

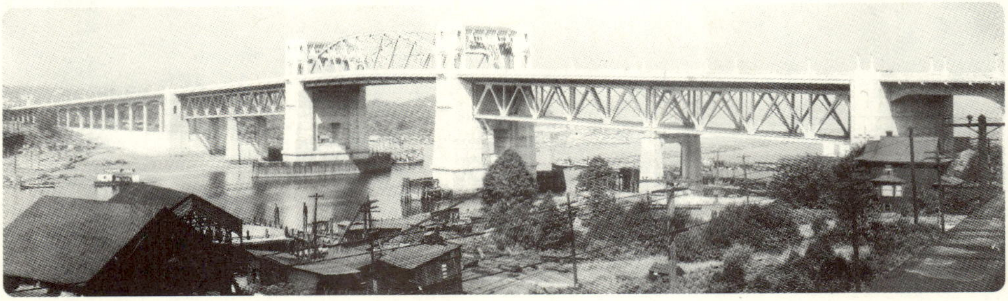

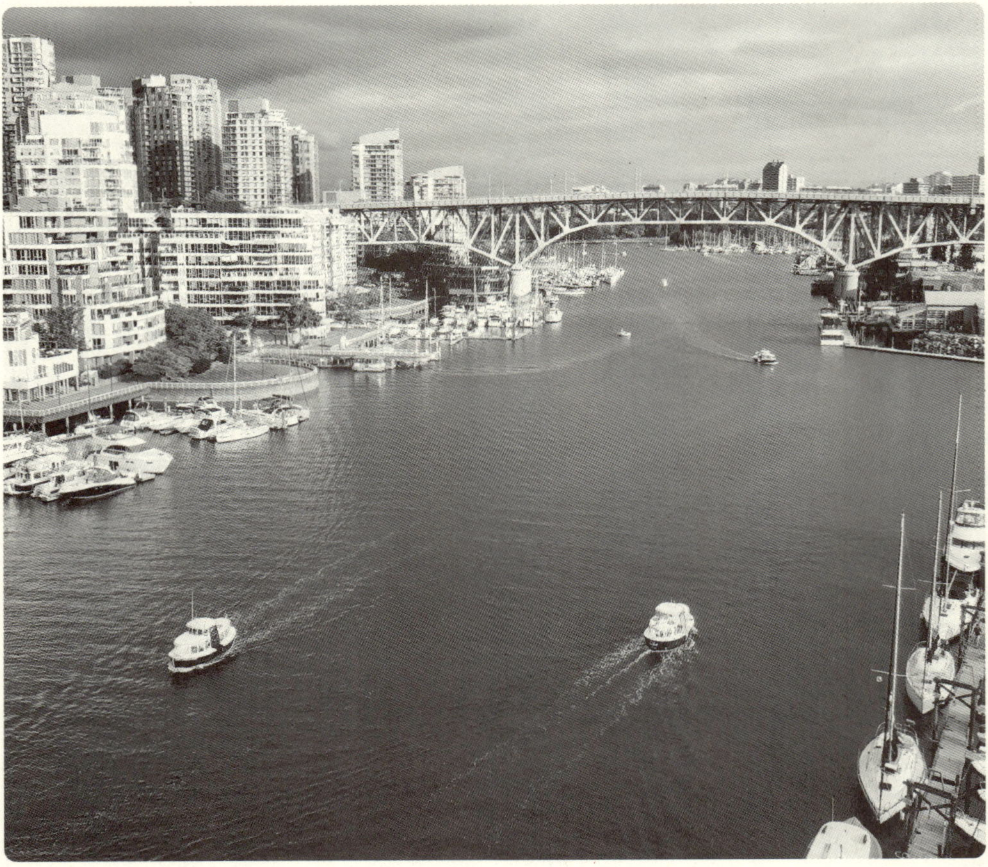

TOP TO BOTTOM: Burrard Bridge just after its completion, looking southeast, 1932; Burrard Bridge, looking southwest, 1933; passing ferries, looking east to Granville Street Bridge.

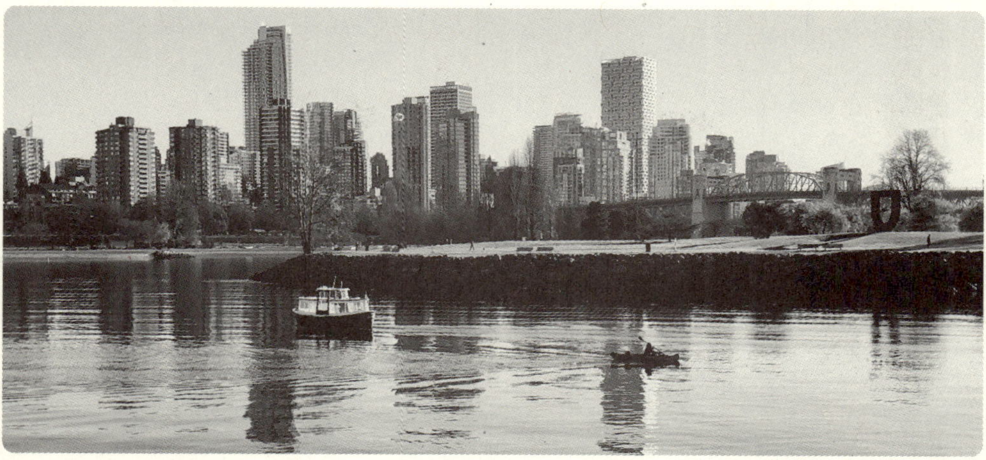

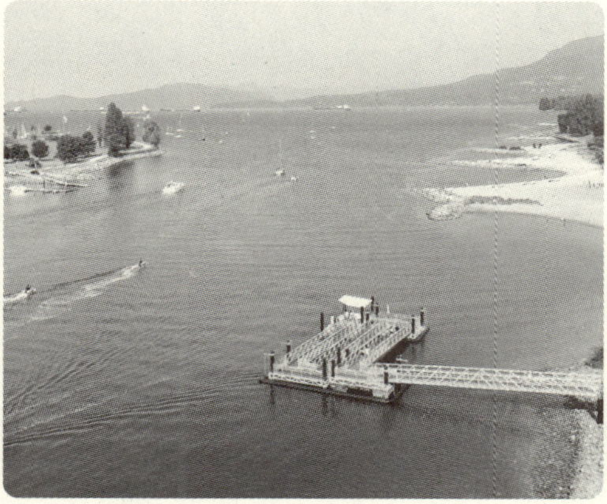

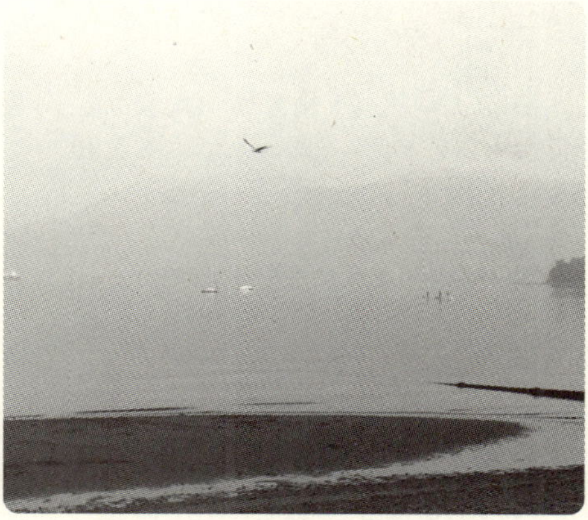

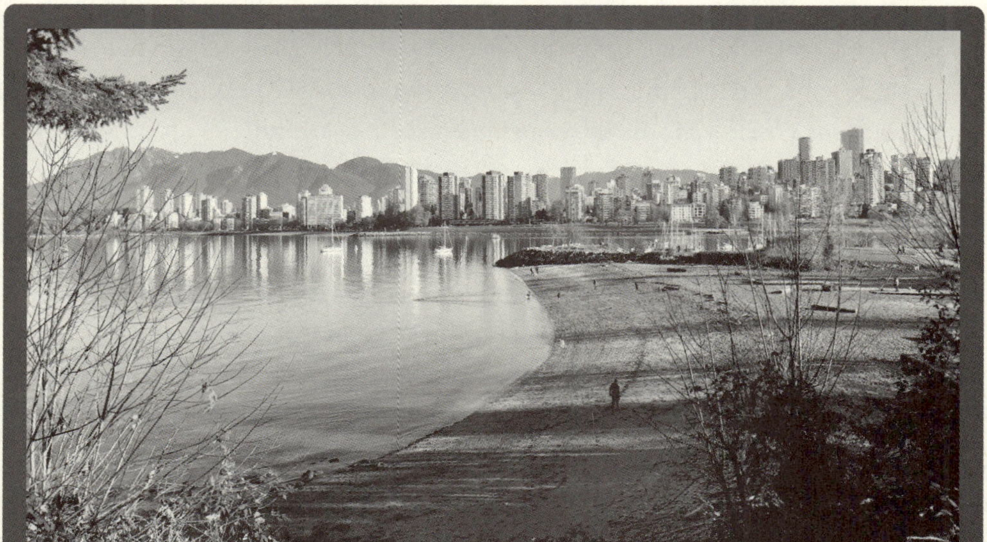

CLOCKWISE FROM TOP: a ferry and a kayak at Kits Point, downtown to the north; a gull in fog at Kits Beach, looking northwest; Hadden Beach, looking north; looking west from Burrard Bridge.

Fisherman's Wharf

OPEN ARMS OF THE HARBOUR

A NEW DAY ON FOOT—no bus, no car—and I'm following the Seawall on False Creek's south side. A gull nibbles crab, and crows are shucking mussels with a rhythmic *clack-clack*. From the walkway I find the False Creek Harbour Authority, where a gangway leads to public fish sales: spot prawns, tuna, and salmon. A sign reads "Fisherman's Wharf Harbour Office." Moths flitter between shrubs, and there's an echoey gull's cry with the peep of another, their tones like an out-of-tune choir.

With an eye to the birds, I consider the neighbourhood from an imagined sky view. This is the region of Fairview, sandwiched between Burrard Street in the west and Cambie Street in the east. Another south border of West 16th Avenue and a north edge of water. Here the area curves with False Creek, as Granville Island extends like a thumb, hitching a ride toward the sea.

Which today is jade green, a flat mirror. I have company too. An untimid crow hops beside me, nearly slipping between my legs as I walk. Sun strikes the Harbour Office door, and I think of previous walks when I used a time-travelling app to visit an imagined Vancouver in 1948. As

I scrolled city streetscapes on my screen, a lit door indicated that with a touch I could travel to *there*, learn a story, and be immersed in new places. A door glowing in light just like this.

The glass entry swings inward, no ding of a bell, just a smile and "good morning" from Turk, who's standing behind a short counter, wearing a crisp blue Harbour Authority cap. Behind Turk is Nicole, running office admin, who offers another smile, and without even calling ahead, I'm welcomed and shown around.

"We're a non-profit," Turk says. "And we take care of the commercial fishers. This all started in 1952, I think." He grins, facial piercings adding a gleam. "Everyone's welcome here. And our harbour's a healthy one, thriving. The only one here in the city. There's Steveston, of course. But here, in the city, the harbour, it's like a fishbowl, a good one, and we're at the heart of it." He strikes me as someone who likes what he does and seems happy to help.

On a wall is a calendar outlining seasonal catches: salmon, shellfish, and whitefish. Turk elaborates on what I'm looking at. "The commercial fishers are aging out: buyouts, buybacks, retirements. You used to be able to make a living just fishing salmon. Not anymore. There's young fishers coming up, sure, but they have to diversify: salmon, prawns, halibut, lingcod. Otherwise you need a separate day job to get by. It's mostly trollers now, line fishing, hardly any trawlers anymore. Although a few gillnetters still go out to get sole."

There's optimism here, pride of place. JC, a skipper, saunters in, leans on the counter, and joins our visit, while Nicole keeps working. No doubt this is what she sees every day, anglers talking fish and unwinding world problems.

Turk leads me to a few open boatsheds for a further look around. It's quiet, organized. From the sheds I move to the pier, check out boat names: *Native Nations*, *Estevan*, *Sundog*. Vessels in highly polished steel, some frosted in spume, others in Mediterranean hues. There's a gentle palette exchange with the water at the moment, blue boats on green water. If I had a jeweller's loupe to my eye, I might even say sapphire and emerald.

A few of the boats I can see are trawlers, which Turk said still fish for sole. These boats stand out, equipped with stern-driven spools for nets. Most of the vessels, however, have the vertical spears of long fishing poles, line gear for tuna and salmon. A few decks are stacked with round and square traps, equipment for crab and prawns.

What sounds like a castanet party ramps up, more crows cracking mussels on concrete. The tide must be dropping, revealing a buffet. There's something about these birds—they look ancient, with thin ruffled feathers and bald spots. I think of what Turk said, that anglers are older and aging, and wonder if it's the same across species.

He tells me a bit more about what the marina now offers. "We've got space for boaters to shower, do laundry. There's recycling, and we're keeping things clean. You know, care for the environment. Around here it's a healthy one. No restrictions or memberships. Everyone's welcome."

A sentiment that seems to pervade, and I find myself feeling just that: welcome.

"For a long time the feds ran things around here," Turk continues, "but they ran it poorly. You'd get staffers assigned here based on seniority. Folks from the Prairies, next on the pecking order, handed this, not knowing the first thing about it. But now it's well run, by a board of directors, commercial fishers. Occasionally the feds come in for large-scale things: infrastructure, dredging, and such, although we don't need to dredge here. Not anymore."

With thanks, I carry on, extending my saunter past bright painted sheds, each rolling garage-style door painted with fish designs: salmon and tuna, crab and prawns, geoduck clams, an octopus too, plus a fierce-looking lingcod, razor teeth lining its jaws.

Turk's back at work in the office but pops his head out the door and catches my eye, keen to share more. He points me toward the marina's common room space, where a bookshelf is laden with books. A lending library.

"Good pulp in there. Lots of romance," he laughs. "Out on the boat, a long stretch, you read anything!" He waves an arm. "Go on, take a look around. Everything's open."

A quick browse of titles—spy books and sexy man-chests—then I walk down a pier and strike up a conversation with Carolyn. Her spouse, Alden, is hosing and scrubbing their boat, a forty-two-foot trawler built in 1978 named *Argo Navis*. The boat's nautical blue, trimmed in white, with rich polished gunwales of hardwood, what looks like mahogany. Their dog, Archie, presses against my leg. There's a dock cart, the marina version of a wheelbarrow, loaded with gear.

"Heading out, or coming in?" I ask.

"Just got back. Two weeks away," Carolyn says.

"Where've you been?"

"Over to Comox. Then up the coast. Powell River and Desolation Sound."

"Sounds nice."

"Yeah, we saw whales. Took the kayak out." Now I notice their inflatable kayak jammed in the cockpit. "Got out in the dinghy as well."

At the stern of the boat is their dinghy. A RHIB-style motorized tender.

"Do you fish?" I ask.

"Not as a trawler, no. Just recreational." The boat, she explains, is owned by four parties, equal ownership, one-quarter per party. "But we fish from the dinghy," she adds. "Casting and jigging for salmon and cod. And throw traps for crab and for prawns."

"What do you think of the water here on the coast?" I ask.

"Oh, it's relaxing. Every time out feels like a holiday. You understand, we're not fishing for a living. But it's peaceful being on the water."

Together we peer from the pier. Minnows riffle the water, adding a sheen to the green. We exchange smiles and waves, and I leave them to it—unloading, repacking, and scrubbing.

From the marina I follow the shore west to Seṅáḵw, where songbirds chitter in low branches. The inlet looks perfectly clear and healthy. Maybe it's the absence of boats, a turn of the tide, or maybe the efforts of people like Turk and Nicole.

I glance back to where *Argo Navis* is moored. Its deep blue is what I associate with old sailor's eyes, a life lived at sea. Not under it, like Nemo, but riding the water on days like this. Halcyon. I can almost, *almost* reflect warmly on those frightening days of high wind, when every sea lump, whaleback, roller, and even dirty bastard felt like a friend.

The False Creek Ferry *Spirit of Shelagh McInnis* toddles by, bobbing southwest from the Aquatic Centre toward the pier at the Maritime Museum. A few cyclists and joggers make their way around Vanier Park, while two picnickers sit on grass in a pocket of shade. Pleasure craft burble beneath Burrard Bridge, aiming for open water. Gravel scrunches underfoot, the ground chalky white. The Bard on the Beach Shakespeare Festival is in full swing, with red flag-topped tents adding a medieval flair.

At the False Creek Racing Canoe Club, I stop and visit with Lesley. A sign behind her reads "Canoe, Kayak, Outrigger, Dragon Boat," and I ask her which craft she prefers.

"OC," she says. "Outrigger canoes. I came from sailing, a sailing background. And with sailing, you need wind. But when you're paddling, you can go out anytime, which is nice." She nods at the water, still calm at the moment. "False Creek tends to be calmer. I'd say 90 percent of the time it's calm water. Unless an easterly kicks up, then everything on the inlet is choppy. In English Bay you get more swell, more chop, although this morning it was nice and calm there to start."

I ask for details, how the paddling works, and she runs through a primer.

"There's specific terminology: Paddles down, paddles up. Draw left, draw right. Hold the boat. That sort of thing." A smile. "Like being a midshipman, even though you do it all from the stern, from the tiller, which I did when I started OC. They figured I knew what was what from my time as a sailor, so they put me on tiller. You think it'd be easy, just another big tiller. It's not!" She shakes her head.

Bringing to mind a memory of watching a novice steer a boat the way Lesley described. A long multi-paddle outrigger. The slightest shift of the big steering paddle—the tiller—caused the boat to veer radically. No smooth turns or transition, just a violent tack that spun the boat in a tight little circle. The race route, however, was straight. Watching it play out was cringeworthy, a craft of such beauty mistreated.

"You should give it a try," Lesley adds. "Give OC a go. We get all ages and ranges of paddlers. We get a lot of breast cancer survivors joining our groups. It's excellent for fitness, reconditioning the upper body and rebuilding muscle. Plus the camaraderie." A grin, then a frown. "We take E. coli counts into consideration as well. The water can be ... you know." She shrugs. "Some people wear masks. Me, I try not to splash. Keep my mouth closed. Part of the experience, I suppose, paddling in the city. Even one with fairly clean water."

I wasn't always aware of E. coli counts. Just made a point of not gulping seawater when swimming and doing my best to go where the bay widens and the water perhaps has more turn.

I enjoy English Bay swims, same as Seraphim "Joe" Fortes, the beloved Vancouverite who lifeguarded around here. On my walks from the West End toward Stanley Park, Joe was there, in a way, his name on a library branch and a restaurant. Joe was a Black Caribbean immigrant who arrived here in 1885, when the city was not yet Vancouver but Granville. He rowed forestry supplies across the inlet, servicing logging camps. Even beyond his work, Joe loved the water, the beach, and the bay. According to Places That Matter,

> Joe defied the prejudices of the time, endearing himself to Vancouverites as the city's first Official Lifeguard. He also patrolled the area every night as a Special Constable of the Vancouver City Police. Thousands paid tribute to Joe at his civic funeral on February 7, 1922.[29]

If Joe's experience swimming these shores was the same as my own, he'd have clambered over seaweed and rock. There are pockets of sand, but I tend to choose private coves, avoiding the beach where sunbathers gather, preferring a sense of seclusion with the feel of coarse seabed below. I love being submerged while still in the midst of the city, high-rises nearby with the smell of a vendor grilling onions for hot dogs. Even with others close by, I can find separation, that immersion and oneness that only come from a dip in the sea. Yes, it's an inlet with islands beyond, but it's still, in its way, open water.

My most recent swim was at Kits. A quiet morning, and apart from a heron and a seal, the whole beach was empty. Sun snuck above the pavilion, adding warmth to the water, as much mental as physical. And I let myself float on my back, easy in saltwater, but a good mental shift just the same. A bit of air in the lungs, a tilt of the hips, and then gentle, shallow, but meditative breathing. That sense of connection and weightlessness the same as when I was diving, but with direct contact of ocean on skin, no equipment or gear. Just the aid of the saline, my lungs, and my mind. I could've stayed there and drifted all day. In a way I felt it was a seance with Joe. Peter Pantages too, founder of Vancouver's Polar Bear Club. Not that the water was icy, but it was that same feel of channelling others known for their love of the water.

Now, however, still on land, still in Kits, I skirt a forest of hardwood, cottonwoods mostly, where a sign warns of coyotes denning nearby. I can't imagine much wildlife apart from birds lasting long here as the construction around Seňáḵw continues. It was just a short time ago that I saw a coyote right there, maybe the one with the den, standing on the raised slope of land that served as one end of the swing bridge for trolleys and railcars, a wood crossing that once crossed False Creek on a diagonal from Granville Street to Burrard.

Now that last lump of land, which resembled a rampart that neolithic builders might have used to hoist standing stones, has been carved neatly through. The earthen lumps could pass for a trigonometry equation. What was previously an oblique triangle has been hacked into one wonky rhombus with a separate equilateral sibling. Making me realize that I owe Mrs. Hadland, my grade school teacher, an apology. I *did* end up using trigonometry, sort of. It just took fifty years.

The coyote I saw had stood at the highest point of the dirt ramp that's now gone. The colour of the two, the earth and the canine, were identical: buff cinnamon tones. Had the animal not turned to watch me with a piercing amber-eyed stare, there's no way I'd have seen it.

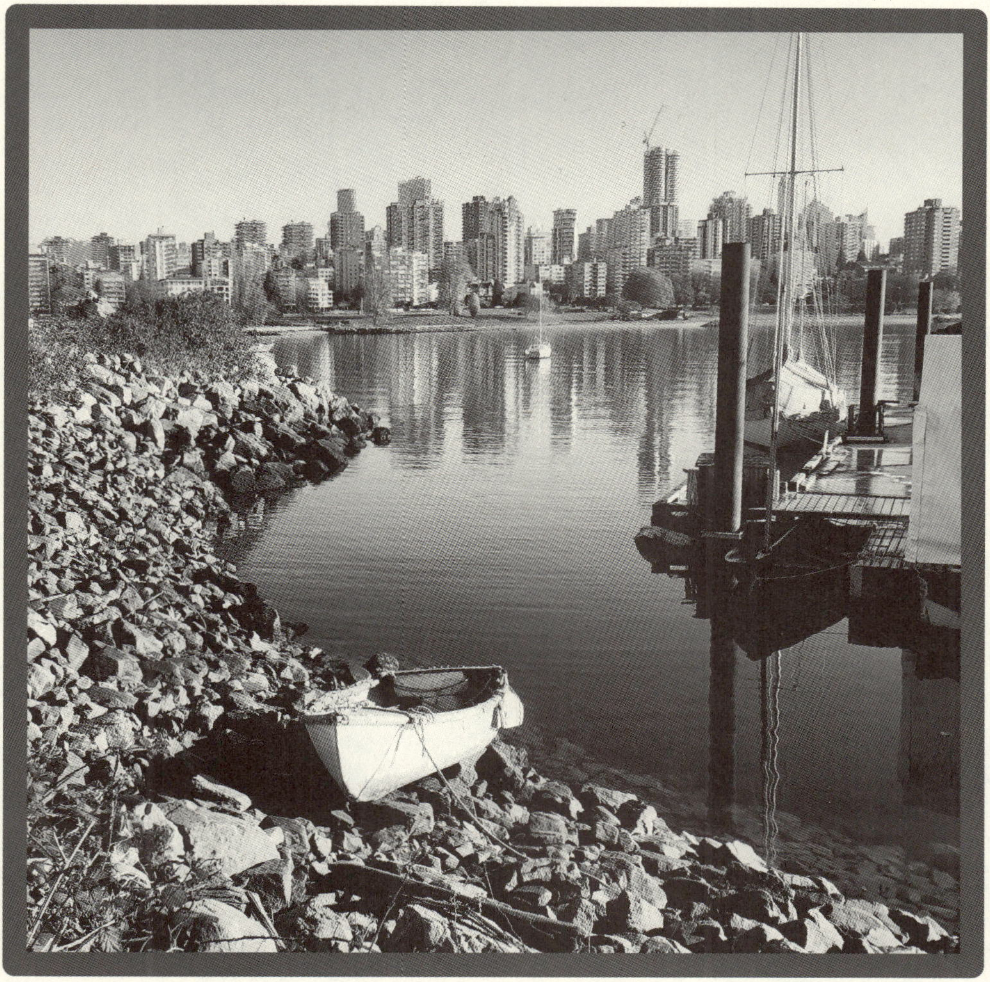

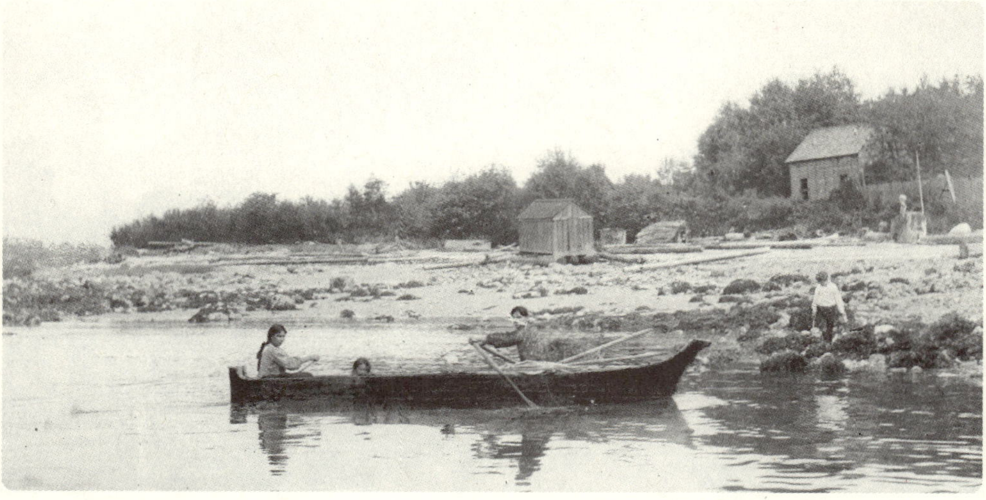

TOP: a rowboat at Elsje Point, near the Vancouver Maritime Museum.
BOTTOM: August Jack rowing and Swanamia paddling at Snauq, 1907.

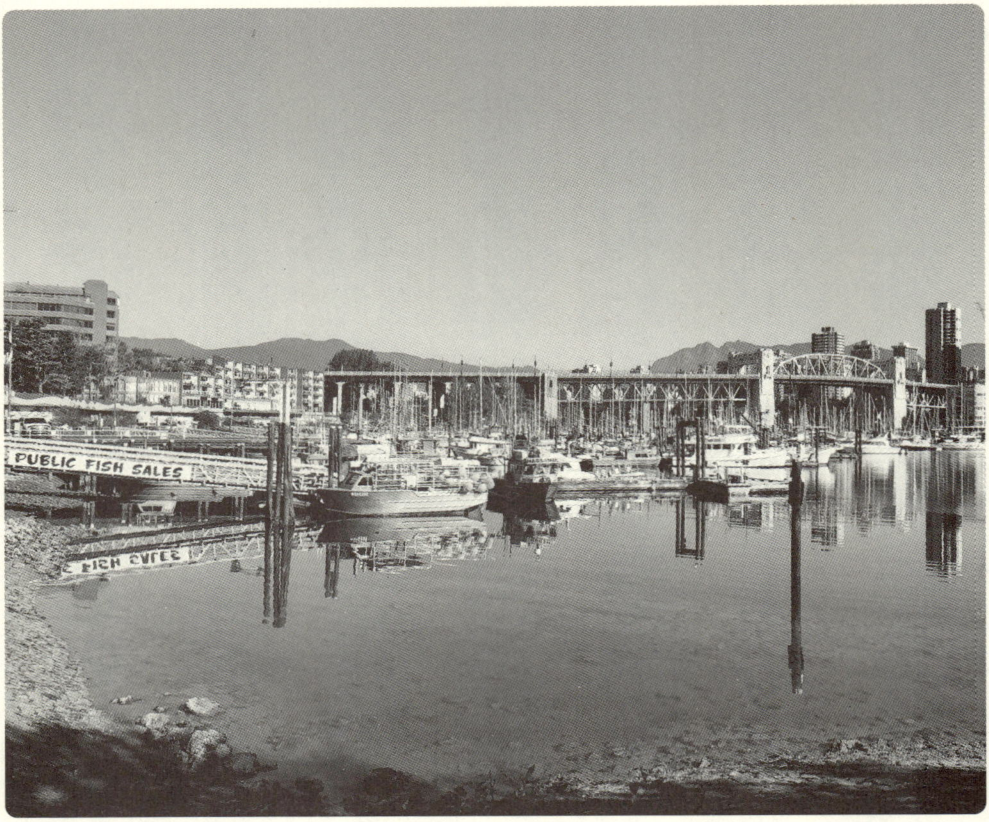

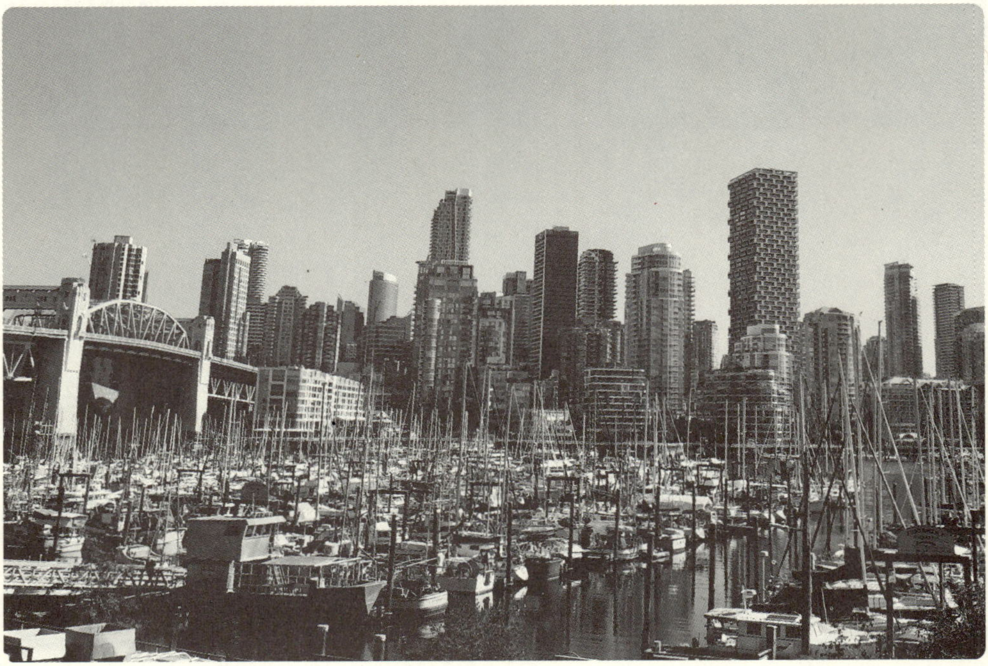

TOP: Fisherman's Wharf, False Creek, looking west.
BOTTOM: Fisherman's Wharf, looking north toward downtown.

Granville Island

NORTH BY NORTHWEST AND A BIT EAST AS WELL

BACK TO MY WATERSIDE WALK, now onto Granville Island with Burrard Bridge to my left and Granville Street Bridge spanning above. I'm here to visit with CBC's Margaret Gallagher for her radio show *North by Northwest* and to discuss these *Perfect Day* walks. We're treating the interview as its own little stroll, sharing stories as we re-examine a place we know well, an efficient way to glean fresh perspectives and see old locations anew.

Margaret arrives on a bike, her burgundy helmet reflecting the sun. She locks up her ride, and together we walk to the iconic spray-painted artwork called *Giants*, six concrete silos transformed into people, some facing north and some south. Each painted person wears vibrant clothes, trousers and hoodies. Ground-level pass-throughs give some of the forms a squat version of legs, making the personae even more realistic.

These behemoths are the creation of OSGEMEOS, Brazilian brothers Gustavo and Otávio Pandolfo, and this is one of many Biennale art installations around Greater Vancouver. The Vancouver Biennale is a non-profit organization whose objective is to exhibit unusual multimedia art in public spaces to create fresh-air urban museums. *Giants* may be the grandest example.

Together we admire the piece, playful colours on a vast concrete canvas. The paint is now weathered, as though the giants' clothing is faded and worn. A part of me wants to spruce it all up, until I remember a lesson learned from a Haida carver. The artist made it clear that when it comes to natural or spiritual art, and totems in particular, pieces aren't always meant to be "restored" but rather to return to the earth, like fallen trees that become nurse logs to nourish their surroundings. "Maybe it stands for one year," he'd explained. "Maybe one thousand. That's not for us to decide."

What the artist said resonates, as Margaret and I are now at a carving shed, having turned west from *Giants* to Ocean Artworks, a public multi-use space. At various times it's an artist's studio, a performance venue, even an event bar with a small skateboard park. But most frequently, this space is known as the carving shed, a place where Haida carver Clarence Mills has worked for two decades off and on, shaping cedar into totems and masks.

It's what an anthropologist might call a record of moieties: social, cultural, or ritual groups or divisions. I consider these totems as timelines, straight-edged family trees. Each vertical carving a narrative, blending present-day stories with legend and lore. At the uppermost point, whether raven, eagle, or thunderbird, each apex forms another thin place, literally and metaphorically. A lineage blur where corvids and clamshells and gods interweave, every story touching the sky.

Consistent with that blurring of space, just behind us to the south is a remnant of Vancouver Mural Festival. In its way, like *Giants*, it's a somewhat temporary piece that's still here and likely will be for years. The mural is another vertical installation, this one wrapping a support pillar of Granville Street Bridge. Indigenous in design, the painting features a salmon, a hook-nosed beast with the look of a sockeye. Salmon are the perfect encapsulation of time: the seasonal, cyclical nature of birth, maturation, departure, and return. That transition from freshwater to salt a reminder of clean resources and stewardship too. In a word, sustainability.

Next to the salmon, running the height of the support column is an unmistakable star blanket design, this one in yellow and red. And I wonder if these are the colours of the garment draped on the shoulders of Joe Capilano in the black-and-white picture I saw. Like so many vintage photos, the absence of colour creates its own nuance of shadow and mood.

The last place where I passed a star blanket design was in Vancouver's Downtown Eastside. The mural adorned the side of a building, ten storeys high. Redevelopment brought that wall down, but the mural was saved, in a fashion, reimagined as a new building wrap, no longer vertical but horizontal, bringing the whole to street level with a call to awareness of the fentanyl overdose crisis and the need for ongoing change.

Each image lingers: the prescient gaze of the Chief, cycles of water and land here at the flow of False Creek, an arm or "reach" of the sea. Bringing to mind a quote by author Robin Cody: "On the water, a reach has arms, the opposite of normal."[30] Where I am, either applies, the reach of the inlet, this arm, almost in arm's reach of the art.

Margaret and I add a zig to our zag, turning north, where we slip between buildings on the boardwalk to the edge of the water. In front of us, False Creek runs west and east; we're directly under Granville Street Bridge by a boat named *Relief*, with a historical plaque on display.

The boat has an interesting past, having been a rum-running craft, with a stint as a Canadian Naval Reserve vessel, but mostly the ship's been a troller, fishing for salmon and halibut. Brass winches, now patinaed soft green, were used to haul in the lines.

By the hull of the ship, which today throws a southerly shadow, we have a good view of the water. Sun dimples the surface in glints, and it takes no imagination to envision this craft launching west, aimed at inviting low swells that await just beyond English Bay.

Before turning back, Margaret asks what else we can see here, at Seńáḵw or Snauq, "the place inside the head of False Creek." So I mention that this was where August Jack Khatsahlano grew up, harvesting shellfish and hunting for ducks.

Our conversation shifts to what the new development of Seńáḵw might mean. And I think of that salmon circling the base of the bridge with the star blanket design, another kind of cyclicality. Land that was solely Indigenous, then appropriated, then roughly redrawn with new dotted lines, is now a place of community growth, mixed-use residential and commercial with income-assisted housing as well. I see this as a form of renewal, or a version of sustainable management. And yes, stewardship too.

Ahead of us, around Granville Island Public Market with its art installations, produce, and fish, is a commemoration of the tugboats that make much of the city's water-based industry possible. Ubiquitous profiles that rumble their way through the inlets, tucking cruise ships and tankers in place, not to mention hauling barges and booms. Unglamorous and essential high-horsepower cogs in the wheels of commerce and industry.

Past the small tribute, we reach the westernmost edge of the market, which happens to be the final bit of the first building around here, part of the tinworks of BC Equipment, heavy manufacturing to support the forestry and shipping that dominated this reinforced island of silt, which at the turn of the twentieth century was known as Industrial Island.

As we finish our walk, I ask Margaret about her own experiences around Vancouver shores and learn that she was part of a crew that navigated much of this coast, from Burrard Inlet's North Shore to the east edge of False Creek, where the waterway truncates at Science World's dome. This was the passenger ferry and tour operator Harbour Cruises, which has its own integral history going back to 1911, having been a ferry service on the Fraser River before shuttling tourists and commuters from North Van to here. Now the company operates three vessels: MPV *Constitution*, a stern-driven paddlewheeler that looks like it belongs in the pages of Mark Twain, plus the yachts MV *Harbour Princess* and MV *Britannia*.

Margaret smiles as she recounts her time on the water, twelve trips a day across Burrard Inlet and around Stanley Park to English Bay, perhaps the same route of those earliest map-makers. The MV *Hollyburn* in particular resonates in that nautical history. Constructed in 1936 and purchased by Harbour Navigation in 1945, the stout wooden ship resembled an elongated tugboat, with round portholes on the waterline, a large passenger deck, open air at the fore, coverage and seating in the aft. The main run of the *Hollyburn* was not unlike today's SeaBus, a north–south shuttle from downtown to North Van. The same journey as the first settler-based ferry, operated by John "Navvy Jack" Thomas.

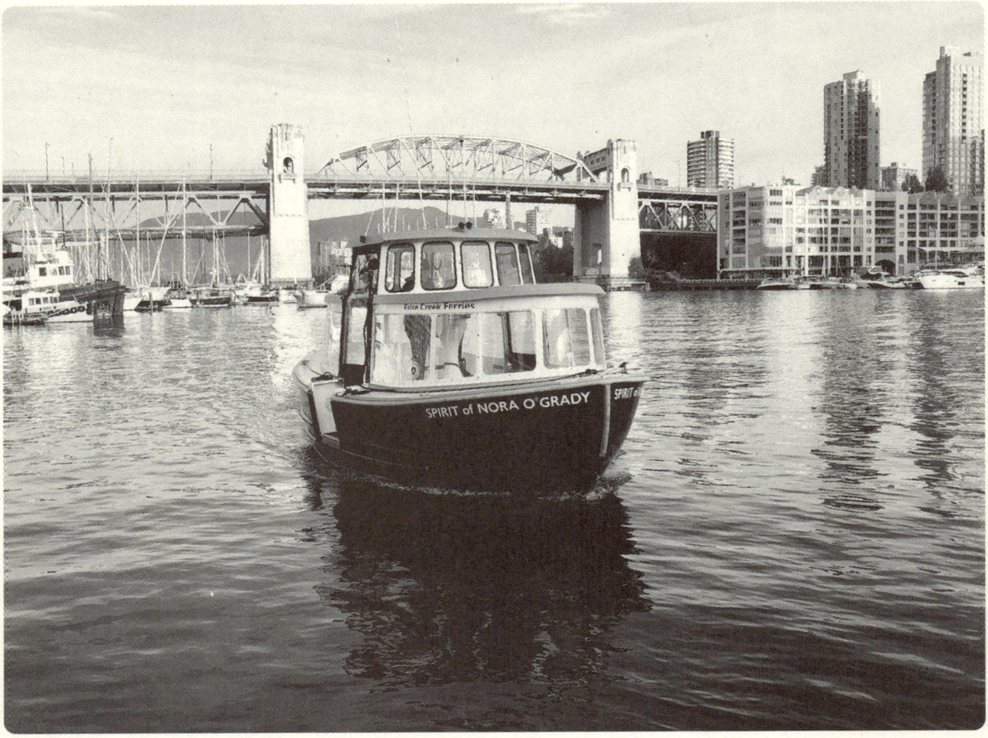

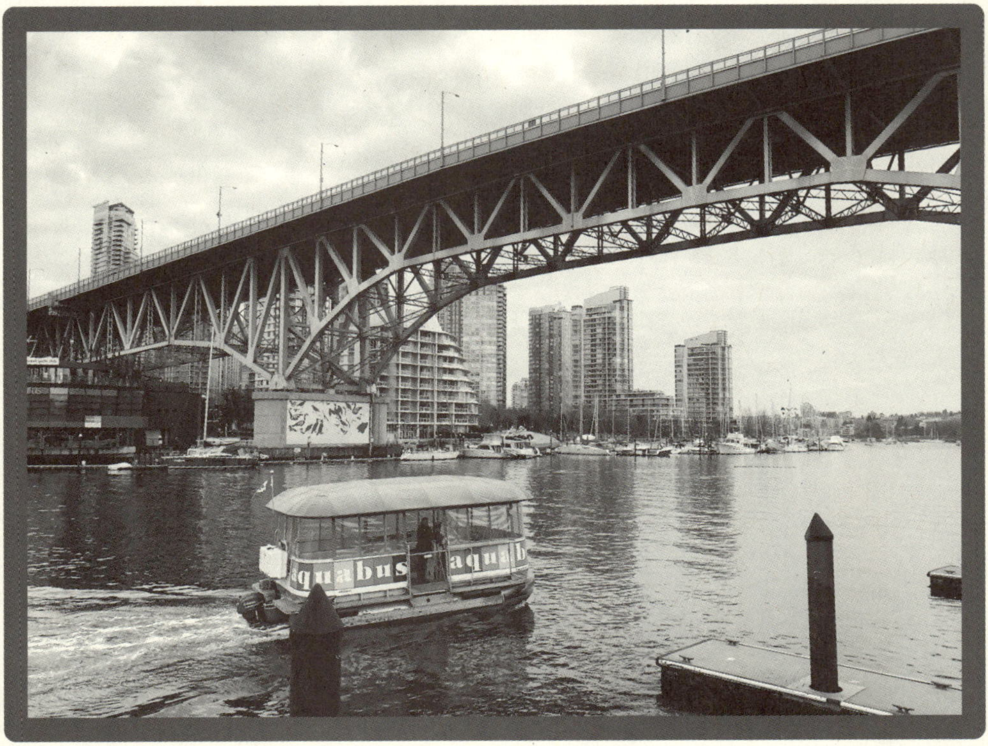

TOP: a False Creek Ferry arriving at Granville Island.
BOTTOM: an Aquabus under Granville Street Bridge.

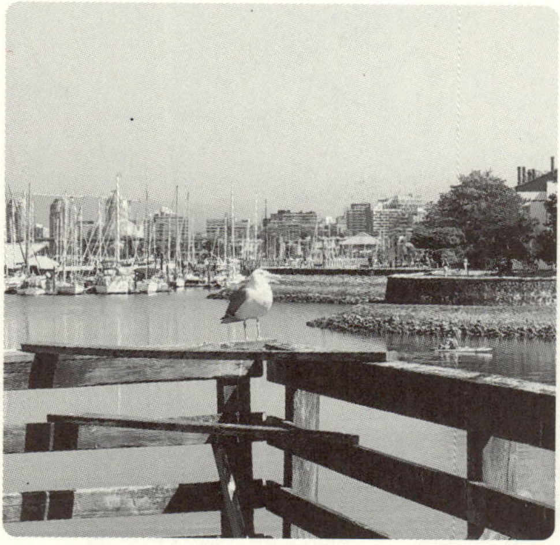
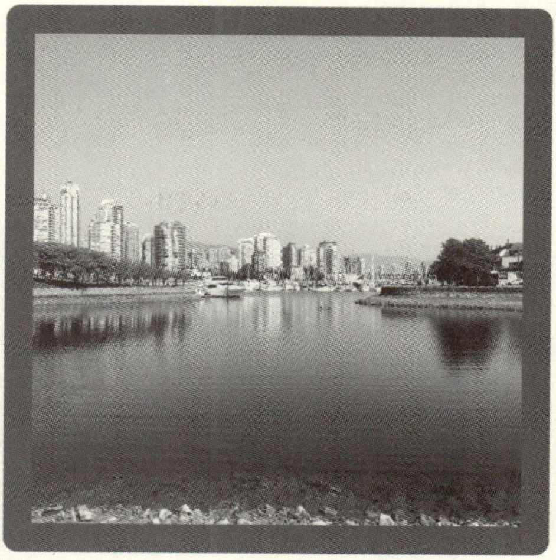
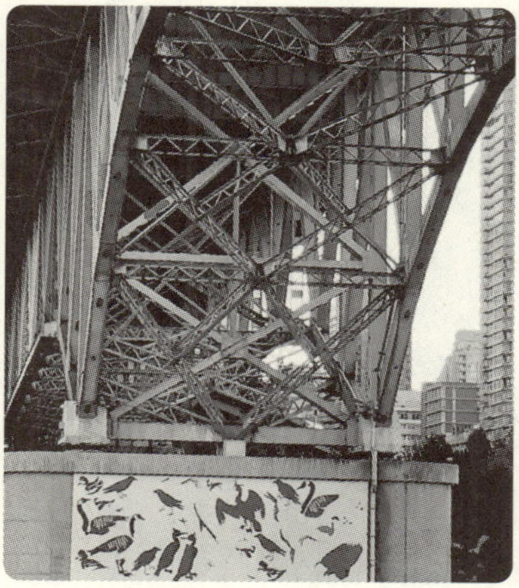
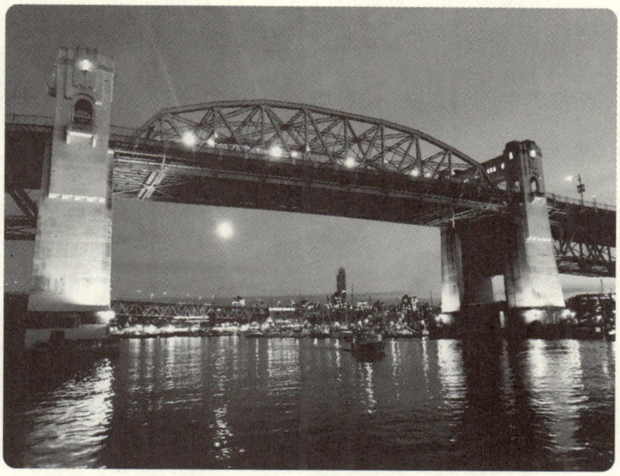
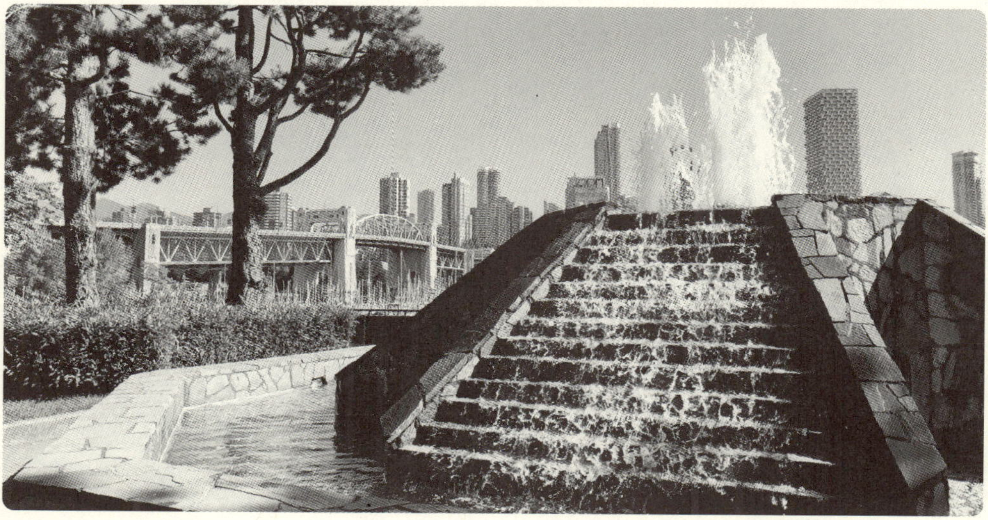

CLOCKWISE FROM TOP LEFT: a herring gull at False Creek, looking east; looking toward Yaletown from Granville Island; a False Creek Ferry in moonrise under Burrard Bridge; a water feature near Fisherman's Wharf, with Burrard Bridge beyond; under Granville Street Bridge.

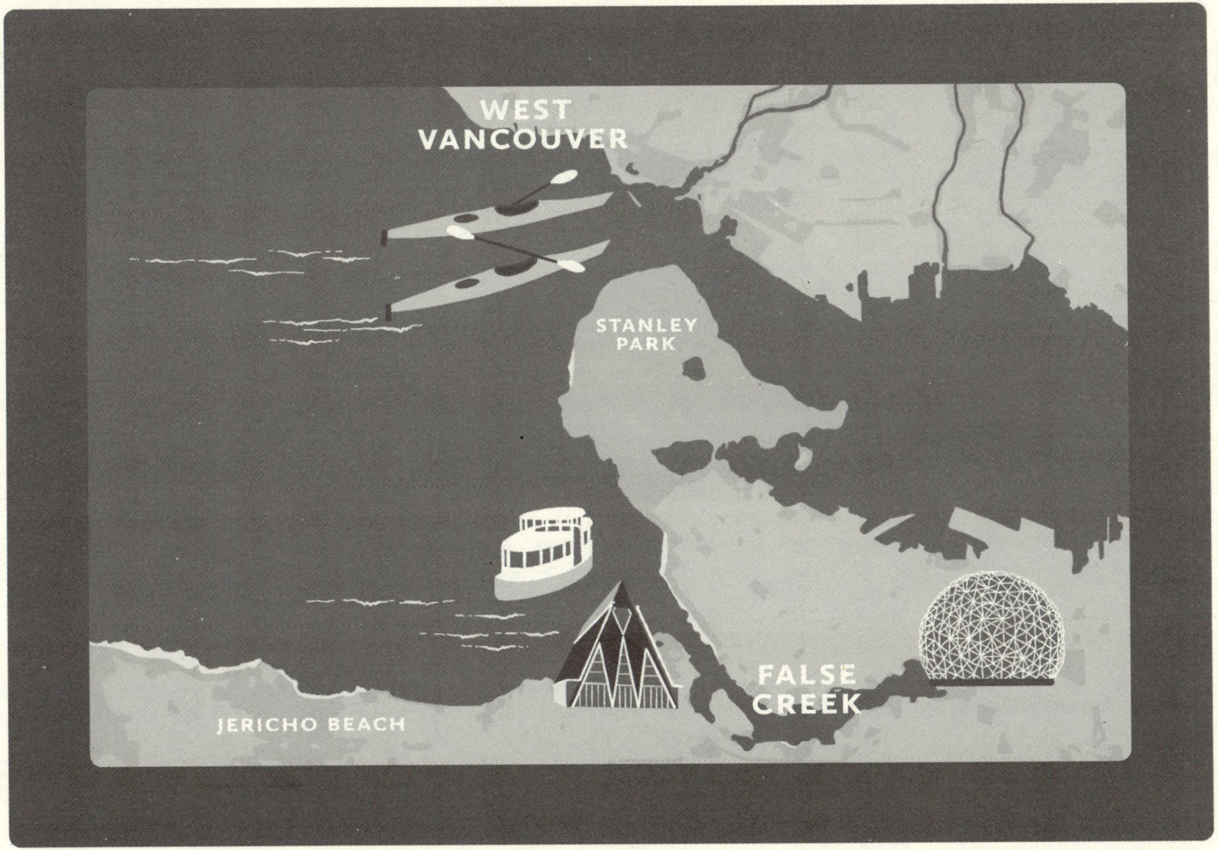

WEST
VANCOUVER
STANLEY
PARK
FALSE
CREEK
JERICHO BEACH

CONNECTING CITY SHORELINES

Who's Navvy Jack?

AN AMBLESIDE AMBLE

RETURNING TO THE North Shore Spirit Trail, I've picked up the path in West Van, walking in soft sunrise light, a peach hue to the sky. And apart from the wake of a passenger ferry roaring to Coal Harbour from Nanaimo, the water is morning-time calm. There's a good volume of walkers and a few joggers, all enjoying a view of Burrard Inlet and English Bay. To the east is Lions Gate Bridge, while Stanley Park does a passable impression of a long green-backed turtle. Prospect Point fronts the north head of the park, and if I squint, I can see Siwash Rock on the park's northwest corner. From here, the columnar stone almost centres the park to resemble a sundial gnomon.

Ambleside Pier spears the bay, tall at the moment in low tide. Beyond that, fishers cast at the mouth of the Capilano, about thirty anglers standing in waders, resembling fence posts.

Someone bustles up in a bright T-shirt with the enthusiasm of a fresh volunteer.

"Are you coming to the barbeque? There'll be music!" she says, rather loudly.

"Huh?"

"The Coho Festival! Come join the fun!"

I respond with a positive sound. Truth is, I didn't realize that was today.

Coordinated by the Coho Society of the North Shore, the annual festival has been happening since 1979, a celebration marking the season when salmon return from saltwater to fresh. A public barbeque is one of the main attractions, along with entertainment, a play space, and an open-air garden. A feature is the Stewardship Zone, where exhibitors demonstrate clean water practices, with a focus on "rejuvenating, maintaining, and improving" streams, rivers, ocean, and forests.[31] Members of the Squamish Nation offer a welcome as part of the festivities, and the Squamish Ocean Canoe Family begins the event with a traditional "Blessing of the Salmon." All of this takes place here, at Swá wi, or Ambleside Park.

Eating a slab of salmon does appeal, but I hope the coordinators aren't relying on the anglers standing there in the river. I don't see much action right now.

My stroll takes me from Ambleside into Dundarave, all of which is West Van, with railway tracks tracing the pathway and shore. At one of the pedestrian crossings, two crows stand on a directional sign. One side points west, indicating Ambleside Town Centre. The other aims east, marked Dundarave Village. Each crow's chosen a side, so it seems, one looking west and one east. No doubt they're a couple, arguing about directions.

A painted banner hangs from a street lamp, Coast Salish imagery of two women with long flowing hair. The dark outlines resemble peaked mountains at sunset, when hills shift from purple to black. Beneath the women is a wide sweeping band with the look of spread wings, what could pass for a phoenix about to take flight. A wash of blue centres the art, a depiction of water, where three canoes cut through swirls of blue-green. It looks like a permanent exhibit, somewhat faded, but it could serve as a welcome sign for the festival now. A visual of water and land, the First Peoples, the motion of paddles through surf.

Past Hollyburn Sailing Club, I watch workers lug buoys to the water, likely for lessons. I cross Millennium Park, then John Lawson Park, where a tanker slides by close to shore. The vessel becomes a trompe l'oeil, as though the ship's about to heave itself onto the walkway.

Art is on display in a loose market of paintings: acrylics, oils, and watercolours on paper and canvas, depicting mostly nature, flora and fauna, with stylized views of what I'm walking by now. An address on Argyle Avenue indicates the former home of Navvy Jack Thomas, where a placard and a quick search online offer a slice of the person, this place, and that time.

Navvy Jack, otherwise known as John Thomas, arrived here from Wales in 1860. Considered a BC pioneer, he built his home on this spot and became something of a bridge between places and people. He ran that first ferry across Burrard Inlet, linking West Van to downtown. His home housed the region's first post office, as well as the first church and wedding. As an entrepreneur he came up with a new blend of gravel and sand, the makings of concrete, the name of his inventive mixture still used today.

Jack became part of multiple Musqueam, Squamish, and Tsleil-Waututh family trees. He married Rowia of the Musqueam Nation, granddaughter of a prior Chief Capilano. Building further regional ties, Rowia and Jack's children and grandchildren married Squamish and Tsleil-Waututh partners. One of their grandchildren's spouses was Chief Dan George.

I can imagine it as a totem, a diverse moiety line, with roots running deep through this real estate and finding the water. The result: a quilting of Indigenous and settler families, community leaders, and a link to Jack's ferry, which sutured a young growing city.

Now I'm on a small concrete patch where the Spirit Trail, which is paved along here, meets with John Lawson Park. It was Lawson who planted a holly tree next to a creek on his lot. The tree and the creek, also known as a "burn," inspired him to call the place Hollyburn. Some signage and a reference online show that what's left on this sliver of Argyle Avenue is little more than a memory of Lawson, indicating, more than anything, the notion of change.

A history of change may seem obvious, yet inherent in that is evocative narrative. Naturally, things change, but the *pace* of that change adds mystery, engagement, surprise. Even the trail I'm now walking shifts with the pulse of the sea. Fluidity clings to it all, and I imagine those family tree lines, people and land, might be the only true constants.

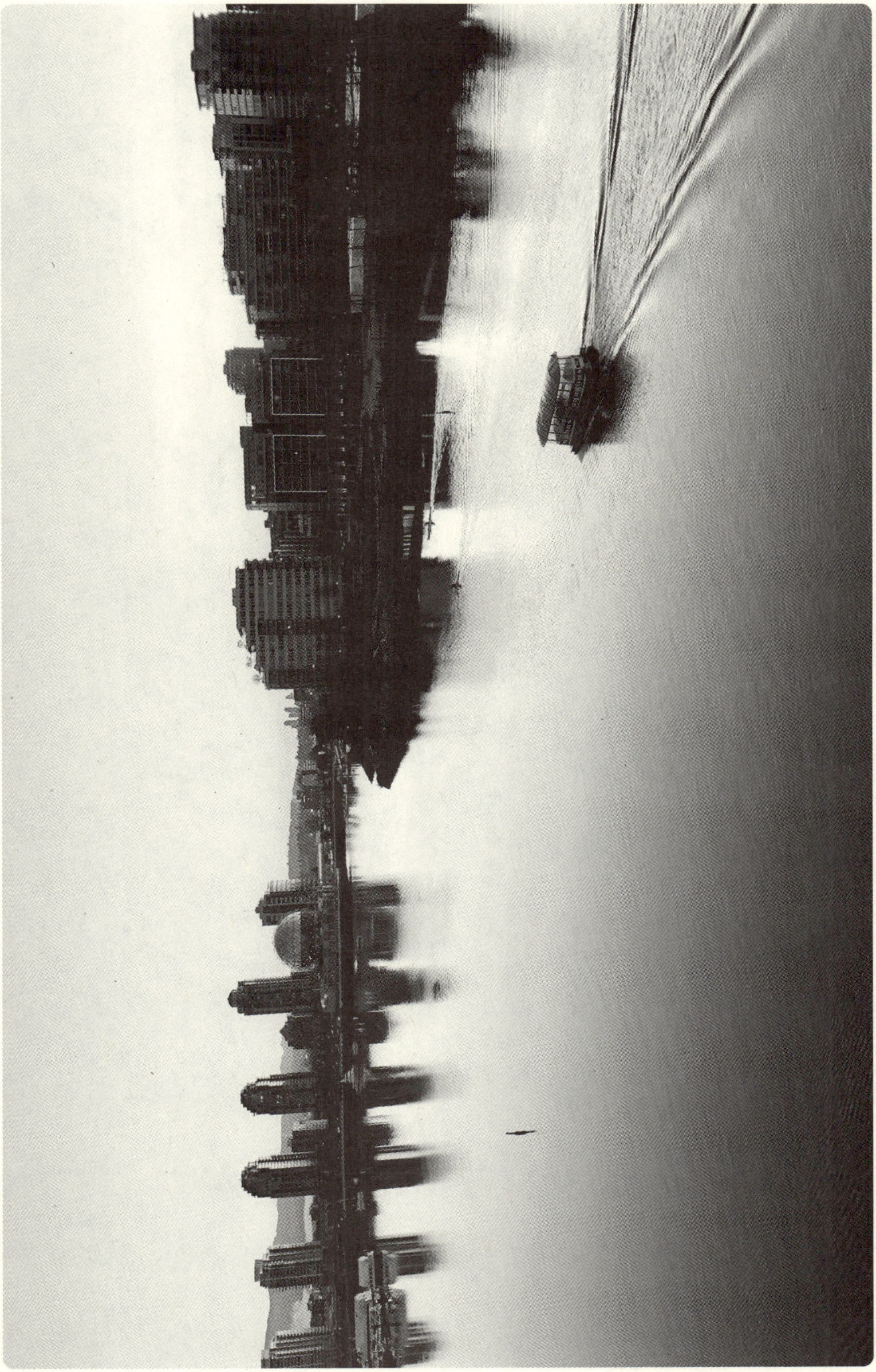

An Aquabus at sunrise bearing east on False Creek.

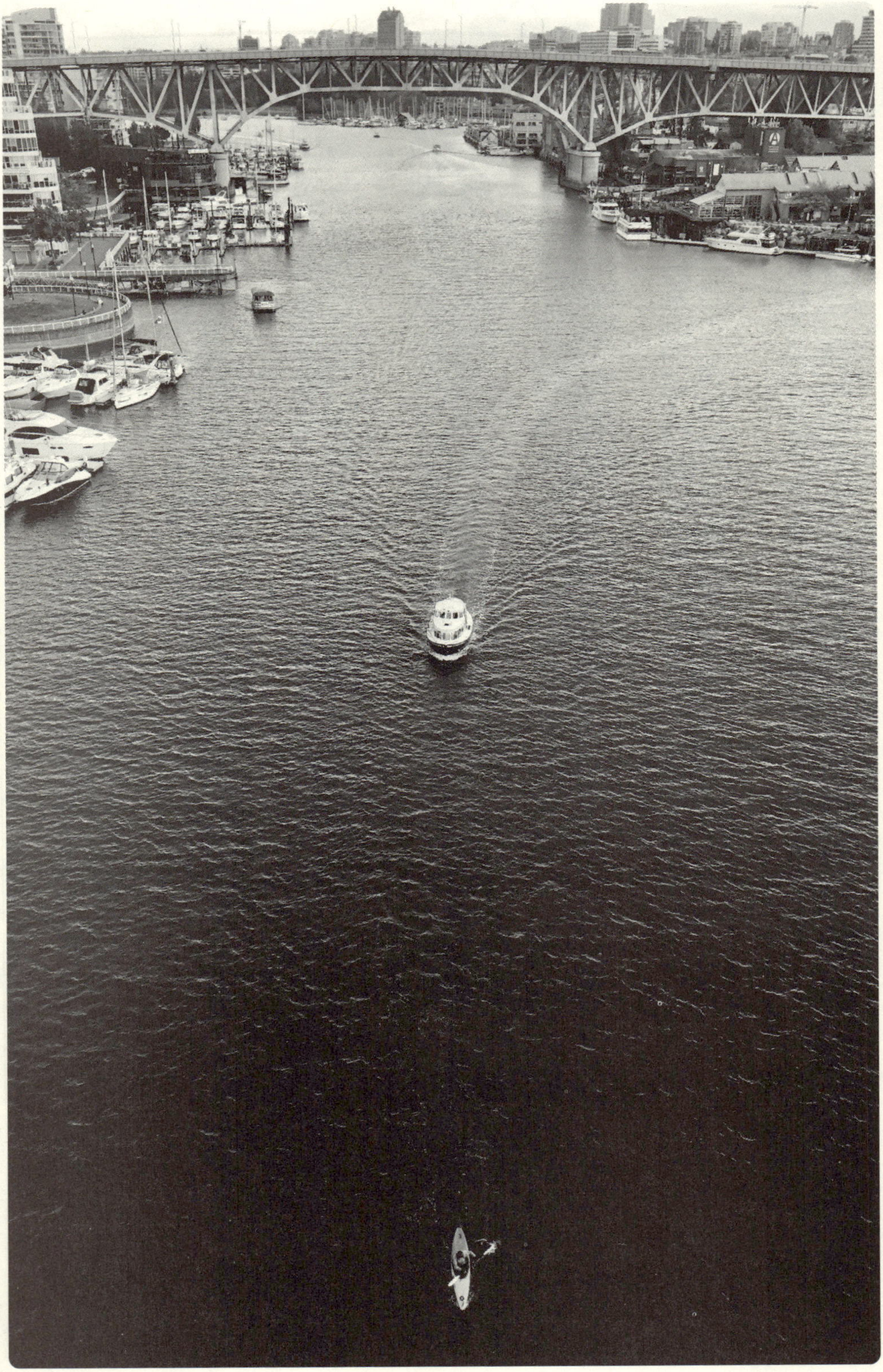

A False Creek Ferry and a kayaker bearing west.

Paddling False Creek

WATER SAFARI

IT'S MIDDAY IN THE BLAZING SUN, and it only makes sense to be on the water. I'm at the east end of False Creek where Science World catches the light with the look of a mirror ball hung for a dance. Over the water, BC Place is agleam, its roofline of spokes resembling a crown. A SkyTrain squeals, and the water's invitingly calm. Descending an access ramp to the dockside, I'm at the Creekside Paddling Centre jetty, where an array of outriggers, kayaks, and dragon boats jut from the pier like bathers dipping their toes.

A heron watches all this from the roof of a shed with a mortician's gaze. Walking the pier like a shopper, I choose a three-metre kayak the colour of ripe tangerine that, neatly enough, offers the feel of three separate craft. A long double-blade paddle will be my propulsion, the most common one used for kayaks. In the bow of the boat, I stow a backup single-blade paddle, the type used with traditional canoes. And if I have a spill, a flotation pad can be affixed to one end of the two-bladed paddle; then, by lashing the opposite end of the paddle at right angles to the boat, I can effectively create a single-arm outrigger, making it easier to reboard from the water. And just like that, I have a kayak, canoe, and outrigger too, all in one modest boat.

Devian, who's taking care of rentals today, passes me a life jacket and a collapsible dry bag. Before pushing off, I ask him about paddling here. With the selection of boats on the wharf, the space has the feel of a clothier: Pick a colour, a size, and a fit.

"What are your favourites?" I ask.

He doesn't hesitate. "Oh, dragon boats. Totally."

"Why's that?"

He grins. "Being part of a team, when your catch, drive, and exit are perfectly coordinated. 'Blend,' we call that. You feel the boat actually lift off the water when you're paddling as a collective. That momentum, it's called 'glide.' Which can take years to achieve, but there's nothing better!" His grin widens, eyes twinkling, as though he's no longer here on the dock but out there, skimming the surface in tandem.

My enthusiasm suitably bolstered, I launch from the pier, where a reinforced slab almost meshes water and jetty. A friendly push from Devian and a backstroke from me, and I'm off, exploring once more in the reach of the sea.

Keeping shoreline, Seawall, and piers to my right, I paddle the east end of False Creek in a counter-clockwise direction where the water is shifting from pea green to teal. A few scraps of cloud temper the light, but the sun is still hot. And once again I feel I could be almost anywhere, a resort or a surfside vacation.

There's a sliver of coarse gravel shore where a red aluminum boat has been beached: a small outboard motor and oars. Its owner, I presume, is the man sitting on a rock by the boat, having a coffee and surveying the view. Behind that, stacked and locked onto trailers, are the Voyageur Adventures canoes, replicas of what early fur traders paddled. Every likeness is well done, simulated birchbark with pitch seams and decor on each prow: wolf, beaver, or bear.

I'm sticking with the double-blade paddle, remembering lessons from Robyn: Keep the blade low to the water, use the torso and core rather than the shoulders and arms. Feel the water and craft as one system or whole. A slight swivel with each stroke, a gentle turn of the hips, and in theory you could paddle forever.

Making my way to the inlet's north edge, I slice between tethered boats, a mash-up of pleasure craft taking advantage of free anchorage: sailboats, yachts, and a jerry-rigged houseboat. All this in front of Science World, BC Place, and the building that served as the BC pavilion during Expo 86, its warehouse construction in glass the same colour as the inlet right now. Along the Seawall and shore I see downy fluffs in the breeze, goose feathers in delicate swirls, the look of a just-elapsed pillow fight.

If I were to beach the kayak next to Science World, I'd be on what's called the Environmental Trail, a short walk that encircles the complex and grounds by the inlet. This borders the future East Park, a proposed expanse zagging south in a Z-shape design, like a treed flick of Zorro's sword.

Paddling west, I pass seagulls and cormorants. A few sparrows and towhees sing from the shore. Toward Cambie Street Bridge the water busies with False Creek Ferries and Aquabuses. There's civility within the bustle—awareness, right of way. It feels nicer than driving. Maybe if this was my daily commute I might find it stressful, but today that doesn't seem possible.

At a break in ferry traffic, I cross the inlet from the north side of False Creek to the south. There's a dock and a moored boat called *Safari*, the Swahili word meaning "expedition" or "journey." Something about it, that name on a white-painted hull, strikes me as particularly alluring. Another pull of horizons.

Behind me, to the north, are Yaletown and Vancouver's downtown, to the east and south is Mount Pleasant, and directly ahead is False Creek's Fairview neighbourhood. Now I'm passing a chunky pleasure craft that's starting to fade, but above its chipped paint is a line of bright nautical flags strung from conning tower and bow. An assortment of gear sits on deck: inner tubes, a faux palm, a giant fig leaf, and a pair of inflatable people, both in swimwear, as though I've stumbled unannounced on their shindig. I'm compelled to look away and can't help but wonder if the party will resume once I'm gone.

Straight ahead is Habitat Island. My last time here, I was on foot, walking its network of trails between seagrass, nurse logs, and birdhouses in trees. A Parks Board sign added detail to this spheroid of land, its outline the same shape as my kayak. When I first saw this skerry on a satellite map, it struck me as a modest version of Granville Island, another oblong of reinforced earth, built-up silt, and stacked stone. Only here, rather than industry, the objective is to welcome in nature. According to BC Parks,

> Deep layers of soil have been added to the area to provide nourishment for new trees to grow. Boulders and logs commonly found along the coastlines in this region of British Columbia provide a home for plants, small animals, insects, crabs, starfish, barnacles and other creatures. Surrounded by water at high tide, the island is also a sanctuary for birds.[32]

A quick pass of the island, linked via causeway to shore, and I paddle alongside the Seawall once more, by the footbridge that spans where I'm paddling. With a sharp pivot, I slide the boat through the pillars supporting the walkway above. The tide at the moment is low, and mussels cling high up the concrete. Three metres above my head, people are walking to and from lunch, sightseeing, exploring—but all that disappears. Here, in a weird blend of the constructed and the natural, it feels isolated, removed. All I hear is the drip of water from the edge of my paddle, the lap of tide against stone, and the coo of pigeons nesting in overhead beams.

My visual of the walkway pilings is like the underside of a high pier, a hallway of water and columns. It looks like a loggia, something fronting an Italianate gallery. Angled light, meanwhile, makes the water increasingly green, the hue of fresh olives. The tideline too adds a tone, a clean line between light and dark. Above the high-water mark, the concrete shines as if recently scrubbed. Below are the colours of steeped tea and peat. And I feel as though I've stumbled on another kind of Habitat Island, only this one is corridor shaped, designed to be used as a gathering space.

From the underbelly of the Seawall, I return once again into sun. The breakwater here is huge cubes of granite raised into stacks like a staircase designed for a giant. Someone's seated there, eating a sandwich. A non-giant. They wave. I wave back. Just ahead, an Indigenous raven design has been added to a vertical face of the rock, the stone serving as a canvas. The artist must have timed their work with low water, and I suspect the image gets hidden when the tide's at its zenith, during neaps and full moons. The painted raven looks to the west, toward open water. Like the concrete silos of *Giants*, this bird too has been humanized. Its shoulders and wings, scapulars, coverts, and tertials, have humanesque eyes in the swirl of each feather. With the soft splash of surf and a shoreline of mussels, I can't help but envision another clam filled with people about to pop open, maybe to repopulate the world.

Time to swing back to the pier, but Devian is helping a couple launch a kayak, a bigger sibling to the boat that I'm in. I give them plenty of space and do another lap of this southeastern corner of False Creek, and I'm glad that I do. For another discreet bit of art has revealed itself, something I'd never see from the land. Each wooden piling supporting the seawalk has been painted with a salmon in white, as though they're negotiating fish ladders, making the same frenzied leaps that I saw when the coho and chinook put on their show by the Stanley Park shore. By paddling with the curve of the walkway and angling my head to one side, the fish become one of those flip-book cartoons, single frames that leap to life with a shuffle of pages. Only here it's a series of stills placed on vertical logs, like a circle of salmon-topped totems.

I ease the boat back to the dock. Devian helps, and we haul the kayak onto the pier. I thank him and head west, finding my land legs again. Along the Seawall, just east of the Cambie Street Bridge, I find an eerie discovery: a submerged sailboat stern tied to the shore with a rope and a chain. The sun's now high in the sky, and the boat nearly glows in its liquidy grave, a luminescent lime green. Unlike the dive wrecks in Howe Sound, sunk right-side up, this vessel looks murdered, sprawled on its side. I can envision a chalk outline around it.

Two men stand at the lip of the walkway, pink graffiti under their feet, sizing up the wet ruin. I join them, and within moments we're chatting like part of a sailing crew. Colin and Dan are their names. Colin's local. Dan is from Ottawa, where he sails the Gatineau River.

I nod toward the sunken boat. "What do you make of that?"

"That's a twenty-five-footer," Dan says. "Probably snagged its keel, mid or low tide. Then the tide rises and the boat fills with water. I've seen it before. Almost happened to me once. You get these small craft, inexperienced boaters. A seven-to-one ratio is what you need for your anchor rope, chain, or whatever. For each metre of tide depth, you need seven metres of line to account for the movement. In deepwater, most vessels don't have enough rope to account for that." He furrows his brow, remembering. "The time I got stuck? Snagged the keel? I got lucky. A big boat came along and hauled me to safety. But in here? A cheap boat? People abandon them. Not worth it to try to recover. Too costly. Easier to walk away."

Colin and I slowly nod. I suspect our heads look like buoys.

"I sold my son my last boat," Dan says. "Three thousand dollars. The motor alone is worth more that that! Now he sails it over by Second Narrows. We sailed there together around Deep Cove. Big tides, twelve foot or more. Need a lot of rope there!"

The three of us stare a while longer at the wreck. Understanding how it got there doesn't make it less eerie. The green glow adds a mood. I imagine a body down there, the sightline looking upward to here. A sway of current shifting colours, the light. Where we stand, we might look disjointed, a squiggle with each wave, ripples running up legs into torsos. Even in the sun I feel a slight shiver.

We shake hands, and I leave Colin and Dan still watching the wreck as though it may yet come to life. Remarkably, a short distance ahead, I encounter another wrecked vessel, tethered yet sunken, this one crudely lashed to a pillar of the Cambie Street Bridge. Ironically, it's at the base of the blue-painted stripes of the art installation *A False Creek*, by Rhonda Weppler and Trevor Mahovsky. The same work that caught my eye when I walked on the north side of False Creek. This art, with its depiction of rising oceans, takes on new meaning next to this boat, which could pass for an ark that didn't make it. The artists' statement shared by the city describes this interpretive look at projected sea levels increasing from four to six metres as a result of polar melt. A sobering thought in a city surrounded by sea.

Leaving the wrecks and the artwork behind, I move west, following the Seawall as it meanders toward Granville Island. Past Charleson Park and Spruce Harbour Marina, beyond the fixed piers, where a few dozen boats are at anchor. I hope they have plenty of rope.

One multi-mast craft flies a Jolly Roger. On another, a wind meter spins in the breeze, westerlies now gusting in warm air. A heavy-hulled catamaran shifts on its anchor line. Some of the sailboats, houseboats, and powerboats appear to be permanent residencies, while others look rarely used. Through it all, passenger ferries burble in their rainbow and blue-and-white polish. In the bustle, I witness a microcosm of nature, a rise of the tiniest minnows. Miniscule flashes and soft splashes. *Bloop. Bloop*. A short calm, and then, *bloop*.

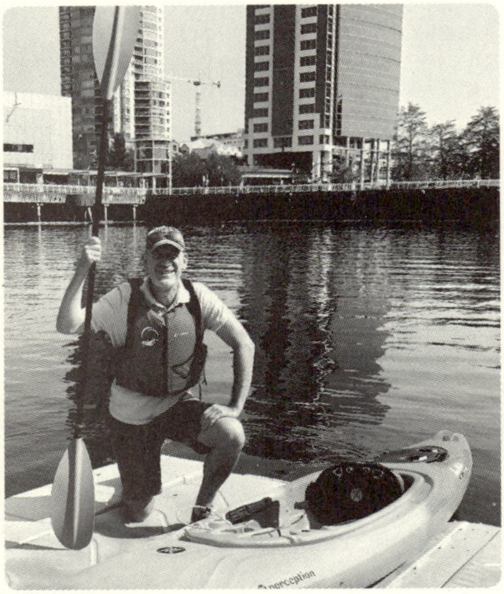

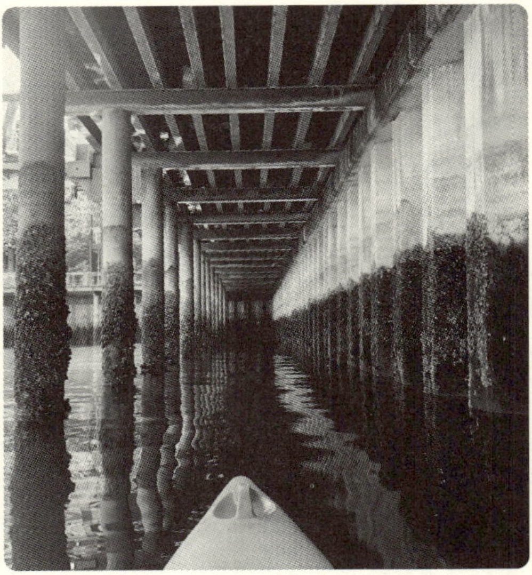

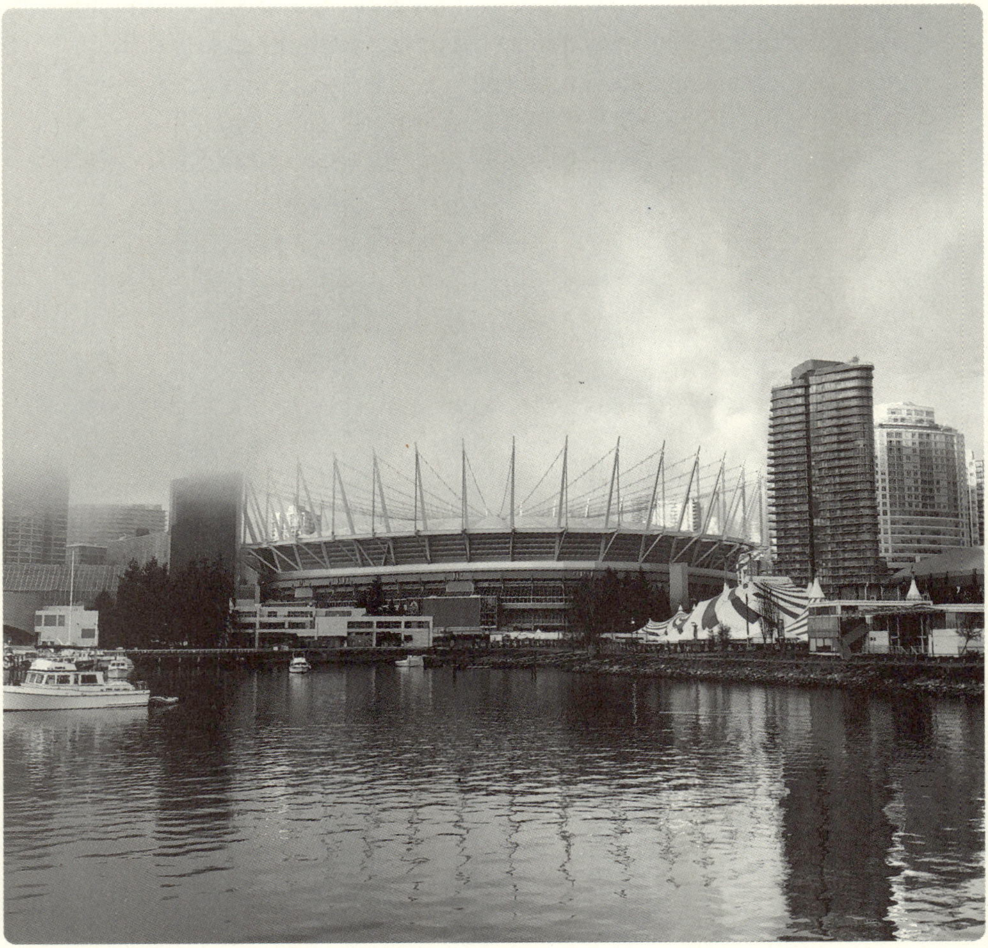

CLOCKWISE FROM TOP LEFT: paddle prep with a kayak at False Creek; paddling under the seawalk at Olympic Village; paddling toward BC Place stadium.

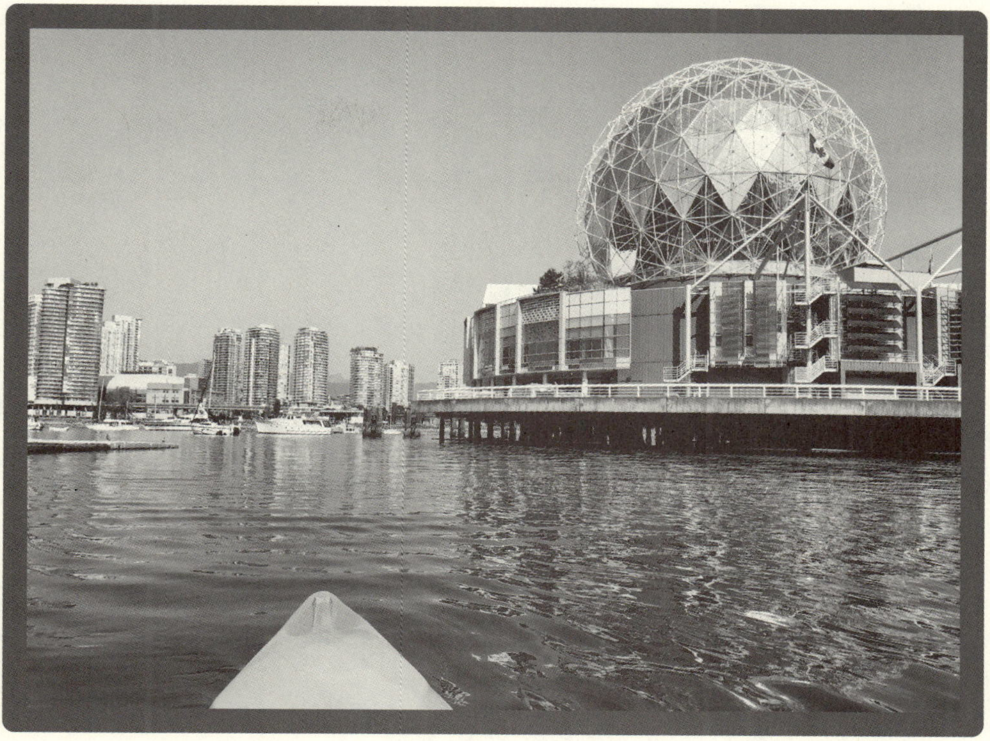

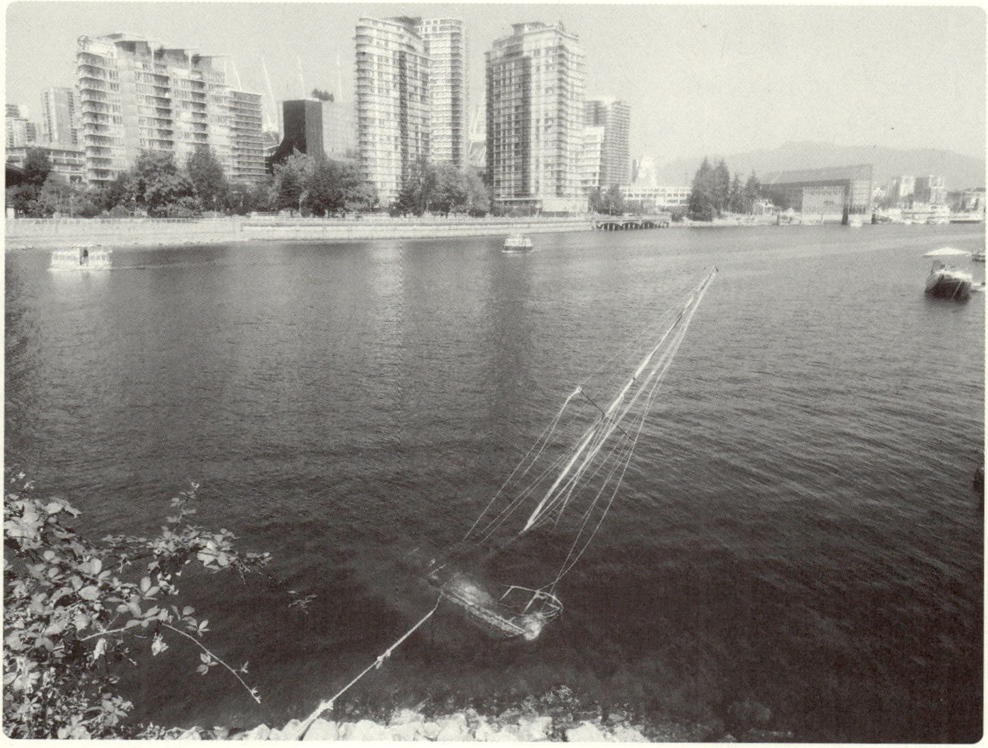

TOP: view of Science World from a kayak.
BOTTOM: the sunken sailboat at False Creek.

St. Roch and O Siem

RE-EXAMINING MARITIME HISTORY

THE SUN'S VANISHED FOR THE DAY, I suspect, although it's only late afternoon. The sky is bright but awash in chalk cloud, an inversion of sorts, as I walk to the Vancouver Maritime Museum to spend an evening pretending I'm at sea. I've received an invitation to join a small landlocked crew aboard the *St. Roch* and to further explore the museum. Apparently snacks will be served.

My route takes me along regional boundaries—Fairview, False Creek, Kitsilano—in a pie-shaped city slice with a northerly view, as though I'm navigating Trivial Pursuit game pieces. Aptly enough, the primary colours here are green and blue, same as the game categories Science and Nature, and Geography, with that hint of a diluted sun the pale yellow of History.

When I walked here before, my focus less on water than on land, I felt one of my companions was trekker Robert Macfarlane. Something about this light, the obverse sky, brings to mind his writings, when he too walked beside inlets and found the same blur of a shoreline. He referred to a "soft bluish silver haze ... causing sky, sea and land to blend and interfuse, producing a new country that was neither earth nor sea."[33] Precisely what I see at this moment: an oddly inviting neutral zone where the ground is simply a portal.

I pass the Museum of Vancouver, the H.R. MacMillan Space Centre, the Vancouver Academy of Music, and the City of Vancouver Archives. Across the road is the False Creek Racing Canoe Club, where I learned that OC is more than a place, a TV show, and a movie.

When Macfarlane had that encounter, the flip-flop of weather and water and land, he detailed how the visual affected his sightings of birds, as gulls appeared twice their size. The image of that magnified cod comes to mind, but right now I see only crows. Normal-sized crows. But with impeccable timing, two ravens take flight, passing over Seńákw and providing me my own glimpse of magnified birds, these oversized corvids, same as on my Spirit Trail wanderings. Never before have I seen ravens in the area, and I can't help but smile, wondering who else is here with me.

The *St. Roch* is tonight's feature, sporting its reinforced hull of Douglas fir with ironbark eucalyptus and its nautical stories. It's the main exhibit around which the museum was constructed in 1959 and is now a national historic site. Parks Canada offers an overview of this RCMP schooner:

> In 1942, under the command of Sergeant Henry Larsen, she became the first ship to cross from the Pacific to the Atlantic by the Northwest Passage, having made a 27 month voyage from Vancouver to Halifax along the northern edge of the continent. Two years later she returned to Vancouver via the more northerly deep-water route. Making the east-west journey in only 86 days, the *St. Roch* was the first ship to complete the hazardous journey in both directions.[34]

In other words, after Roald Amundsen made the first recorded transit through the Northwest Passage, the *St. Roch* was the first to do so the opposite way, from west to east. And in an exploratory version of doubling down, the *St. Roch* did it again, returning from Atlantic to Pacific via an alternate northern route, making it the first ship to complete the journey both ways. Then, for good measure, the ship circumnavigated North America, the first vessel to do so, going through the Panama Canal before retiring here. I imagine finding the old ship in a rocking chair, a blanket draped on its lap, with nothing more to do than enjoy this pleasantly unfrozen view.

The *St. Roch* was built in North Van at Burrard Dry Dock in 1928, another link of Vancouver shores, from the same stretch of coast where settler ferries were launched to connect the North Shore to downtown. The dock too serving as a timeline through subsequent city names: first Gastown, then Granville, now Vancouver.

It's tempting to revisit that line of transit, North Van to downtown. From Indigenous canoes, paddling to the scene of Vancouver's Great Fire, followed by Navvy Jack's ferry, then Harbour Cruises hauling commuters and tourists, to the present-day shuttling of SeaBuses. But for now, I have plenty to see and learn aboard the *St. Roch*.

It's only as I enter the museum that I realize the scope of what's underway: a complete makeover of exhibits to decolonize the museum. Along with this overdue shift is an update in tech, intended to surround items in a shimmer of Northern Lights, a reinvention of this maritime space. The room is filled with curators, designers, and dignitaries as well. I find myself at a high standing table with a government official, a deputy something-or-other who seems determined to consume the charcuterie table. I wonder if I should notify the Guinness Book people, let them know some sort of record's being broken. But instead I excuse myself to explore the museum.

High on one wall is an Inuit kayak, skin stretched on a slender wood frame. It's narrow and long, a hunting craft built for speed, quite the opposite of the orange boat I paddled between passenger ferries. Under the A-frame of glass that houses the *St. Roch*, I slow down to take it all in. The boat resembles the *Gjøa*, the vessel Amundsen sailed through the Passage on a three-year journey completed in 1906. When I saw the *Gjøa* in Oslo, it also had a purpose-built space, and I feel the same feelings I felt there: remoteness and icy memories clinging to portholes and planks. At a glance it resembles yet one more ark, this one successful, and real, with a high rounded hull to push icebergs and floes, intended to partner with shifting sea ice.

I do a lap around the ship, where supporting displays are raised in glass cases: little models of snowshoes, a dogsled, and an umiak (a family-style kayak), all crafted in leather and wood, the same materials the full-sized items are made of. Reminiscent of that miniature carving at the MOA, the first model for *The Raven and the First Men*, another illusory shifting of size.

Next to these pieces is a carving in soapstone: a hunter, a seal, a walrus, and a bear. *Hunter and Hunted*, it's called, created in 1968 by Pierre Karlik of Rankin Inlet. At another display two Arctic fox furs lie in dead lumps, one brown and one white, indicating how the animal changes coats with the season. Oddly, I hear Nana's voice: "Never wear white after Labour Day." Clearly this white-coated fox, trapped in winter, never met Nana.

There's even a modest-sized model of HMS *Discovery*, George Vancouver's ship. The intricate sails and ropes—sheets and lines, all in miniature—make my head swim. Each passerby becomes Gulliver.

By a window, an inukshuk looks east. The display's set on a pile of boulders, adding a natural element. Traditionally, inukshuks, or inuksuit, served as spiritual conduits. Landmarks as well, to aid navigation, beacons in the mist and the snow.

Another case is filled with tools made of wood, bone, ivory, and stone: adzes, harpoons, a blubber oil lamp, and the smooth, rounded curve of an ulu knife, perfect for skinning and flensing, slicing and chopping. Next to this are more soapstone carvings in cold polished grey.

Then an igloo display, another model, the winter shelter cut vertically in half, as though Gulliver took the ulu and sliced this dome home neatly in two. Inside, a tiny person is seated on a raised bed of skins. Tools and weapons lean on a wall: bow and arrows, harpoons. Furs are being stretched and dried, and a stone pot sits by the bed. It looks cozy, a stationary version of that temporary-permanent home of Craig and Mr. Mann, the vast world beyond—only here I imagine it scored with a frosted howl of wind.

To warm up, mentally, at least, I return to the main room and visit with Rebecca Duncan, language specialist and translator for Sḵwx̱wú7mesh Úxwumixw, the Squamish Nation. We chat briefly about a range of things, principally about being here by the water at Snauq. Then the spotlight's on Rebecca, as it's her task to welcome and greet the gathered visitors. She begins with the traditional Salish greeting of O Siem, expressed physically with palms open, arms inward and up. This salutation is equal parts tribute and salute, a show of thanks too. Which I liken to the first words we learn in new languages—*hello, please*, and *thank you*—extensions of manifestation and gratitude.

Rebecca's knowledge, patience, and manner resonate with the care of an Elder, an echo of those lessons of leadership, who best to lead going forward. Adorned in a cedar-bark hat, she plays a frame drum that has the look of a Celtic bodhran. Holding the beater, or mallet, she begins with a lesson in the musical art.

"I'll start with a paddle song, which is in a way like a prayer. And the beat goes like this." She strikes the skin of the drum with the beater.

Boom ...

Boom ...

Boom ...

Boom ...

"This beat, you know it's a paddle song. The same tempo as paddling. But this ..." She hits the drum double time. *Boom. Boom. Boom. Boom.* "This accompanies a story or dance. Maybe tales of Raven or Eagle, a mask dance as well. And this ..." She doubles the tempo again. *Boom boom boom boom.* "This means it's a party!"

A round of laughter.

"That's celebration," she says with a smile. "But tonight, it's a paddle song. You see, we're all in canoes. Many different canoes. Your own canoe. Your family canoe. And community, that's another canoe. Each canoe, we all paddle each day. Personal. Family. Community. It takes balance and care. Remember, this is a maritime city."

She then makes eye contact with each of us as she plays and sings a traditional paddle song, the story shared in the cadence of propelling a boat. In the Salishan, I pick up *Snauq*, the one word I identify. The message, however, is clear: welcome, caring, balance.

Afterward we move to another room for further explanation of the re-envisioned museum, which will include canoe carving in a working studio reminiscent of the space Margaret and I explored on the other side of Seṅáḵw, or Snauq. There's to be greater focus on storytelling through immersive and sensory exhibits. I note a few sound bites as curators and politicians take turns addressing the group.

"In spaces like this, context starts with a map." (This I understand.)

"We want less light to better preserve each display."

"When you see the *St. Roch*, we want you to think less 'ship in a bottle' and more 'ship in the Arctic.'"

"Including more voices, an Indigenous perspective. Seeing history through an Inuit lens." (Again, an emphasis on decolonizing exhibits.)

I read a record of the ship's crew, a sample of those aboard for the *St. Roch*'s epic journeys: Ole Andreasen, William Cashin, George Dickens, "Frenchie" Chartrand, and a special mention of Joe Panipakuttuk, the Inuit hunter who, along with his family, helped to guide Henry Larsen, the skipper, through the Passage.

The event shifts again as we meet Maarta Kyak and Deborah Kigjugalik Webster, both of northern families directly connected to Joe Panipakuttuk when he sailed with Larsen. Maarta and Deborah share their stories through video, highlighting the Inuit role in what was otherwise a sovereign excursion. In a back issue of *Nunatsiaq News*, I discover a succinct synopsis of what we're discussing.

> In 1944 the tiny Royal Canadian Mounted Police vessel *St. Roch* headed north from Halifax, bound for Vancouver via the Northwest Passage.
>
> . . .
>
> The vessel put in at Pond Inlet to pick up an Inuit family who would assist the crew on its passage. Joe Panipakuttuk was a hunter who had been born at Igarjuaq, a whaling and trading site just east of Pond Inlet, in 1914. He was accompanied by his wife, Letia, three children under 10 years of age, and his mother, Panikpak ... who insisted on

bringing her granddaughter Mary Panigusiq, whom she was raising. Joe was also accompanied by his 15-year-old stepson Aariak ... Larsen considered Joe and Aariak natural-born seamen. Seventeen sled dogs were also loaded in Pond Inlet.[35]

The article includes diary entries written by Panipakuttuk.

I remember I left Pond Inlet on the RCMP boat in the summer of 1944, on the 17th day of August. On our way we stopped at Nalluaq where I got two dogs. Captain Larsen obtained two narwhal tusks at this place. I shot one bear when we were leaving. On crossing Lancaster Sound from Nalluaq a very heavy gale set in.[36]

Panipakuttuk's account resumes three days later.

We arrived at a small island off the west end of the big one we had been sailing alongside ... It is said that in the old days some white men got lost and the head of the expedition was never found although many ships had called here searching for him. The name of the man was Franklin. On the island I saw some stone markers and graves of white men.[37]

Putting the party at Beechey Island, where Sir John Franklin and crew landed and wintered in their futile attempt to escape from the north. It would take the better part of another century for researchers to locate his wreck, the ill-fated HMS *Erebus*. A vessel horribly named for the Greek god of darkness and gloom, the offspring of Chaos. They might as well have named the ship *Doomed*.

Panipakuttuk noted that Larsen and crew erected inukshuks at a number of places where they stopped. I assume those built by the settler sailors were intended as landmarks rather than spiritual conduits. Then again, maybe not. Perhaps the environment and time spent with locals influenced their thoughts and behaviour.

In spite of a lifetime of hunting, Panipakuttuk had never seen muskox. One record noted in the article has Larsen pointing toward Melville

Island, letting Panipakuttuk know that muskox were there. To which Panipakuttuk wrote,

> I went to where he directed me … I searched the land with a telescope and saw no sign of live animals. All I could see were huge rocks. Mr. Larsen said that these were musk oxen, these very things I thought to be rocks. So I looked again through the telescope and the rocks began to move. We got near the musk oxen and I found out that they were carrying something on their backs. I thought to myself they must be carrying their little ones, but I soon learned that this was part of the animal. When you see musk oxen for the first time, they have such a huge back on them![38]

To add a superb visual to Panipakuttuk's notes, here in the museum, a broad-backed taxidermied muskox stands next to a window, keeping an eye on parked cars. A sign tells me he's named Bruce. Which transports me to a previous Arctic adventure, when I trekked southern Greenland. In Narsarsuaq, a cook had prepared muskox with peppers. By the time I arrived, however, the muskox was off, so instead I had whale and reindeer (Arctic surf and turf). I never thought to ask if that muskox had a name too.

Another *St. Roch* account written by one of the crew refers to Panipakuttuk's mom:

> One time in the Passage we weren't sure where we were. Even Larsen was unsure. Then the Eskimo woman [Panikpak] looked at the coastline and checked with the chart. "That's where we are," she said. And that's where we were![39]

Reminding me of Ashley Samsone's reference to wayfaring. This is a fine example. Only the white crew believed they were sailing the unknown. In fact, they were navigating a place known intimately by generations for millennia. Apparently the Inuit community liked Larsen and called him Pallursi, a word to describe someone with eyes that slope outward and down at the corners. The squint of a mariner.

I take another look around the *St. Roch*, while away to the west the sun's come out to set, taking a bow in maritime reds, forcing me to squint in a manner that might resemble Pallursi. Meanwhile the aroma of the old ship lingers, evocative and intense, an earthy essence of canvas, lacquered timber, and a hint of bridled humanity.

In a tight wood-and-brass cubicle, I stand at a captain's bridge simulator, which gives a sense of displacement, aligning another vertical realm. Something about it exudes *Heart of Darkness*, Conrad's fictionalized version of delving into jungle, uncertain and fearful. Only here, at the helm of *St. Roch*, there'd be no hippos or crocs. Maybe a narwhal or a beluga, exhaling amid riddles of icebergs.

The evening winds up, the crowd thins, and I leave under that sailor-red sky, the weather now stellar. Sun dogs fan on the water in amber and crimson. And I stand for a moment next to the *Ben Franklin* submersible, let my mind sink with the sun toward the sea, everything splashed in bronze-gold.

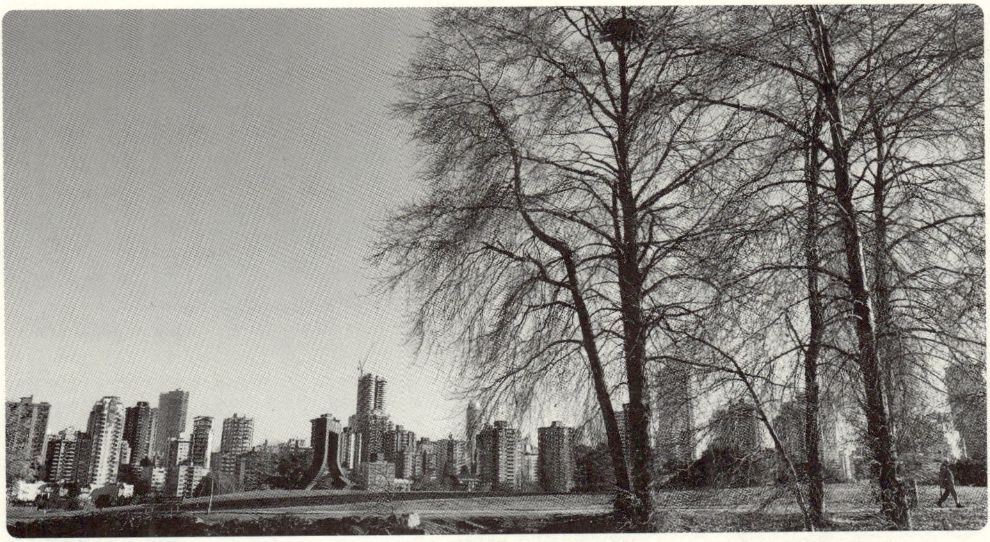

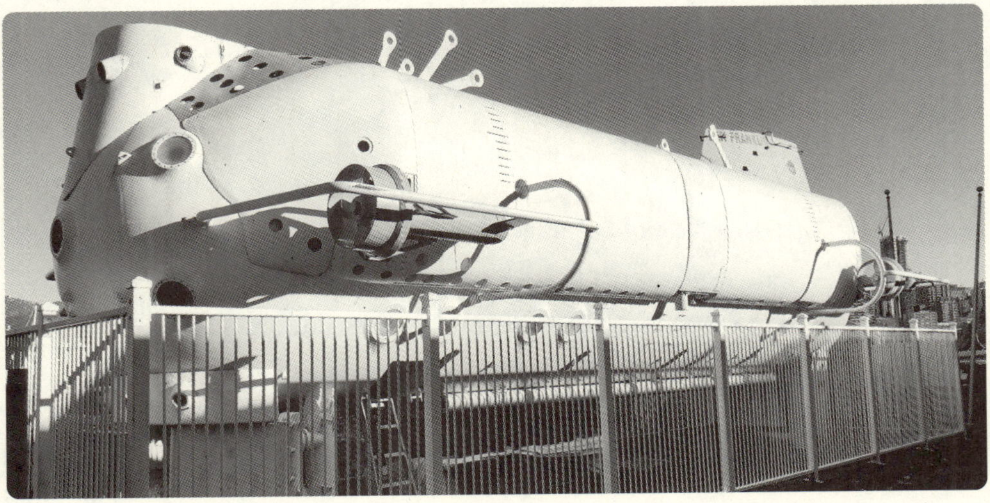

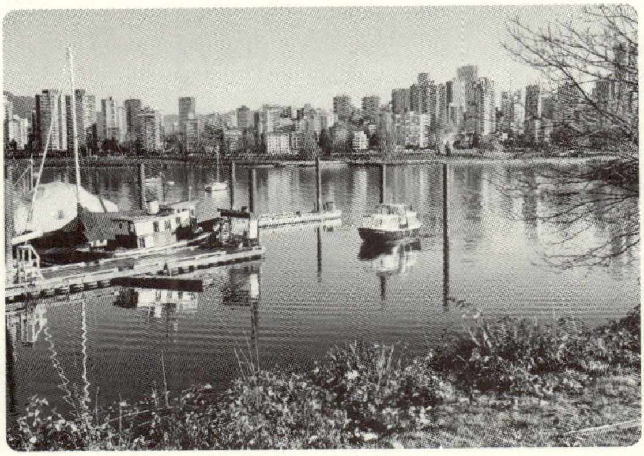

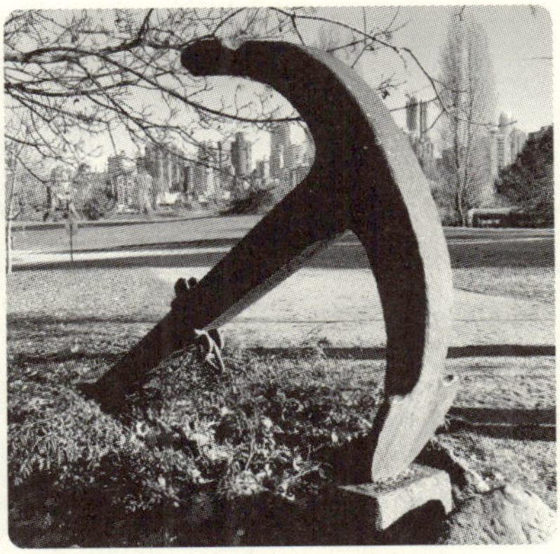

CLOCKWISE FROM TOP: a bald eagle's nest near the Vancouver Maritime Museum; the *Ben Franklin* submersible beside the Vancouver Maritime Museum; the ship's anchor next to the Vancouver Maritime Museum; a False Creek Ferry arriving at the Vancouver Maritime Museum.

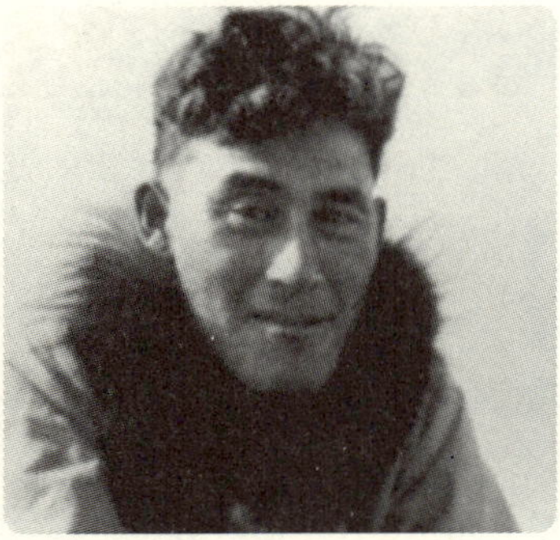

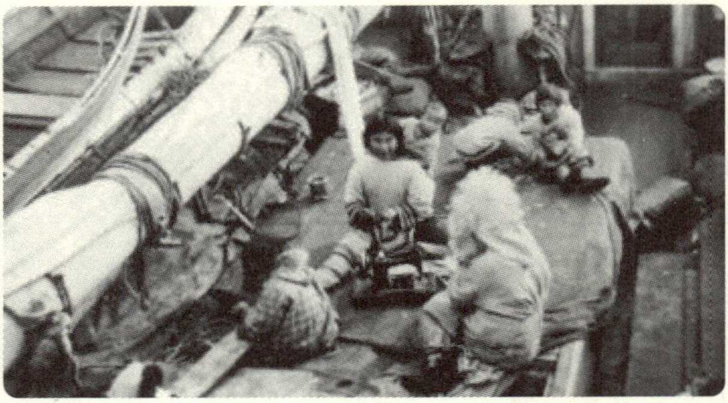

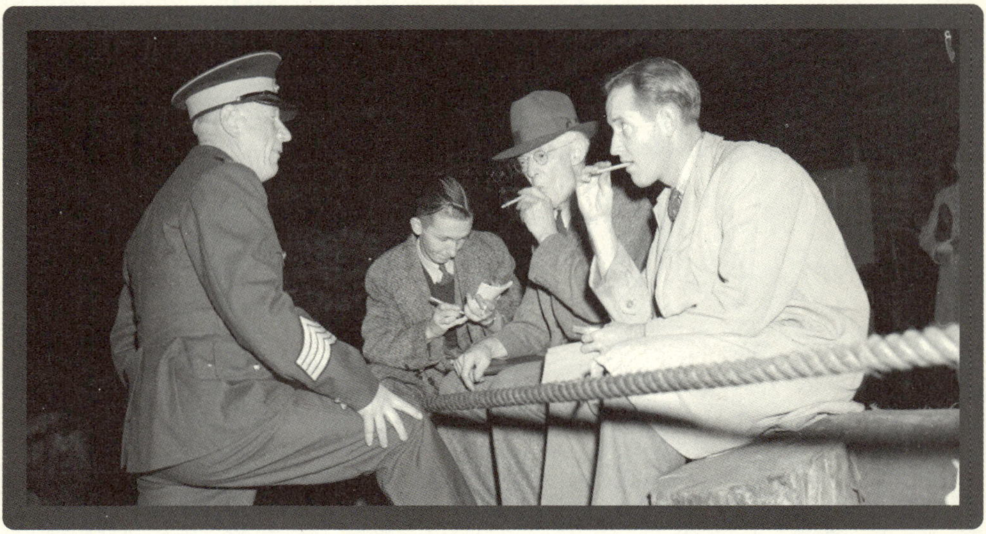

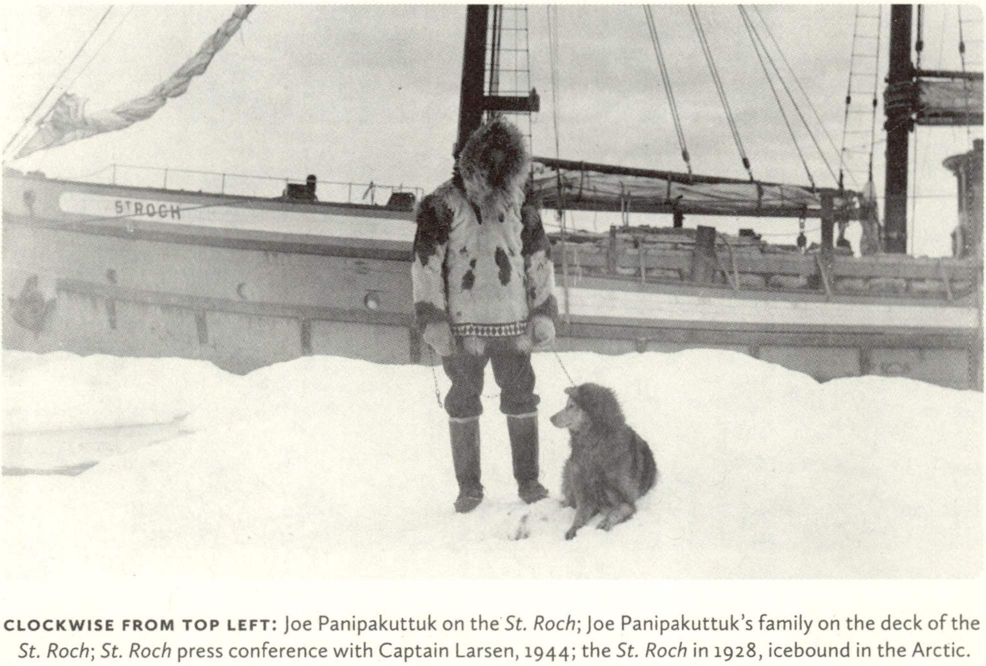

CLOCKWISE FROM TOP LEFT: Joe Panipakuttuk on the *St. Roch*; Joe Panipakuttuk's family on the deck of the *St. Roch*; *St. Roch* press conference with Captain Larsen, 1944; the *St. Roch* in 1928, icebound in the Arctic.

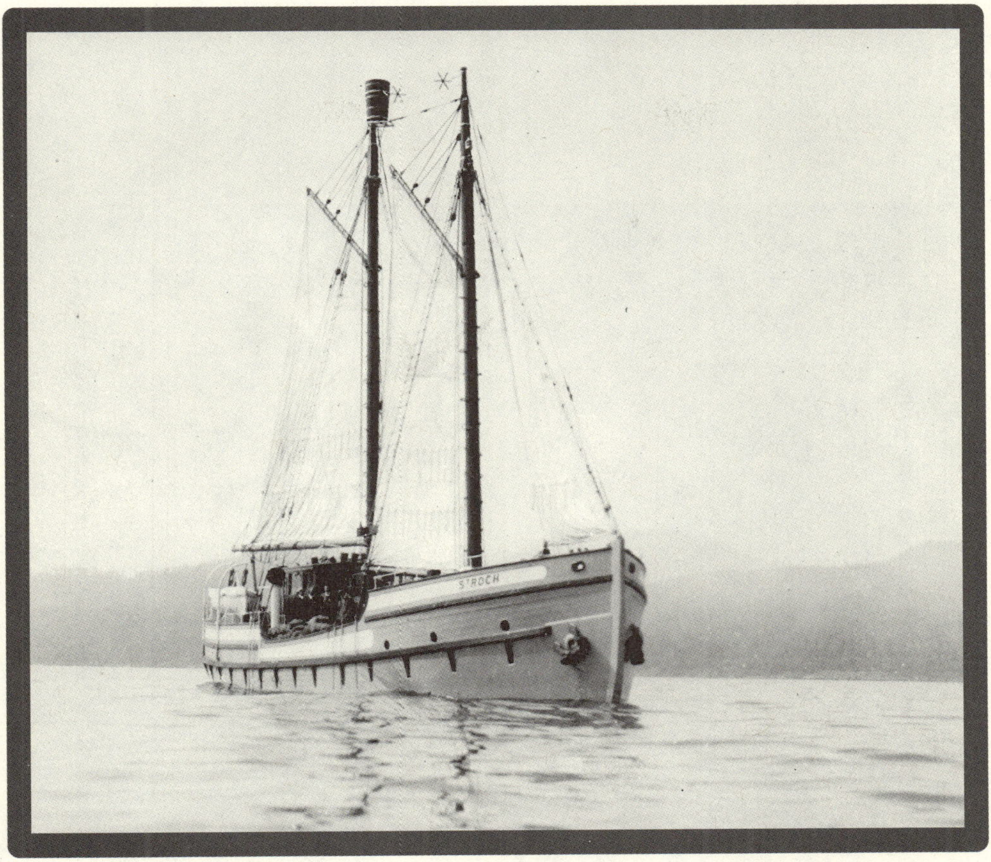

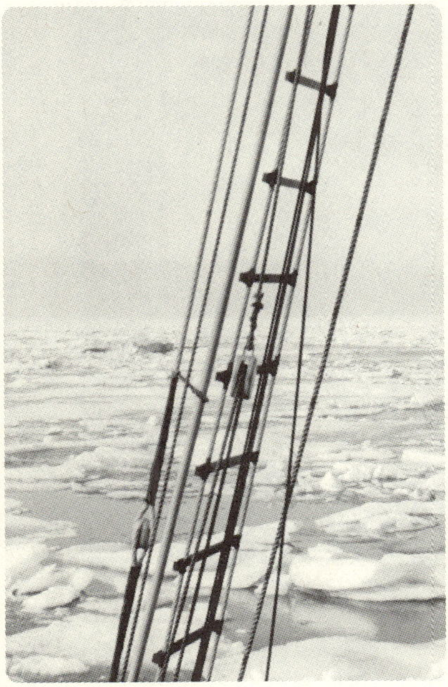

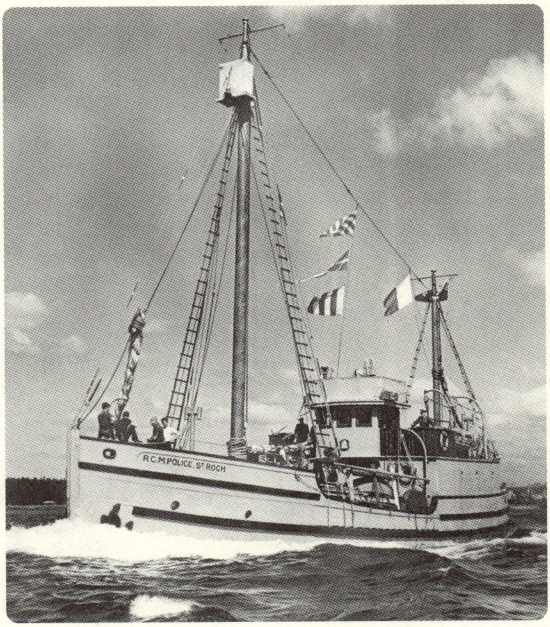

CLOCKWISE FROM TOP: the *St. Roch*, 1928; the *St. Roch* leaving Halifax, 1944; the *St. Roch* returning to the Northwest Passage, 1944.

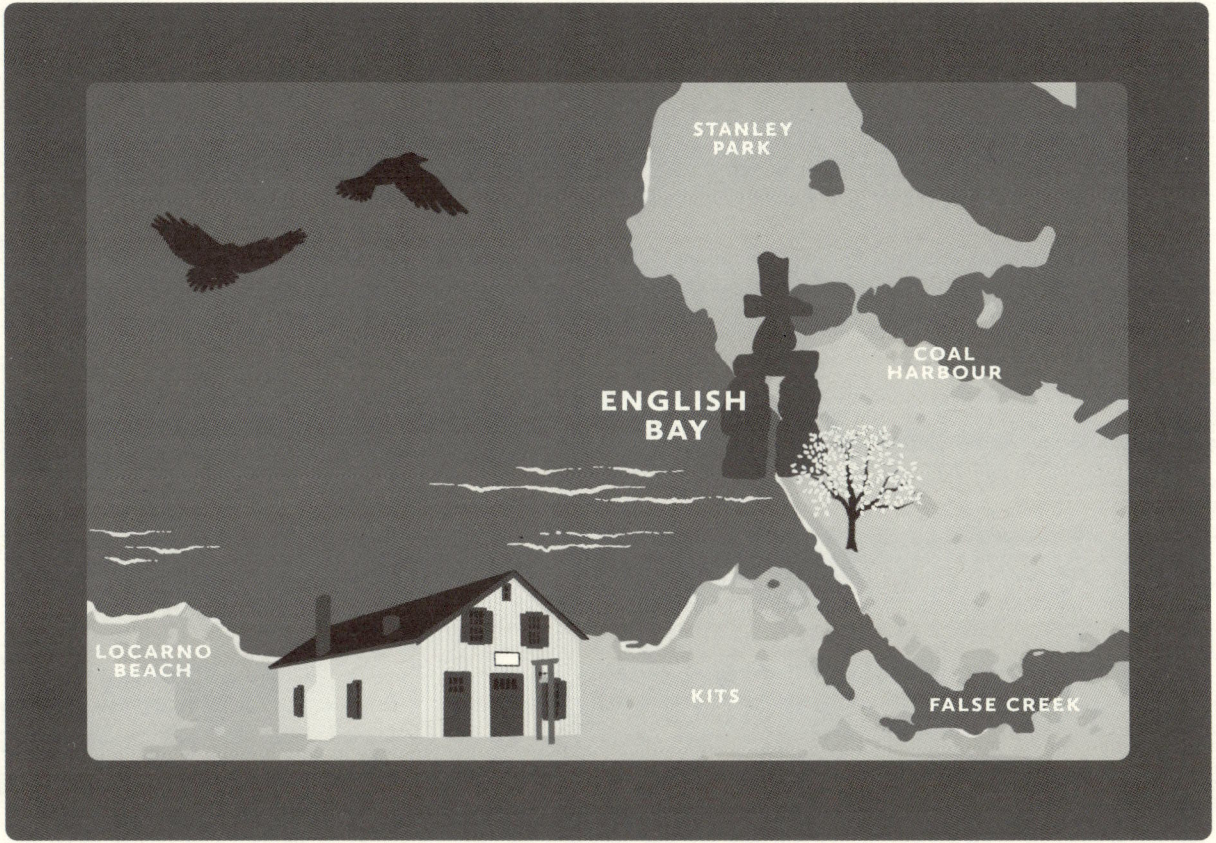
STANLEY PARK
COAL HARBOUR
ENGLISH BAY
LOCARNO BEACH
KITS
FALSE CREEK

ENGLISH BAY BOUNDARIES

Tributaries

INLETS, CREEKS, AND A DEVILISH TALE

A DIVERSION TODAY: Rather than walking the water, I've taken shelter from an overcast sky in a diner a short stroll from the beach. On a wall, a print of Van Gogh's *Starry Night* grabs my attention. Considered by many to be the Dutch artist's magnum opus, the oil on canvas was painted in Southern France in 1889. A few things resonate: The view, which is not unlike what I walked through to get here, looking east before sunrise. The swirls in the sky, twirled brushstrokes that resemble a whirlpool or waves. The colours too—the heavy blue of indeterminate water and air, as though still deciding whether to gust into gales or settle into a lingering calm. In front of an imagined village, Van Gogh added a shrub much like a flame in the half light.

The painting reminds me of a mosaic in Vancouver's Downtown Eastside, a piece called *Phoenix* that depicts the city's Great Fire of 1886, when Squamish paddlers launched from Burrard Inlet's North Shore, going *toward* the inferno to aid and to rescue. Like many Indigenous legends, it's been passed down not only orally but with music. Another paddle song, the tempo of blade pulled through water. In this I hear mallet on drum, *booms* in four-four pacing that glide that Devian spoke of, when a boat joins the song, skimming the surface in flight.

I wonder if news of the destruction of the New World town of Vancouver reached the south end of France, if Van Gogh had any notion of a distant bird rising from ashes. True to his art's name, in the painting, there are stars. Whether he saw them for real as he worked is unknown. Each spin of light has a hint of those yellows he loved, the same tones as his *Sunflowers* painted in Paris and Arles. At a glance the stars resemble the swirls you might see when a snake puts you under its spell, those cartoon depictions of hypnotic eyes.

The twirls of light on the dark also look like a fireworks display. The same scene that I saw from a tour boat launched from Coal Harbour. Another work event, this one purely for pleasure. A brief burble while enjoying Vancouver's Celebration of Light, the summertime fireworks show that occurs on a few separate days. Each show is sponsored with VIP seating on shore while the rest of the city crams along bridges and beaches to enjoy bright explosions above English Bay.

Another departure as I make my way over Ironworkers Memorial Bridge, this time heading north to meet with a fellow explorer—adventurer, author, and filmmaker Frank Wolf—for a chance to visit, have a beer, and swap stories. What makes this apropos is that Frank spends much of his life on the water, paddling a canoe or a kayak, occasionally pulling oars in a rowboat. He knows the water, its moods, and its appeal as well as anyone.

Later, with a pint in hand, I ask what our coastlines and water in particular mean to him.

Frank's response is to smile as though I've offered him a piece of his favourite dessert. His look, by the way, is pure mariner: woolly beard, stout cap, and blue eyes that I want to call lapis.

"That's easy," he says. "Escape. Being on the water represents complete freedom. It can be therapeutic as well. Times, I'll paddle from Whytecliff to Bowen. I do that in the kayak. There's a feeling of ritual.

I've worked with groups there as well, individuals dealing with mental health issues. Like a retreat, exploration and healing. It could involve meditation. Maybe microdosing mushrooms as well." He chuckles. "Now *that* can be an adventure. Journeys within journeys." He takes a sip of beer. "You can step off, on an island, and instantly you're in another world."

I write that one down.

"Even around here," he continues. "False Creek. Granville Island. You find 'creek critters,' people living rough on their boats. It becomes their world. I've seen squatters, junkies, thieves. Like *Mad Max*."

Which strikes me as a parallel with the "squatters" who for years inhabited False Creek shores, mostly the north side—settler workers, coopers, and loggers, labourers, and tradespeople—when Granville Island was still Industrial Island. People called the shanty settlements "hobo jungles," the residents "shackers." The shacker population swelled during the Depression as False Creek's tinworks, shipbuilding, and logging came to a virtual standstill.

"A guy I know," Frank adds, "interesting character. Brilliant. He works on wrecks at the boatyard on Granville Island. Salvaging, servicing, reclaiming, and rebuilding boats." Bringing the image of those sunken vessels to mind. "Think of the layers of stories, each boat: people, journeys, and lives."

And I feel the same sense of unease as when I stared at the wreck in the shallow blue-green. Questioning if I'd seen it move, if only slightly. As though it were almost, almost still sailing.

Close to home once again, for a run heading west by the shore. Behind me, the tapering east end of False Creek is what the Salish would call X̱áywá7esks, "narrow passage."[40] More toponyms from times when map-making, like storytelling, was oral. The beauty of such descriptive, detailed place names is how they result in geographic specificity. Places are singularly identified. Comparisons become unrequired. Learning each place and its name, like a poem or song lyrics, results in its own form of wayfinding. Actual songlines. The same process Ashley Samsone described as she'd cut through a forest, considered a form of memory map. Resulting in what I consider, cartographically, as stepping-stone paths: from way*faring* to way*finding*, then eventual signage, the indicators or blazes of way*marking*.

Now, however, pigeonholed by linguistics through street signs and satellite maps, I'm running on a multi-use path where pedestrians and cyclists share asphalt, gravel, and grass. Next to this are thick laurel hedges with clusters of gnarled cedar. Near Kits Beach, I learn the Salish name for this stretch was X̱epx̱páy̓em, "having red cedar."[41] Leaving me to believe that apart from the houses and condos, it's been like this a very long time.

Finches *chit-chit* in shrubs as a fat full moon is descending. The tide's high, and the thin strip of shore has a paving of oysters and clams. Sun glints on West End high-rises, and on the bay is a brig, its profile the same as HMS *Chatham*. I take it all in, as much as I can. Then do a double take at where a pole protrudes from the water, something I've not seen there before. And I realize it's the top of a mast, another wreck in the inlet, maybe caused by the big full moon tide.

Continuing west, I pass a string of parks adjacent to Point Grey Road intersections. One at Trafalgar, one at Stephens, one named for city park advocate Margaret Pigott. Then Tatlow and Volunteer Parks. On earlier *Perfect Day* walks, this space was undergoing construction, a makeover, and revitalization. Now it looks mostly done: pristine fences, a creek bed lined with smooth rocks, a path with places to sit. At the shoreline somewhere is a stone the Coast Salish used to hone adzes and knives: Ts'mts'ámels, "tool-sharpening rock."[42] For the life of me, I can't figure out which hunk of basalt or granite it could be. Maybe multiple stones served that purpose.

I survey the space, an hourglass of treed green, the stream bed now carving a gooseneck into the sea, and then find a city description of what I'm now seeing:

> The Vancouver Park Board is restoring a small segment of a historical stream in Volunteer and Tatlow Parks originally known as "First Creek."

> This project is a unique opportunity to daylight the stream and connect the existing stream in Tatlow and Volunteer Parks to English Bay and improve access to the beach and shoreline.[43]

The synopsis continues, highlighting enhancements including rainwater management, an accessible ramp, native plantings, and a bird habitat with pollinators and water-based species. It's part of an initiative called Weaving the City Together, a reconnection of landscapes, water improvement, and ecosystem enrichment. The city's goal is to adapt to climate change, restore wild spaces, and "Seek Truth as a foundation for Reconciliation."[44]

I didn't realize a creek ran through here; most of it had been buried and clogged, exactly why the space was ripe for revitalization. Like the green space around Habitat Island and Olympic Village, a kind of O Siem or rewelcoming to all that lived here before.

Rivers in general come to mind, which so often define a landscape, channels of exploration and trade that formed much of this country's settler-based past. Every search I began on this topic seemed to steer me toward surveyor and cartographer David Thompson, as though I were back on a raft plunging down rapids, the explorer at the mouth of each river guiding my wanderings to where fresh and saltwater commingle.

Having lived most of my life by a lake or the sea, I'd always been mystified by rivers. Something about surging runnels and eddies, whether frothy and fast or murky and slow, left me slightly unnerved. Rivers caused drownings and floods, that was what I knew. So I tried to unwind all of that, to find the beauty and calm in the channels that carve through the province. And with a small trailer in tow, I spent a season exploring BC rivers—a few big ones, that is. What I considered reverse-engineering Vancouver shores by heading inland to headwaters. Memories, however, tend to pair with the rivers I followed, some pristine, others muddied.

I began a new journal with a Kerouac line from *On the Road*, "Let us sleep by rivers and purify our ears."[45] A sensation I longed to experience. And so, with my little mobile apartment, much like Craig and Mr. Mann, I ventured out, in this case following the water inland from Vancouver.

I began with the Fraser River, on the south of the city where Borden made a name for himself at c̓əsnaʔəm, the Musqueam village in what's now South Van. Here the river splits around Sea Island, home to YVR, Vancouver International Airport. Iona Beach Regional Park tops this extension of silt, a green space that quite appropriately resembles an emerald-cut gem. If you happen to be airborne in a plane at this point, seated by a window, the park offers a visual surprise, as the long twinning points of Iona Jetty and North Jetty give the oddly shaped park the look of an oversized prawn crawling into the ocean.

To the east, still in South Van, the Fraser breaks again around Mitchell Island, former agricultural space that's now fully industrial. Farther south, dun-coloured arms carve their way through Richmond and Delta, making more sediment islands. At the Port Mann Bridge, another confluence offers more options north along the Pitt River, or east, the route that I chose, to follow the wash of the Fraser.

I could've also treated Simon Fraser as a river-based guide, but by the time I reached Kamloops, where the Fraser River shakes hands with the Thompson, I'd learned more about both explorers, and it was images of David Thompson I retained. Perhaps because Fraser was first and foremost a trader, exploration fuelled by industry, while Thompson seemed more driven to explore, communicated through his cartography.

Called "the greatest land geographer who ever lived," Thompson's work reset a bar in map-making.[46] To this day, two centuries on, his charts remain nearly flawless. Maybe it's that melding of science and art that appeals, another maker of maps who saw water as the primary element, with land simply there to contain it. Or it could be the nickname he earned, the Stargazer, a moniker given by the First Peoples he travelled with through Canada's Prairies and foothills, the Blackfoot Nations of the Kainai, Piikani, and Siksika.[47]

Thompson was fluent in multiple Indigenous languages, a lover of the land and its people. As he travelled, he sketched what he saw, navigating with nautical instruments. His note-taking was constant, calculations involving the sun, moon, and tides. Measurements made with a compass, protractor, and sextant contributed to his Stargazer handle. I like to believe if it weren't for the demands of sponsors and business, he too would've made maps by toponym, charting by narrative, paddle, and beater.

His vocation, however, didn't start in this manner. Prior to this, Thompson worked as a clerk and apprentice, later for the Hudson's Bay Company. When his apprenticeship contract concluded, the usual completion or retirement gift for employees was an outfit of tailor-made clothes. But Thompson instead asked for surveying tools, like a budding scientist requesting a chemistry set rather than socks. And in a rather grand send-off, his employer presented him with all the map-making gear he'd hoped for, as well as a new worsted suit. For Thompson, Christmas came early that year.

In an interesting footnote, Thompson used the new kit to create his first drawings at the same time George Vancouver was aboard the *Mexicana* admiring Spanish maps of what's now West Point Grey and False Creek in 1792. Thompson, however, drew his earliest charts around Lake Athabasca before heading south. His travels took him across the continent's northwest, tracking the river now bearing his name, a river that joins with the Fraser to meet the Pacific. I imagine it all cinched together, sketched in free-flowing lines. Thompson's Indigenous nickname, Stargazer, and his new garb their own form of star blanket, a link to celestial skies and the unending flow of water that led me to the spot on a map he created.

A few vivid memories remain of that season of my own river transit. One is fishing for brook trout near Princeton, meeting point of the Similkameen and Tulameen Rivers, on one quiet, cold, late-season morning. At a bend in the Similkameen, the fish were in flight, soaring in speckled rainbows. But not one would respond to any fly that I offered. Working a wide stretch of river, I tried every lure that I had: mayflies and gnats, Tom Thumbs and Doc Spratleys, even a small woolly worm. Repeatedly, nothing. The trout nosed my lures, gave the odd nudge of disdain, but none would bite. After a few hours in the icy dawn, I could no longer feel my fingers or hands and made my way to a diner, where I spent several minutes simply holding a hot cup of coffee. The best coffee that ever existed.

Another memory surfaces, this one surreal. It took place farther east, where Thompson veered south to explore the Columbia River. I was having a cowboy-style bath, splashing river water over my head, when I noticed a prawn floating by, looking like Iona Park from above. A decent-sized specimen, bright and pink, it looked freshly plucked from the pot. Then another went by. I was confused. These looked like jumbo shrimp swimming by, in BC's Southern Interior. Until I realized there was a person upriver, another camper, I guess, throwing up prawns they had eaten. I just happened to be downstream as the vomit went by, romantically heading to sea.

With a shudder and a chuckle, I decide that I've run far enough and slow to a walk, continuing west from revitalized Tatlow and Volunteer Parks. Up ahead is a spot I've been meaning to visit, the Old Hastings Mill Store Museum. Opening hours are limited, so spending time there hasn't felt easy. But if I'm honest, I suspect I've avoided the space because it's known, so I've read, to be haunted.

Even here I feel Thompson tagging along, for he too had his own eerie tale to tell. Not a ghost story as such, but a face-to-face visit with Satan. In his personal journal he wrote of the experience, which he clearly found more than unsettling. According to the handwritten notes, Lucifer came into the cabin where Thompson was camped near a south BC river. Oddly enough, the devil sat down and played him at checkers. Stated Thompson,

> I was sitting at a small table with the chequerboard before me, when the devil sat down opposite to me, his features and colour were those of a Spaniard, he had two short black horns on his forehead which pointed forwards; his head and body down to his waist (I saw no more) was covered with glossy black curling hair.[48]

As they played, Thompson noted, the devil lost every game.

> He got up or rather disappeared. My eyes were open, it was broad daylight, I looked around, all was silence and solitude, was it a dream or was it reality? I could not decide.[49]

Leaving us to determine for ourselves what it was, who it was Thompson saw. His journal, by the way, was shared posthumously, never intended to be made public. He wrote solely for his own records in the same way he drew maps, with care and scientific precision—observations, calculations, and facts. Making the story far more intriguing.

There's something, mind you, about the devil and board games. When I trekked across Europe as part of my *Gone Viking* excursions, I encountered multiple places of worship with a chessboard affixed to a wall. Often affiliated with Templars, a checkerboard or chessboard hung on a diagonal is known to keep the devil away. Apparently the Prince of Darkness finds the pattern confusing. So when I read Thompson's account of the devil repeatedly losing at checkers, I have to admit, I wasn't surprised.

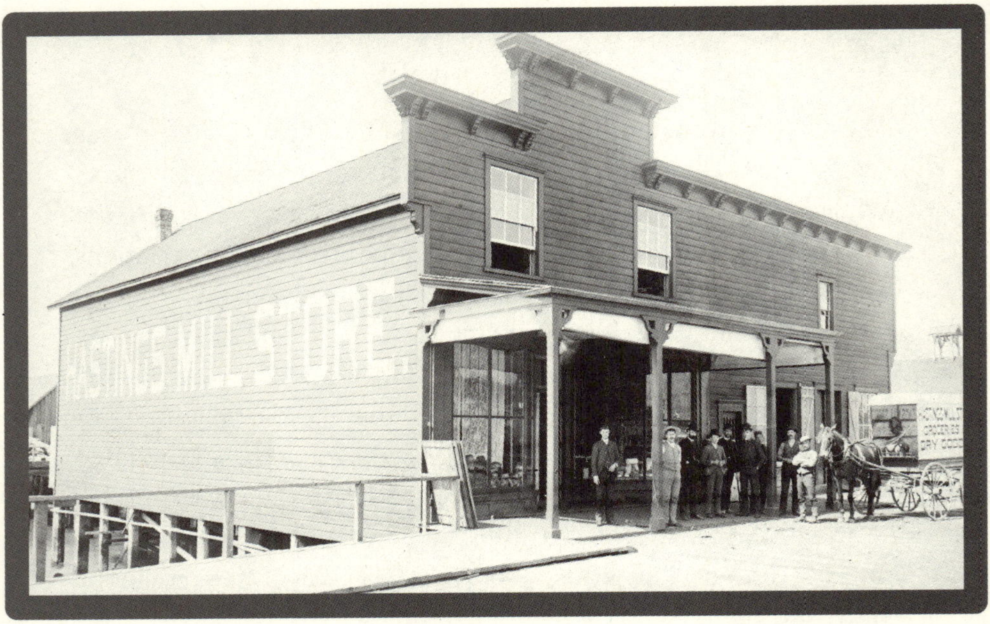

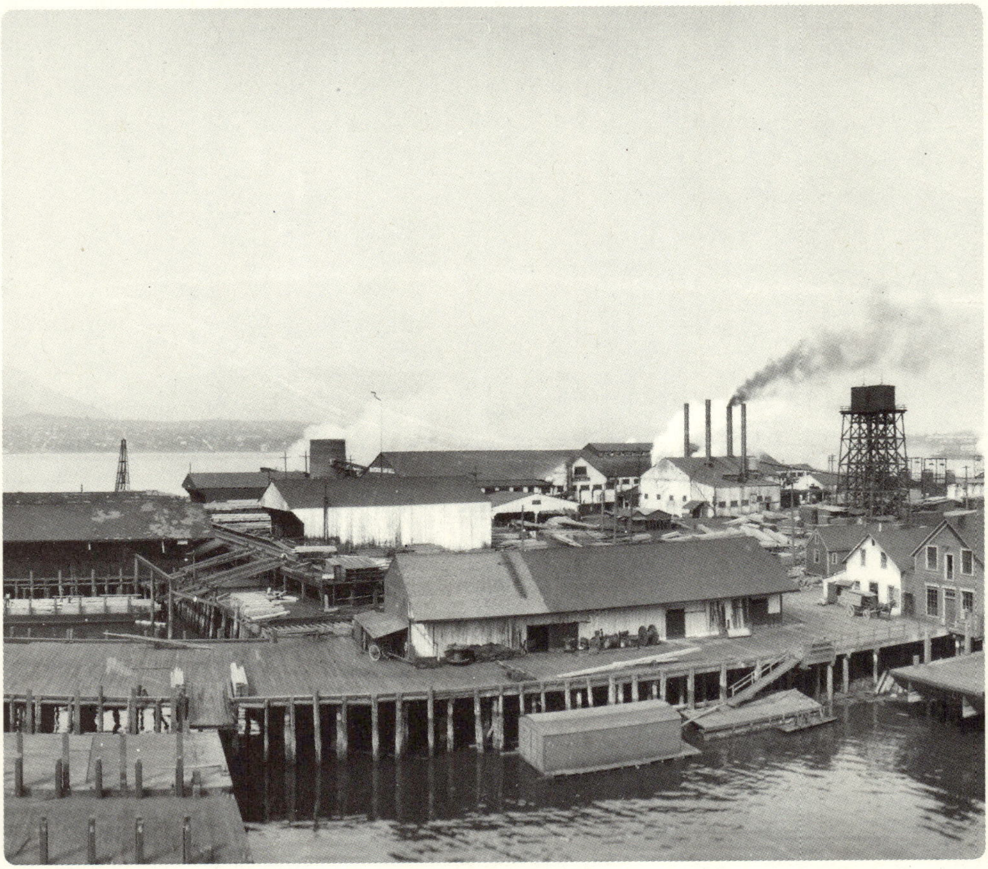

TOP: the Hastings Mill Store, 1888.
BOTTOM: Hastings Mill, 1913.

The Floating Museum

VANCOUVER'S OLDEST BUILDING, THE OLD HASTINGS MILL STORE

I START BY walking the grounds here at the corner of Alma and Point Grey Road, dense with cypress, maple, sword fern, and azalea. A sign, "Hastings Mill Park Museum," sets a tone. Attached are two notices, one for a "Film Noir Movie Night," the other for "A Haunted Evening." On the poster are graphics of bats, as though it's always Halloween here. Adding to this, a murder of crows have just surrounded the museum, cawing in unison, and I almost need to force myself forward, my legs feeling not unlike how they do when I exit a boat.

There's a mosaic on the walkway, black and white stones in a windmill design. At a glance it could be a propeller. The building itself is substantial, two sturdy storeys that could pass for three, white-painted clapboard with windows and doors trimmed in red. A brass bell hangs by the door, fixed in place. The front entry resembles a slab of parquet, flooring flipped up on end. Benches offer a view of the inlet, where a clump of white sails indicate a lesson's now underway. From the Yacht Club, a nautical pinging of rigging on masts adds a suitable score.

Before heading in, I read a plaque placed by the City of Vancouver, this being a heritage building.

> As a survivor of the Great Fire in 1886, the Hastings Mill Store is Vancouver's oldest building. It was built in 1865 as the general store for the Hastings Sawmill Company at the foot of Dunlevy Street near Gastown. This was also Vancouver's first post office and later served as a library and community centre. In 1930 the building was floated to this site and the Native Daughters of British Columbia opened it as a museum in honour of the province's earliest pioneers.

A thick slice of settler history here in the timber and beams—library, post office, community centre, and general store—coming from the port and downtown via water. Another doorway that could well be lit up like the ones in my time travel app. All I have to do to return to the past is to enter.

Pushing open the heavy red door, I'm greeted by Anita, a smiling curator who in turn introduces me to Theo, an enormous black Newfoundland crossbreed. The huge dog presses a nose to my leg with affection, leaving a warm string of drool. Without prompting, Anita describes where we're standing.

"This building was built at the Port of Vancouver on pilings like these." She indicates the floorboards and beams. "Solid old-growth planks. See here, the darker wood is from the original construction, 1865. Whereas this lighter wood"—she points to the other side of the floor—"tongue in groove, is the newer panelling from 1930."

Like an usher, she steers me to an alcove, a clutter of dusty items with photos and an actual hansom, a two-wheeled carriage that would've been pulled by a horse. It looks like it rumbled straight over from 221B Baker Street, and I expect Sherlock Holmes to pop out and declare Theo a hound.

On a small TV screen, a video plays on a loop. Old-timey music huffs from a speaker, the scratch of classic reel films. And I watch grainy footage of the museum crossing Burrard Inlet to here by barge, hauled around Prospect Point past Stanley Park and through English Bay. The same water now filled with tankers and white-sailed Hobie Cats. The next sequence is perhaps the most impressive: the engineering feat of hoisting this structure up the embankment to where it now sits. A hundred years ago, this shore was a cliff nearly twelve metres high. The method of raising the building, however, looks much the same as the method used to lift homes nearby. Now, to add one more storey. Then, to simply set it in place.

There are several photo displays of Vancouver's Great Fire on June 13, 1886. One vintage newspaper headline simply states, "Black Sunday." Another shows a hand-drawn map, an aerial city perspective. The downtown is halved, the West End all forest, the east of downtown labelled "CPR Townsite," False Creek probing farther east than it does today. "Vancouver" is written on the map as a note, almost an addendum, with a thick arrow pointing to Gastown. The arrow highlights the spot where the port is located, where the fire was most fearsome.

Next to this is a stylized version of the same city map, this one with paint on the image. What's now Coal Harbour, Stanley Park, the West End, and south downtown are the green of a heavy pine forest. CPR Townsite—the cleared land—is shown in off-white, with each "hot spot" of burn clearly labelled. "Fire Enters. Clearing Fires. Dense Mass Dry Fallen Trees." Then a blood-red inferno engulfing Hastings, Cordova, and Water Streets. At what appears to be the epicentre, "City Wharf" is surrounded in flame. Just east of Main Street is one more label: "Fire Ceases to Rage." And at the north edge of the burn, "Hastings Sawmill."

Despite a touch of the sensational, the drawing makes my skin crawl. It is, I realize, an accurate depiction. There's no hiding the innate terror of an entire city being consumed within a half-hour. Even here in the cool wooden space, a mizzle of light rain outside, a part of me can almost detect a faint whiff of resinous smoke, as though the fire left a charred creosote scar. I wonder if the darker wood, the original planking that Anita pointed to, could hold memories as well as aromas. There's a personality here, that's for sure, a trace of perseverance and obstinate hope. Community too. But no sign of ghosts at the moment.

Now, with the annoyingly catchy old music fixed in my brain—morose ragtime played two speeds too slow—I do a more thorough search through the exhibits: photos of the store on its floats with its tugboat and barge; a few more of workers standing next to the building as it leans like the Tower of Pisa; and old bric-a-brac, kettles and irons and pots. There's a milk jug, a grater, a pitchfork, a plough. Fierce-looking sawblades, little and large. And a fabulous map on the wall of Vancouver in 1890. The drawing is beautifully done, a soft 3-D angle making it all very lifelike. Thompson, I'm sure, would approve. The north–south gridwork of streets, skewed slightly east, looks the same as what I might find in a satellite view even now.

I see tools to make bread and equipment to turn logs into boards. Weirdly, these heavy implements look much the same. Now I find a series of black-and-white photos, time travel hung on a wall. There's a great shot of Swanamia, spouse of August Jack Khatsahlano, also known as Mary Anne. She's paddling, steering, at the stern of a long dugout canoe, which at the same time is being rowed by a man seated toward the bow. Between the two, a toddler peers over the gunwale. Based on the age of the photo, the location, it could be her eldest, Emma. All three look directly into the camera. It's a wonderful capture of motion as the canoe passes the shore of Seṅáḵw. Behind is a shed, a small version of the building I'm in now.

Next is another fine photo. This one is of Chief Joe Capilano, taken in 1906. Joe stands with a North Van ferry dock delegation, the send-off to Joe's meeting with King Edward "to address Indigenous territorial rights and the outlawing of the potlatch," according to museum signage. The venture was unsuccessful. In the photo, however, there's hope. Determination. Perhaps thirty people in all, six wrapped in star blankets, a stirring collection of Elders.

I do one more sweep through the exhibits and spot an overview of the building, describing where it originally stood at the foot of Gastown's Dunlevy Street. The old structure was to be demolished until it was saved and floated to here. Another story of rescue.

Then I come to a shelf where a homburg sits, caringly placed, as though just removed from a head. It's a felted beaver-fur hat, cleverly displayed near a rivet from the HBC steamship *Beaver*. In another odd circle of life, this sits next to a painting of the wreck of the *Beaver*, keeled at the base of Prospect Point's stony cliffs.

The *Beaver* was the first steamship to operate here, fur trading in the Pacific Northwest. For a time the ship served as a tugboat, then a survey vessel, drawing more maps from the water. Having chugged along this coast for a half century, the *Beaver* finally capsized, wrecked on the Stanley Park shore. Human error, tough tides, testy reefs, and apparently the great amount of booze consumed by the crew on that day all played a part in the mishap, which occurred in 1888.

The room opens up as exhibits accumulate, overwhelming in the volume of displays. More models of boats, with kayaks and canoes made of cedar. I see stone knives and arrowheads, some of which likely were sharpened on the rock called Ts'mts'ámels. There are mortars and pestles, baskets and spoons, some of wood, some of stone. And a vivid 1778 drawing by John Webber of the village of Yuquot, Nootka Sound, with buildings on a midden platform of shells, the same visual that may well have greeted travellers to Seṅáḵw or ċəsnaʔəm.

There's a picture of Joe Fortes, standing with staid pride by his cottage, impeccably dressed in a dark suit and a neatly brimmed hat. His pressed shirt is buttoned all the way up, and he's wearing a vest and an ascot. He leans on a low wooden fence fronting the garden, with a quiet confidence that makes me wish I could speak with him, to hear his story first-hand.

From here I come to a wall lined with paddles, some carved from cedar, some painted with red and green patterns depicting chinook salmon. Others are plain polished hardwood, their natural deep grain the extent of decoration.

I find a pair of now-and-then photos of Vancouver, taken in 1891 and 1923, the camera having been placed in the same location for both shoots, the heart of downtown. If I had to guess, I'd say it's where Robson and Granville Streets meet. Both shots have a northerly view. The North Shore mountains are unchanged, but the city skyline is low. There's no mistaking a bustling urban centre, just without skyscrapers. No Marine Building, no cruise ships. But in the shot from 1923 there's a tall-masted brig on the water, a doppelgänger of what's now anchored in English Bay. Along with this, small craft are rounding Deadman's Island while a chunky little vessel is beelining across Burrard Inlet to downtown, likely one of the West Van passenger ferries.

Feeling I've done this space justice, I give Theo a pat and head to the heavy red door. Behind me the scratchy video starts a fresh loop, the same miserable music, and it occurs to me I still haven't seen any ghosts. Then I realize maybe what's haunting this place aren't apparitions like Ebenezer's unwanted houseguests, but rather the very things I've experienced: a hint of ashen odour in the flooring, the essence of paddles pulling through sea, a knowing smile from Joe, and Swanamia holding my gaze from a wooden canoe as she passes the shore of Seṅák̲w.

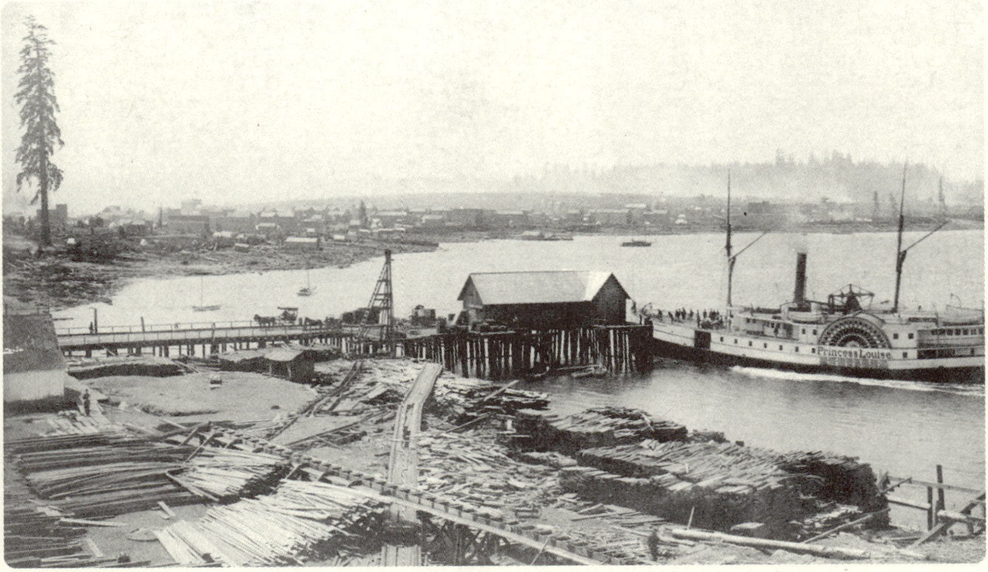

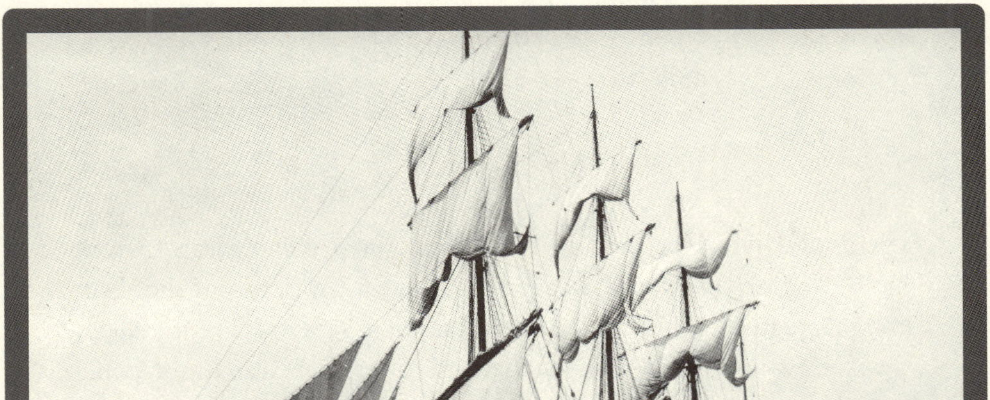

TOP: Hastings Mill, looking west, 1886.
BOTTOM: loading lumber at Hastings Mill, 1918–28.

Around English Bay

WATERSIDE ART AND THE WORLD'S SMALLEST MOTORIST

ANOTHER INVERSION TODAY, but not on a map. A cold weather front has moved in—low cloud, heavy rain. A day for waterproof shoes, an umbrella, a hood. For my visual notes, I admit, it's ideal, as I ventured out this same way yesterday, following the north edge of False Creek, going west. Picking up, more or less, from where I paddled the orange kayak, from Cambie Street Bridge toward Granville Island, with English Bay spreading ahead. Feathered friends for yesterday's walk were pigeons and gulls, cormorants too, as the sun rose in warm peachy tones that spoke of a promising day. Opposite to today's cast-iron sky.

Where the inlet's spanned by the art deco of Burrard Bridge, I enjoyed a unique wildlife display. Under the bridge, to one side, a family of river otters were swimming. Two mature adults with a pup or a whelp, the young otter behaving like any toddler might do, a puppy or a child, splashing and simply at play. The two grown otters, the parents, I presume, swam nearby, partially encircling the youngster, giving it free rein while remaining a protective distance away.

The otters moved on, farther into False Creek, but I stayed near the shore. Behind me, Vancouver Aquatic Centre rose in lumpy, moss-covered concrete with the look of an unfinished pyramid. The shoreline water was particularly clear near the passenger ferry pier, and I noticed a shark swimming next to the beach. *Wait, what?!* Then I realized it was a dogfish, what some call a mud shark—a big one, over a metre long. I've encountered these when fishing for salmon, as many anglers do in these waters. Fishers I know *hate* these fish. If they take your lure and get hooked, rather than shaking like game fish, a dogfish spins like a blender on high, twisting the line into nasty, braid-like knots. More often than not, the gear has to be cut and discarded. But here, far from a boat or a hook or a line, the fish was spectacular. As though I'd stumbled into an aquarium (for free) or been transported to a tropical destination. The only things missing were a surfboard and a lifeguard with a zinc-covered nose.

Under today's darkened sky I keep west, above scalloped-sand Sunset Beach. There are cycle lanes on the road next to pedestrian paths, with more walkways next to the shore. On the bay, the horizon's an outline of tankers at anchor, with a cruise ship inching this way to empty itself at the sails of Canada Place.

On the south side of False Creek, near Seńáḵw, is a meld of nature with civilization. A spot where the coast guard has its own access, a kind of marina within the marina, a channel lined with orange buoys. And on each neatly spaced float, a black cormorant stands, wings spread into cruciform. Each one could be a post-fire phoenix or an early Christian in Rome. Somber herons, meanwhile, watch from hemlocks, feather hands behind their backs, keeping their thoughts to themselves.

Continuing west, I pass two Vancouver Biennale exhibits, touchstones from previous walks. First, the steel multi-beamed *U* titled *217.5 Arc x 13* by sculptor Bernar Venet, designed to convey the beauty of raw metal within natural surroundings and the interconnectedness of people and nature. The piece offers a visual frame perfect for photos, and I can't help but liken it to the square of *Gate to the Northwest Passage*, that partial commemoration to George Vancouver. Only here the inspiration is science and nature, that green pie-shaped game piece again, rather than colonial history.

Now I reach the artwork *Engagement* on a slopy grass pitch ringed with trees. The installation is effectively two giant engagement rings, nine metres high, created by Dennis Oppenheim. Made of aluminum and steel, the rings are set with plexiglass "diamonds," oblique shapes that light up at night. When the light is enticing, be it sunny or dark, it feels like a studio set, and I often find myself snapping photo after photo of ships through the rings. Literal engagement through matrimonial bands. Not, I suspect, what the artist had in mind, yet Oppenheim stresses that all pieces are open to interpretation.

Ahead, at the curve of the bay, is yet another Biennale installation, Yue Minjun's *A-maze-ing Laughter*, fourteen bronze statues, each depicting the sculptor mid-laugh, displays of exuberance, hysterics, and farce, all emoting pure joy. Says the artist, "My intention when making this series of sculptures was to use art to touch the heart of each visitor and to have them enjoy what art brings to them."[50] Although it's calm now, on my prior visit wind gusted, fifteen knots off the water. And as I strolled amid the big bronze men all having a laugh, windmill palms gave a round of applause.

One more landmark: the inukshuk crowning the headland, a southwest spit to the shore. The work of Rankin Inlet artist Alvin Kanak, this commanding stack of eight granite boulders was commissioned for Expo 86, a Northwest Territories feature, before finding its new home here overlooking the water. The stacked granite shuttles me over the inlet, mentally, at least, to the Vancouver Maritime Museum, where the small copy of that similar piece faces this way. Paired waymarks framing the bay.

I keep walking and watching. Admiring the sea. Three ravens flap past, *ffwoom, ffwoom, ffwoom*. Again, ravens, not crows. And I wonder what's changed, what's still changing in the environment, or if the big birds are just passing through. Now comes the high whistly cheep of a hummingbird, followed by the exotic hyena chuckle of flickers.

Next I see the greatest thing ever. A tiny boy—three, four years old—drives a very small Audi, just enjoying the road in a weensy, fully powered automobile. The miniscule driver is going about four kilometres an hour, roughly the same as my walking speed. So I'm able to walk along, on the opposite side of the street, and observe for a short while. It's a quiet stretch (a traffic-calmed zone), yet he seems very road conscious, keeping his pristine black car on the right, passing parked cars. Now I see there's an adult here too, keeping pace a modest distance behind. I should mention the car's a convertible; the boy's little blond head catches the breeze. The visual, in fact, is much like those pieces of art, different-sized installations in perfect proportion. Only here it's a preschooler in a luxury German sports car. At that age, I just wanted a wagon!

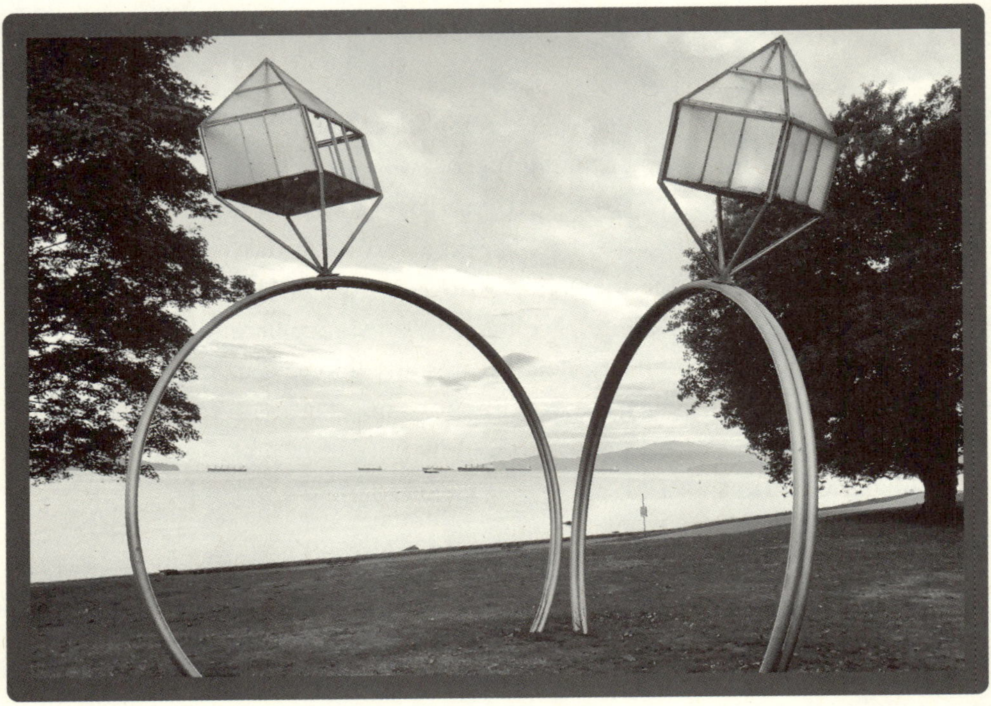

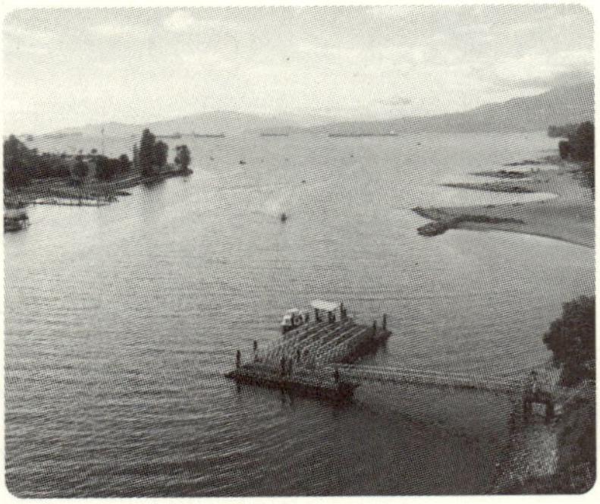

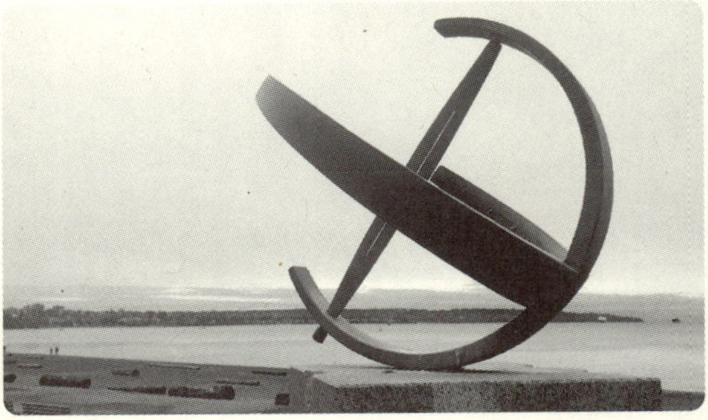

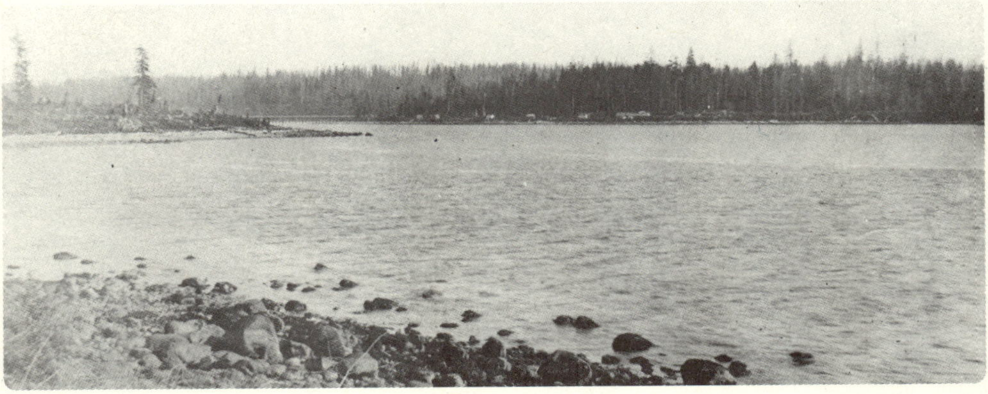

CLOCKWISE FROM TOP: *Engagement* by Dennis Oppenheim at Sunset Beach, looking over English Bay; the George Cunningham memorial sundial at English Bay, looking southwest; English Bay, looking southeast toward Snauq, 1889; English Bay from Burrard Bridge, looking west.

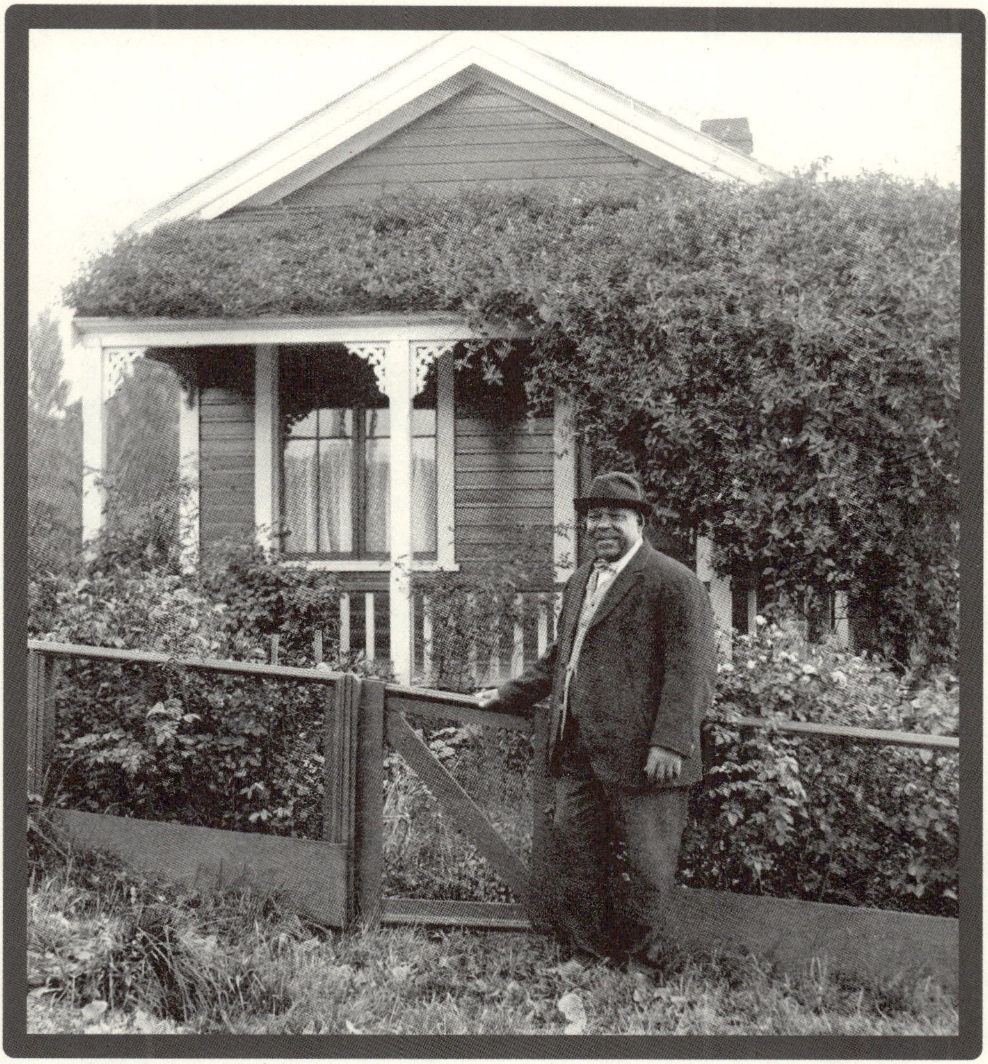

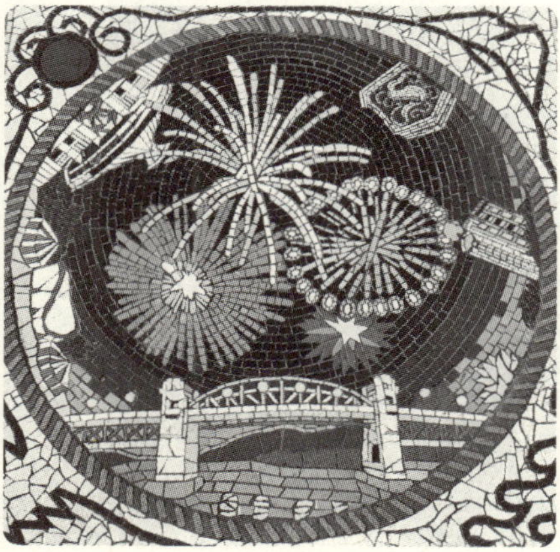

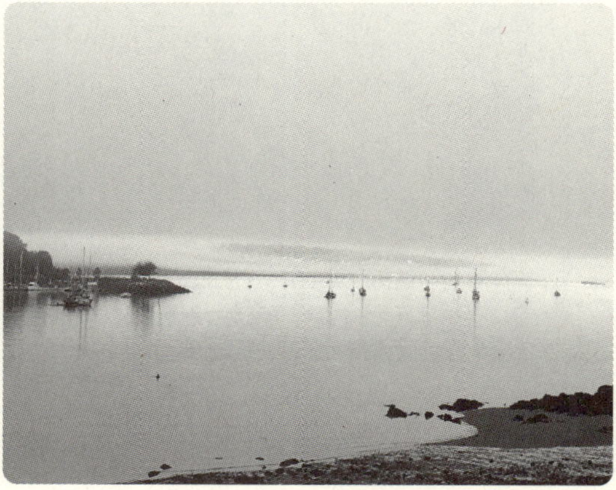

CLOCKWISE FROM TOP: Seraphim "Joe" Fortes at his cottage overlooking English Bay, circa 1910s; sailboats at anchor at English Bay; a street mosaic of English Bay fireworks.

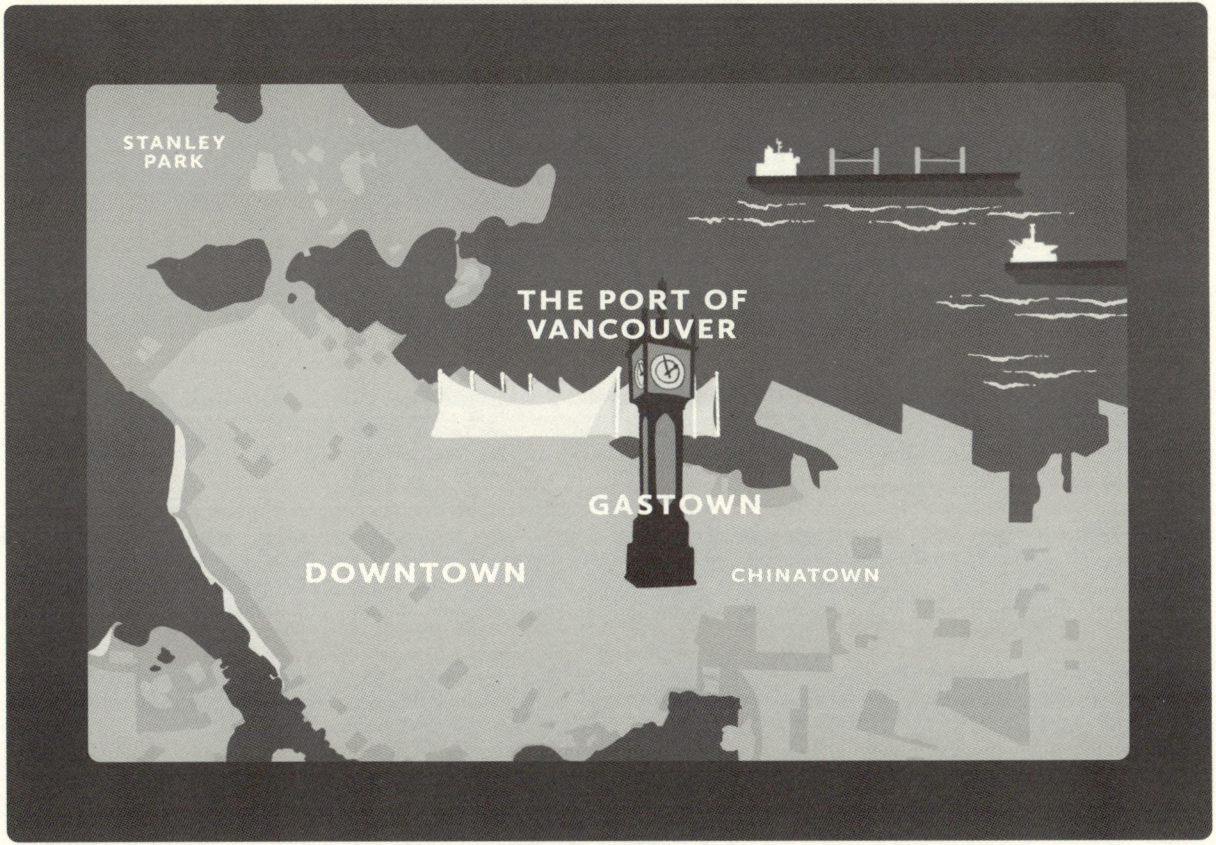
STANLEY PARK
THE PORT OF VANCOUVER
GASTOWN
DOWNTOWN
CHINATOWN

AROUND THE PORT *of* VANCOUVER

Headline News

SELECT WALKS AT A GLANCE

A NEW DAY, a new weather turn. Clear skies to the north and the south, while my easterly view has a great folding fan of high cloud. Nothing with rain, simply streaks adding to an apricot sunrise. Venturing into downtown, the sky opens up, surprising among the high-rises. There's more open cloud, this one a wave, and immense pillows of the same apricot-nectarine tones. On the radio, the on-air personalities are even talking about it.

"Are you seeing this sunrise? Unbelievable!"

I feel oddly connected, sharing a view with detached voices.

It's something about the geography here, a funnel effect with North Shore mountains and other high peaks to the east rising from the Fraser Valley near Chilliwack (an Indigenous term meaning just that, "rising hills"). When weather and wind emanate from the east, our west-facing shores invariably reflect an inversion: angry gusts, chilly fronts, a nasty chop on the water.

The week I spent sailing here—Spanish Banks, English Bay, Jericho Beach—could not have been better for a novice learning the water. Each of the five days offered something new. Sun and southerlies one day, sweeping westerlies the next, then a day of sharp gales from the north. Day four was perfectly calm, while day five brought easterlies—weather like this, a temperature shift, water changing from green-blue to grey as waves raced *away* from the land.

On to the West End, where low cloud hugs the water today. The beach where Peter Pantages and Joe Fortes did their laps now slung in mist at mast height on the bay. Two swimmers go by, each trailing a small coloured float, containers for wallets and keys. Both wear swim caps the colour of work vests. Over their heads, the fog becomes a duvet under which you could hide to read comics at night.

As I watch the two slowly pass, the cloud thickens and drops. No more duvet; now it's a shroud. The inukshuk poised on the headland resembles that photo of Joe Capilano, a blanket pulled around shoulders. And then English Bay disappears. All I can see is a heavy fog drape cinching the water, a Stephen King novel unfolding.

My visibility now is no more than ten metres. No sign of seabirds, although a few geese plod from the shore, cropping grass as they go. Then another fine visual: four Canada geese crossing Beach Avenue in a line on the pedestrian zebra crossing, a perfect *Abbey Road* image.

With coffee and a muffin in hand, I settle in by the water and let my mind drift, mental fog along with the actual stuff. A bit of correspondence as well, a phone call with the *Vancouver Sun*. Reporter and writer Dana Gee and I are discussing *Perfect Day* walks, and she asks me to outline a few to offer a feel for the city. In addition, she asks what motivated me to explore in this manner, why I'm walking and writing. So I do my best to frame these excursions in reply to her five *W*s.

"Why did you want to do these books?" she asks.

"I want to ensure that there are great travelogues emphasizing that we can travel where we live, minimize carbon impact, and still have an adventure, irrespective of available time, money, or accessibility."[51]

"What surprised you when you started doing the research?"

This takes some thought, for what I learn as I walk is at times overwhelming, but I do my best to make my answer concise. "I'd say how much history—ancient and recent—is present and available where many of us live and work, commute every day, and often take for granted or easily miss."

"And who's this book for?" Dana asks.

To this I say something I've said in the past regarding my travel memoirs, although it's still true for these walks. "These books are for readers who love armchair escape, travel, and memoir, but they're excursions that can easily be enjoyed, relived, and personally experienced by anyone."

"What can long-time Vancouverites take away from these books?"

"That there's so much underfoot, history and culture, within easy reach. Even rare flora and fauna wherever we live in the city, or where you're coming to visit. This book is a refresh for locals, encouragement and a challenge to take a new look around, because where we are is ever changing and remarkable."

"And what can tourists take away from your books?"

I try to top it off with ribbon and a bow. "Tourists can find endless vistas, nature, and art here in Vancouver. Each neighbourhood has treasure. Which makes these books ideal for locals and visitors alike, whether they want a loose guidebook or a fresh take on familiar locales. Making this, I've been told, a perfect gift too." I figure my publicists will love that and wonder if I hear a sniff, even a soft snort, out of Dana. In fact, it may've been me.

With more back-and-forth, we discuss my "favourite" walks. Truth is, I have none. Every route, every day, each venture offers something worthwhile. But newspapers have margins and page counts, so I share a synopsis of citywide walks showcasing Kits, Granville Island, False Creek, the West End, the Downtown Eastside, and Stanley Park.

When the article goes to print it fills a page, and I'm pleased. It offers, I feel, a brief look at what *Perfect Day* walks are intended to relay and encapsulate. Dana seems satisfied too, as does my mom, who buys extra copies.

Still on the north side of English Bay, a few things catch my eye as the fog gradually lifts. There's a puffing red tanker, maybe set to depart. Toward the horizon, the white block of a ferry heads from the mainland to Vancouver Island. Two gulls do ablutions, dipping and dipping their heads, and a man stands in the shallows, filming the view on his phone.

Then a fellow in neoprene launches something I've never seen, a kind of non-motorized foilboard. It looks like a contraption that might be linked to a kite sail, a small stand-atop board with a thin keel and a parallel blade to glide underwater. The overall profile resembles a Roman numeral *I*. The man stands on the top "shelf" of the board, then propels it forward with a bouncy action, leaving him nearly levitating over the surface as the whole thing carries him where a shift of his body directs it. The motion resembles a small trampoline on a skateboard, only here it's a blend of manual hydraulics above and below the water and looks eco-friendly while giving, I presume, a good workout.

Late afternoon on Burrard Bridge, heading south. There's ample space on both sides of the bridge for pedestrians, with views of English Bay and False Creek. Steel railings stand raised and secured, painted black, preventing all but the most determined from accessing the ledge and the water below. A phone box in yellow offers a crisis helpline.

After-work traffic is thickening, and I'm walking directly toward ugly dark cloud. There's a heavy aroma of imminent, threatening weather, a precursor, perhaps, to hail. I quicken my pace, but midway over the bridge, the storm hits. Hard, high-force winds, fifty, maybe sixty kilometres an hour. Dust and sand blow into my eyes, and the inlet's a violent brown-grey. An explosion of crows tornado above me, as though a Goliath scooped up a handful and hurled them into the wind. Magnificent and unnerving black-feathered chaos.

This is the crows' commute too, with end-of-day sun dropping somewhere over angry, dark sea. The birds are on their nightly return to their homes farther east, clustered nests in tall cottonwood trees where Vancouver shifts into Burnaby. A few of the birds simply stop, gripping flags on the bridge; others cling to bending branches above and below. The only colour around, so it seems, is the orange-tinted glass on new builds framing the bridge. Everything else at the moment is monochrome. Now the clouds rend a torrent of water. Not hail after all, but biblical rain, dry to wet in an instant. Passing cars send up sprays, windshield wipers work double speed, and funnily enough, in the saturating cold and high wind, I'm glad I'm on foot and not driving.

There's a pause, a slight hitch in the wind, and the crows carry on. The rain eases slightly, and I can even use my umbrella if I angle it into the gale. Walking home takes the feel of braving the elements, of an explorer breaking ground, hauling gear ever forward. I can relate for a moment, assuming they too had a warm condo and leftover pizza waiting a short distance ahead.

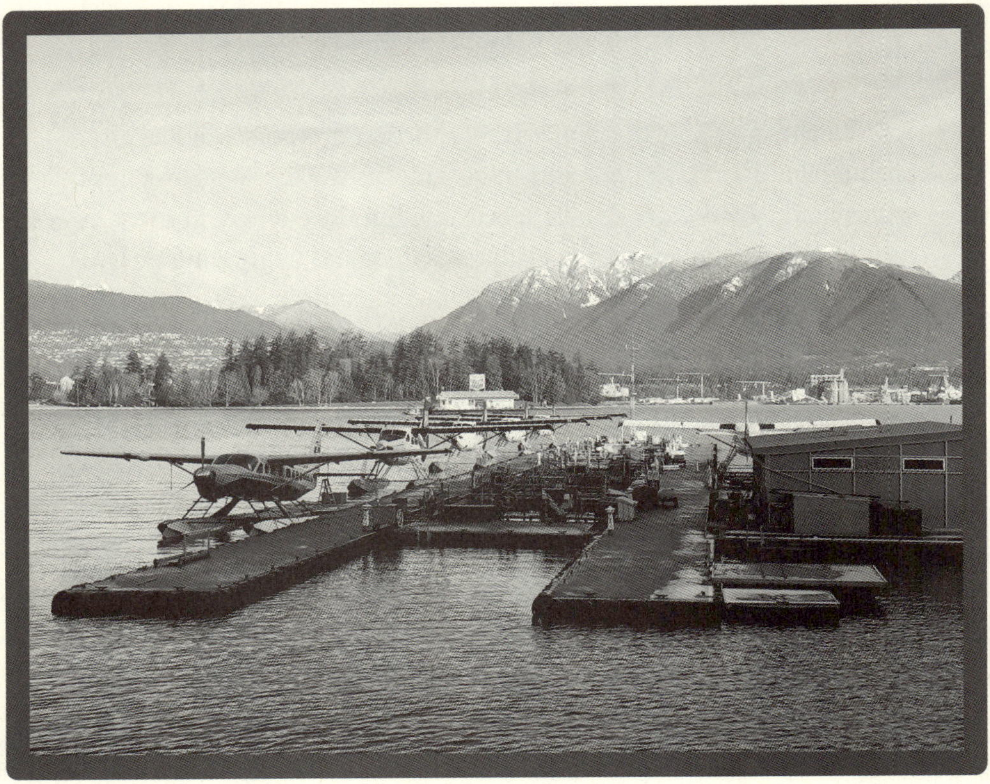

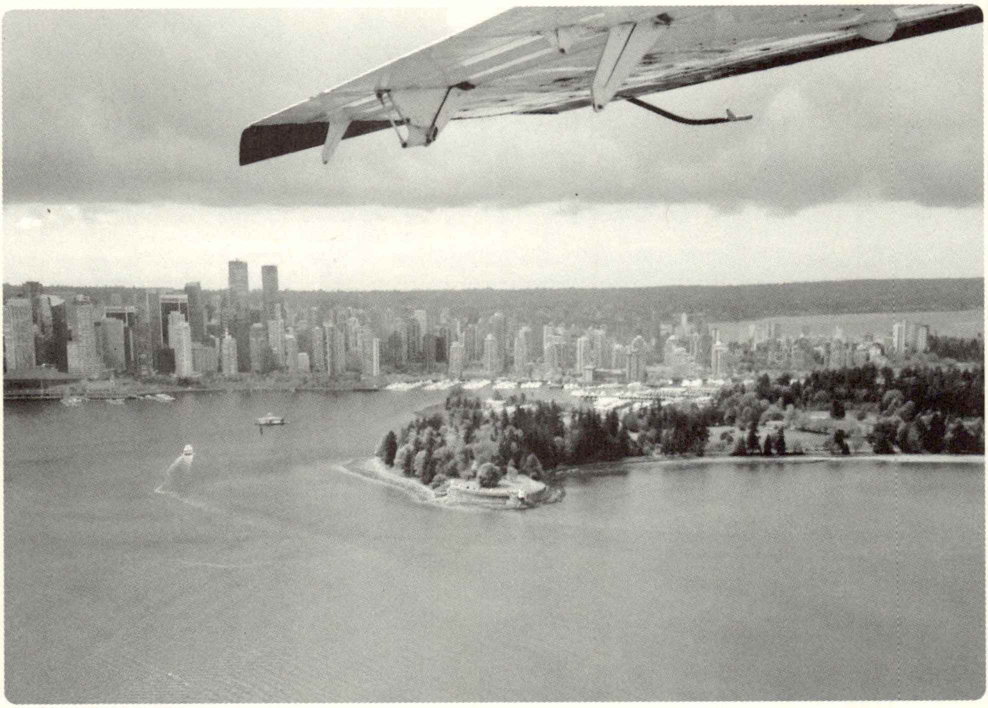

TOP: Coal Harbour seaplanes with the North Shore Mountains beyond.
BOTTOM: flying from Coal Harbour, looking south over Deadman's Island toward downtown.

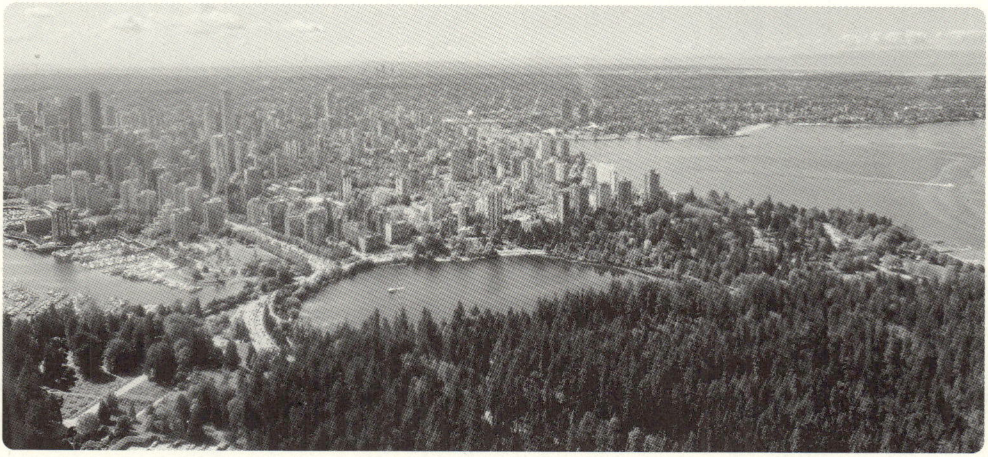

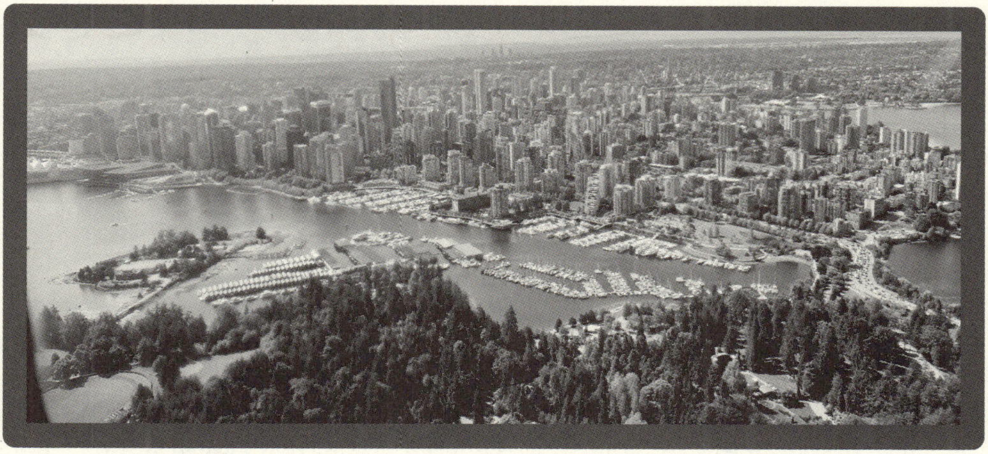

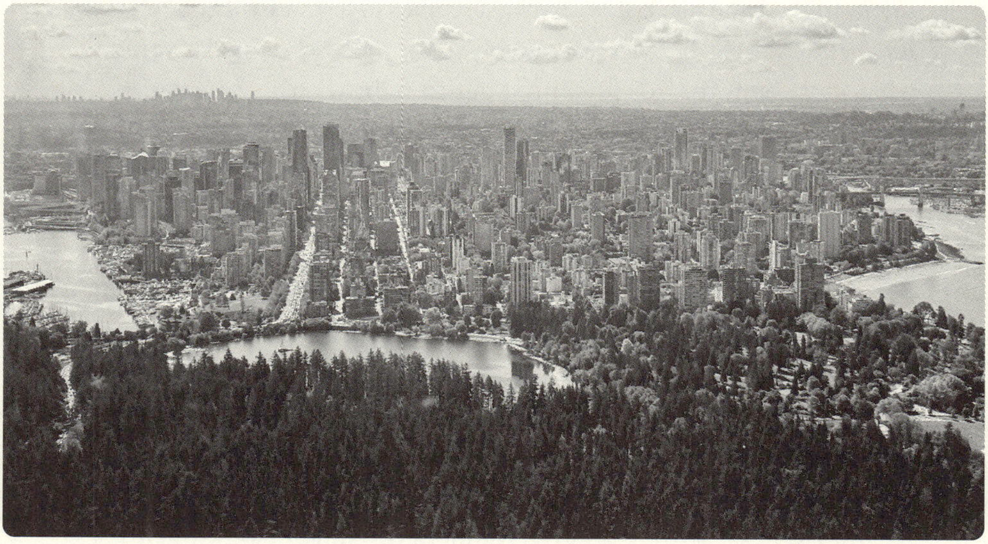

TOP TO BOTTOM: flying over Stanley Park and Lost Lagoon, heading east; flying over Stanley Park and Deadman's Island, approaching downtown; looking south over downtown, from the air.

Water Views

PADDLES AND ANCESTRAL HOMELAND

ANOTHER WESTERLY VENTURE, today beneath scudding grey cloud along Spanish Banks toward UBC's headland. I stop and sit on the sand, watch a tanker ease into the bay—a ship like the one that I sailed around, unending red and black steel. Slowly it comes to a standstill and releases its anchor. A splash, then remarkably, I *feel* the anchor strike home in what must be soft sand stretching out to right where I'm seated, as it sends a residual vibration along the sea bottom and into my own.

On the shore is a line of weeping willows, a shimmer of golden green. Up the bank toward UBC, cliff-hugging evergreens are aggressively pollarded to reduce risk of windfall. Trees take the brunt of the westerlies, a frontline or barbican wall. With a clamber I reach the approach to the Museum of Anthropology, its low concrete structure nestled in a heavy treed copse where a sign reads "Anthropology & Sociology Building."

Through the trees I see land drop to water as English Bay opens onto the strait, my view swivelled almost due west. MOA banners hang from light standards, and the museum sign is framed by dark pine. Beneath hawthorns heavy with berries the colour of rosehips, maples are mixing their colours, the same tones I saw in West Van when I lugged scuba gear to the sea. Along with this is a stand of thin cedar, feathery foliage begging to be steeped into tea. Juncos cheep and scurry through underbrush, and a flicker is having a laugh in a tall tree beyond.

A hunk of granite is embossed with a salmon, and red letters are etched on its partially smoothed side: "Remember your teachings. Welcome to the ancestral homeland of the hən̓q̓əmin̓əm̓-speaking Musqueam people." At the museum's front entrance, I'm greeted by fabric signage of the featured exhibits coordinated by the two curators I've come here to meet: Karen Duffek and Damara Jacobs-Petersen. I'm privileged to be here, as the museum's not open today, but I'm being welcomed in to explore on my own and visit with these experts. Naturally, upon entering a museum after hours, a part of me wonders if I'll have to be cautious of exhibits coming to life, as they do. Things, however, seem placid as a security guard waves me in through a side door, and I take advantage of having the place to myself, a cultural sprawl now wrapped in silence.

The building is an Arthur Erickson design. Heavy, brutalist concrete, with a downward-sloping main entry and a drop ceiling that visually shrinks the entryway. Then there's a grand reveal as the next room opens in every direction, portrait and landscape surrounded in glass, drawing in the outdoors and thrusting those in the room toward what's on display: towering totems, house posts, mythic beings, family lineage, and potlatch vessels for feasting with animals carved in mid-hunt. All of this in a cross-cultural display of Northwest Indigenous Nations. Again I feel that emotion of exploration and discovery that I felt aboard the *St. Roch*, only here I sense something of home. Of stumbling into a community village where, yes, I would ask for permission to land or to enter but would assuredly be made to feel welcome.

Behind me, starting the series of displays is a piece called *Travelling Together*. *Piece*, however, isn't quite the right word, as the exhibit is comprised of many parts shown together as one. But as the name indicates, it's about joint endeavour. Heavy wool blankets are draped on one wall, while a stylized canoe outline faces outdoors and the water. Carved, painted paddles are fixed into position as though the vessel is in motion, propelled by those paddles—the catch, drive, and exit, the blend that I learned of from Devian. It takes no effort at all to imagine those paddlers pulling, a drum beaten to song. Each paddle here is from a different carver and Nation, different eras as well. At the stern is a blunt-nosed broad paddle for steering, that technically challenging role, somewhat counterintuitively leading from the rear of the vessel.

As I sketch and take notes, Damara Jacobs-Petersen, Curator of Indigenous Engagement and Native Youth Program Director, arrives to greet me. Damara's story is as engaging as the paddles on display. Part of the Sḵwx̱wú7mesh (Squamish) Nation, Damara's background includes Sonoran desert studies in the American Southwest, with archaeological digs centred on the Tohono O'odham people. It was then she realized she'd rather focus her efforts on work based on her own cultural background, here on the coast of BC.

"I thought, there's no need to study other Indigenous Peoples rather than my own, and I had a desire to be here, back in the Pacific Northwest," she explains. "The Olympics, in 2010, really thrust the Squamish Nation onto the world's centre stage. Here at the MOA we have a lot of senior curators and designers retiring. People who've been here for thirty-plus years. I don't want to see them go, but we're seeing a shift in engagement, with more Indigenous perspectives."

Consistent with her own history, Damara refers to her lineage and that of her people as "canoe culture." I smile and nod at the display set before us, the paddles mid-thrust.

A grin from Damara. "Kxwu7lh," she says. "That's *canoe* in Squamish." What she says next echoes what I learned at the *St. Roch* exhibit. "Canoe can mean family, community. These words are interchangeable in the Squamish language, effectively synonyms."

I mention the carving shed on Granville Island where I've watched boat builders work.

Damara nods. "It's funny. Around here, dragon boats get a lot of the focus—festivals, events. But the Coast Salish canoe has a much longer history." She indicates the paddles on display. "Even that steering paddle, carved in the mid-nineteenth century. I consider that fairly new. In our culture, two-hundred-year history is contemporary."

As I scribble notes, Damara talks about Squamish writer Justin Neal and his play *Keepers of the Salish Sea*. From a subsequent search, I find this description:

> The play follows Samuel, a Manhattanite whose life has fallen apart due to addiction and career pressures. As he embarks on a recovery journey, he is drawn into a deeper exploration of self and purpose, inspired by the traditions of the Coast Salish canoe journeys. This spiritual voyage becomes the anchor for a story about finding purpose, reconnecting with the land, and tackling the pressing environmental issues of today.[52]

"There's a healing," Damara explains, building on the play's premise. "A connecting through water and the canoe. Part of that canoe community: people and the physical craft, the vessel itself. Which is very much alive, something that gets woken up and put back to sleep. All aspects of our identity."

I consider the paddles, their movement, in brightening light.

Damara indicates the shoreline beyond. "My great-grandma, Lena Jacobs, she lived ninety-eight years. Our family is from the North Shore, the mouth of the Capilano River and along Ambleside. Grandma told me of huge clam beds there. Other shellfish as well. Harvesting sites. 'When tide's out,' she would say, 'table's set.' Food source. Home. Highway. Identity. Who we are and how we exist, connected to shoreline and water."

Together we move through the silent museum to Damara's current curated exhibit, *in Pursuit of Venus [infected]*, a mixed-media installation of artwork and history, displayed with a vast horizontal screen showing depictions of the Pacific Rim Islands in live animation. The visual journey follows the voyages of Captain James Cook, sailing the Pacific tracing the transit of Venus, followed by the contact, influence, and, in no small part, destruction of Indigenous cultures. The visuals and audio are graphic, edgy, and accurate. A clash of idyllic locales and Polynesian cultures with the effects of exploration and settler contact, the imparting of "rules" from elsewhere. The video plays in a loop.

"Ah, here we go," says Damara. "Cook's about to get killed."

We watch, my legs wanting to lead me away, though they're fixed to where I stand. I've read many times of this moment. Even paddled to where it took place: Kealakekua Bay, on the west side of Hawaii's Big Island. The rock there is igneous, much like Vancouver beaches, the only difference being more silica in our aged local granite than in the fresh dark basalt that clings to those comparatively new island shores. But seeing that murder, irrespective of who's "right" or "wrong," is deeply disturbing. Lasting. Another moment in time when things shifted irrevocably.

We return to the main hall, where another canoe, one made of cedar, stands near the exterior glass. With nothing to keep viewers at bay, no stanchions or signage, wires or rope, this is a canoe to be handled, one to receive and impart positive feelings from all passersby, a touchstone in wood. To paraphrase Damara, the canoe is a connection through water—community, people, and the vessel itself—something present and living.

Sure enough, as I slide a hand gently down one of its smooth cedar gunnels, doing my best to emit good intention and thought, the boat feels alive, something to wake gently at sunrise and tuck in at night. Maybe read it a story, stroke the head of the craft as it sleeps.

Returning to the first canoe display, paddles poised around the hull of a canoe outline, Damara tells me more about paddle songs, about the women who powered those craft along with the men across Burrard Inlet in 1886, rescuing those fleeing the city's Great Fire.

"Remember," she says, "We *pull* the canoe. Not paddle. Just like the motion depicted right here, drawing water, moving forward. Think of that drum beat we know from paddle songs. Same as a heartbeat. Songs composed for specific events. In some songs we translate, you can hear, clearly hear the influence of settlers and priests. The mentality, mind you, is Indigenous. But the words of some songs, references to saviours and saints, are all about church. We call that hybridity of culture. Post-contact and colonization: Spanish and British."

The youth engagement that Damara spearheads is considered the unofficial flagship program of the museum, and I mention this as we chat.

"I got a group out," she says with a smile. "Across Burrard Inlet. Same as the voyage that took place to rescue the city from fire. From Mosquito Creek in North Van over to Stanley Park, to Lumbermen's Arch. A tough paddle. The currents there at the narrows—really tough. And we weren't rescuing anyone. Not hunting. Not fleeing Haida raiders. Just a recreational paddle. But everyone there realized, really knew just how demanding that is. How strong our people, our women and paddlers, really are."

I try to imagine that paddle, that pull, almost feel it strain my shoulders and back. Then I ask Damara about where we are; a new Musqueam outdoor display is under construction, a kind of a natural pool or pond, fresh water bridging the land with the ocean.

"Well, we feel deep, deep connections through not just the land but the water and with each other. Using the water to make powerful political statements as well. Taking canoes to and from these events. Political gatherings. Active presence and participation. Building awareness. Again, movement. We have tourists come through who don't realize Indigenous people are still here! That the Coast Salish Nations aren't something bygone. Part of our ongoing activity is letting others know we are *here*. My efforts as well, working for a sense of self as a First Nations person, with deep sacred and ancient connection to and with the water."

Having consumed a generous chunk of Damara's day, with thanks I let her return to her office to get on with her work. Then do a slow loop of the gallery, once more through the Pacific exhibit of Islanders, sailors, and Cook. Watch the captain get murdered again. Still disturbing, but perhaps even more unsettling is the fact that the second time around doesn't affect me as much. *That* really lingers.

On to spend time with the collaborative carving of *The Raven and the First Men*. (Not the tiny original, but the big one.) Unlike the Cook video, however, here the sensory, emotional impact has in no way diminished. I circle the carving both ways, the raven watching its surrounds, guarding while coaxing, encouraging discovery. The people within the large clamshell are uncertain, some curious, some fearful, some already wriggling out, ready to find a new world. Standing directly in front of the piece, the gaze of the raven is piercing. Animate. Timeless. And I wonder what it might see, its gaze passing right through me.

It's the top of a new hour, and I have a new meeting, this one with Karen Duffek to re-examine some exhibits and see how coastal engagement has influenced the city. Curator of Contemporary Visual Arts and the Pacific Northwest, Karen's focus at the MOA is supporting the activation of Northwest Coast Indigenous collections inside and outside the museum. Her research, exhibitions, and award-winning publications focus on the relationships between historical and contemporary art practices, museum collections, communities, and markets.

Having enjoyed Karen's collaborative books peppered with history and Indigenous art, every facet of our get-together, it seems, has the influence of mixed media. Another Erickson-infused reveal to the high-windowed atrium. More time by the "touching canoe," more positive thoughts being shared.

Karen's curatorial responsibility at the MOA encompasses Nuu-chah-nulth, Kwakwa̱ka̱'wakw, and Haida collections, as well as cultural relationships. Documenting historical objects with descendants and originating community members is not only her focus but her passion, as well as working with artists across disciplinary borders.

We circle back to the paddle exhibit, the stylized canoe gunnel hanging mid-air, fifteen paddles poised in the pull. Karen draws my attention to a series of narrated informative plaques, with a quote from Tutakwisnapšiƛ (Joe Martin) of the Nuu-chah-nulth Nation on one of them.

> *Travelling Together*: "The canoe has always played a central role to coastal First Nations—it was our car; the sea was our highway. It gave us access to our hahuuli (territories), and helped us protect our hahuuli. It allowed us to visit relatives."

An echo of what Damara shared: the water as a highway, a home, an identity. Karen reiterates the rethinking of this space, consistent with initiatives elsewhere, much like what I saw at the Maritime Museum. We discuss the notion of collective travel, how collaboration can paradoxically emphasize diversity, which we see throughout the Northwest Coastal areas.

Again Karen directs my gaze to the paddles. "Consider movement," she says, "a metaphor too. Movement of canoes and of paddles: it's suggested, yet subtle. The paddles themselves, old and new, carved by women and men, different woods and designs, new perspectives, an open-ended journey. Moving toward something. Pulling."

I focus on a paddle painted bright blue. It's the work of a young female carver.

"There's been an explosion of young women carving," Karen says. "Here's one from Bella Coola. And more's being done around Terrace as well."

We return to the main displays. "We've been moving these poles and Haida house pieces around the property over the years. Changing views. Now it's being redone to better represent Musqueam culture, creating a Northwest Coast landscape." Our view now is the exterior creation of the earthen mounds, reedy shore grass and a pool, what could be the world's best koi pond. More of a waterscape than a landscape.

Karen indicates watercraft on display. "These are classic Salish inshore canoes. Shallow water and rivers, for two or three paddlers. Smaller and narrower than oceangoing boats. Canoes were designed for the water on which they would travel. Canoe makers are marine engineers. That gets passed on, knowing the water determines or drives the design. It's an engineering feat. The term *carver* can diminish the knowledge and expertise that's required, what goes into the shape, draft, and breadth composition. Freight canoes. War canoes. Whaling canoes. Boats designed for journeys of two weeks or more out on open water."

We move to a particularly tall totem unlike any I've seen.

"Here's a whaler's totem pole by Art Thompson. Whalers were the highest form of revered hunters. Harpooners. They could call whales from Baja. The connection is beyond comprehension."

I think of thin places, spirit awareness, that connectivity with its intrinsically boundless expansion. Believing, no, *knowing* that this is part of that ethos.

We stand by a towering three-sided frame, a carved crosspiece and house posts. "These are sea lion house posts," Karen explains. "Symbols run deep. For example, there are fifty different undersea killer whale gods and mythic beings, including family lineage, all the way back to godlike ancestors. Origin sites, we call these, totems and art. Art can't be separated from people, place, land, and sea. Art isn't just a beautiful thing; it's much more. Art is story. Regalia. And it's lineage, and place, ceremony and rites. Architecture as well. This sea lion house, for example, is the last of the traditional design, including ceremonial space, from the turn of the twentieth century. We can see here supernatural ancestral beings."

I feel it as well, the dense construct of a few thousand years in what we're standing amid. Culture and people being as much of the water as the mesh of ocean with land, the ebb-pulse of bloodlines and tide. With gratitude I thank Karen for this privilege, a window onto a space and the land with the water beyond, that same sense of pull. Both literal and littoral. I take one more photo, shake hands with Karen, exchange smiles and waves with the security guards now playing cards in a corner, and return to a forested path by the sea.

Leaving the museum, I feel another walk is in order to digest this sharing and learning. Here by the MOA, Pacific Spirit Regional Park wraps around the university grounds like a gift wrap of pine, its present a shoreline of driftwood and shells. Signs warn of a drop-off: "Danger. Steep Cliffs." There's a breath of high tide, the bouillabaisse smell of sea air. Wind gusts from the west. Down a cascade of stairs is Wreck Beach, famous for its sunbathing nudists.

A friend of mine made a living right here, hauling duffels of iced drinks down the cliffs in the hot summer months, selling everything that he had, every day, at exorbitant prices. He financed two degrees in this manner. I never thought to ask if he wore clothes while he worked, if "food safety" was an issue. Maybe a hairnet and cap.

Another stop and another mental drift, gazing west toward Vancouver Island. The most recent trip I made there, from Horseshoe Bay to Nanaimo, took place a few days ago. Looking back to this edge of the mainland added a shifting perspective. The highlight of that trip? Sliding past two pairs of leviathans: two cruise ships and two whales. Princess and humpback, respectively. The whales put on a show, flaring their flukes as they dove alongside a ferry heading the opposite way.

From the uppermost deck, seeing the city recede through a pinball display of rumbling ships, tankers, and spume-blowing whales became improvised theatre. Something I'd expect to see from a low-flying drone broadcast on a nature and discovery show. As the city shrank with the inlet, ports, and the bay, it gave, I believe, a true water view. From out there, a few horsepower minutes southwest from the mainland, Vancouver's downtown held a near-perfect profile, the sine curve of a big rolling wave.

On that trip, rather magically, our boat sailed into the sunset. While at the mouth of the Fraser, that giant green prawn kept making its way to the sea. Prior to this I grabbed alternate views of this west-facing shore, one by float plane, the other by Helijet. The float plane went west while the Helijet flew back, humming northeast to the city to touch down by the Port of Vancouver, a kind of transport mixed media. Stanley Park became an oversized landmark, as though wayfinding by evergreen. From the air, Lost Lagoon had the look of a sea monster's eye, watching and waiting for prey. Which of course gets me thinking of fish yet again and the chinook that I shared with old Wink. Both of those aerial view flights—the seaplane, the Helijet—took me over my home at the time, a high-rise in Coal Harbour. The Helijet came in low, almost skimming the tops of Stanley Park trees, while the float plane, bound for the Gulf Islands, took a long sweeping turn from downtown around Deadman's Island before splitting the uprights of Lions Gate Bridge. I fought the urge to raise my arms like a ref indicating a field goal.

From that Coal Harbour apartment, which had a window that stretched to the floor, I could sit on a sofa and gaze directly down to the water. Every few days I'd see Wink diving or making new friends. After I'd trimmed up that freshly caught salmon, I carried it straight up the stairs to my home. Splashed the collar (the shoulder-like piece behind the fish's head) with lemon and salt, tossed it into the oven, and nine minutes later I had one of my best culinary experiences. In my ignorance, I thought I'd eat the collar first, as it's not particularly appealing to look at, unlike those uniform fillets you see at the market. It was only after I ate it, then looked it up, that I realized I was in fact eating what may be the very best part, a perfect balance of moist meat and fat, delicate yet rich. Then I made the mistake of calculating the price per kilo of my fish, including boat charter, and wanted to go back and ask Wink to chip in for his share.

Today I wake to an eagle, its pinched throaty trill, warble-chirp, and glissando. I've relocated to a short-term rental, a fresh view of the water, where a small window offers a corridor glimpse of the sea. Needles and cones frame the outlook, cedar and hemlock punctuating the blue. In the distance is a thin haze, a hint of Monet. Weak tea, then strong coffee, sneakers, a run. Through manicured properties of burgundy maple, trimmed grass, a lone palm, beds of clover, and a high row of sweet gums, the illusion of street lamps with leaves.

Last night, I thought I'd overnight on the beach, get one more perspective. I double-checked the tides and chose my timing accordingly, the moon nothing more than a thumbnail. I settled in where the driftwood had contours and shape, every log like an unfinished sofa. Boondocking, you might call it, or unlicensed camping. But this was just me on my feet, cloaked in a raincoat and toque. I thought I might even see stars, removed from downtown, with less ambient light, like a dimmer descended halfway. But no. Overhead was a pale blue-grey, like a sea upside down on a storm-riddled day. As the darkness unfolded I tried to distract myself from the increasing chill by listening to the sea.

In lieu of counting sheep I replayed terms in my head that I'd picked up like jetsam while walking the shore, mental flash cards of water-based words. One being *af'rug*, a Gaelic expression used to describe the rebounding sound of a wave after striking the shore, a sibilant, truncated tinkle of chimes being grabbed as they blow in a breeze. Another being *klett*, as gutturally terse as what it describes, a heavy stone fixed to the shore, what might also serve as a tool-sharpening rock.

And so I sat shivering, listening to af'rugs ricocheting from kletts, trying not to look at the time. The timing, mind you, was a perfectly paced pulse, water lapping between a paddle song beat and the unhurried tale of a lineage dance.

A few hours in, I gave up. The cold was too much, a penetrating, bone-chilling damp. Or, I suppose, my clothing wasn't ideal. And so I gathered my layers and retreated to bed in my latest semi-permanent home.

Now, under pleasant and determined warm sun, I've trotted along to the edge of the land, where a precipitous drop to the sea offers bluff views of ocean through tall slender pines with high unbranched trunks, as though I'm peering through jailhouse bars, a lock-up for wood elves or sprites. From this viewpoint, however, it's unclear whether I'm outside or inside the cell, and I hope I don't have to fight with a pixie. (Everyone knows pixies fight dirty.)

Down the beach, two distinct lines of round granite stones have been rolled into place, centuries or millennia ago, demarking ancient boat launches and old fishing weirs of the Coast Salish. From the lip of the bluff, I survey this domain with a fleeting, delusional sense of surveying my kingdom. Then a great *ffwoom-ffwoom* sounds above as an eagle (the eagle that woke me?) takes flight from a branch directly above, its flight path an arrow. No recon or whimsy, this is the flight of the hunt, straight to sea. Farther and farther. What can it possibly see? A salmon? A cod? I know that these raptors (when not tracking spawners to Squamish) soar between Salish Sea islands, the sea air their road. Another inversion, I suppose. When the space being traversed is not what's on paper or a screen but rather what's actually there, ocean depths and limitless sky. The vertical realm another topographical squeezing of lines, compressed to a point where they vanish. All that's left is above and below. In this case, two shades of blue: the long curl of breakers and a sky scuffed with clawings of stratus.

Back at my lodging, city centre away to the east, I have tiny new visitors. A hummingbird hovers over cedar while two towhees (mates, I assume) methodically rummage the lawn. The black-hooded male seems perfectly tame, strutting at my feet, its feathers looking freshly salon-coiffed. I give him a nod. Meanwhile, a patch of blossoming clover has attracted a bunny, while a robin yanks a worm from the grass and downs it like throbbing spaghetti.

The susurration of sea finds its way through the trees, a calming white noise. And yet that's not accurate, the sound being much more than ambient. In actuality it's the tonal depth one might hear from an orchestra. A musical blanket, one aural wave, but in layers of limitless parts: every wavelet on stone, brushing sand, touching driftwood and shells, trillions of drops with each surge. Maybe thinking of this as one sprawling thing simply makes it conceivable, the arrogance of perceived comprehension.

I can no longer hear the eagle, but I recall another talk with an expert. Not a birder, mind you, but a man who made his living with trees. Grant was his name. (And still is, I presume.) Grant was an arborist, a tree doctor. And the property strata that we were a part of had determined that one lone, slender fir was a risk. Developers had left the solitary tree for a remnant of green when the land was cleared to build townhomes. But a tree on its own is susceptible to coming down in a gale. And so, for the good of the houses in the shade of the tall pine, the tree had to be felled.

It was a weekday morning when Grant arrived, and we chatted as he prepared for his day. He wore lumberjack spikes on his boots, aiming in, aiming down, like vicious spurs. Then he slung on a heavy leather belt from which hung two chainsaws, giving him the look of a jailer with two large, nasty keys. As he attached this and that, hoisting things into place, it resembled a routine similar to how we suit up for scuba diving.

Grant shared stories of things he'd found when he cleared other timber, which he told me about with a kind of remorse. He was a lover of trees. Bringing down any bit of greenery for him was not so much about commerce but the safety and preservation of forests in aggregate, ensuring trees remained healthy. Wilderness culling for the greater good.

His body language alone indicated the next tale he was about to share was one that still stung. Then he told me about bringing down one huge tree that, unbeknownst to him, housed an eagle's nest. He only realized this once the tree fell. The nest held no eaglets or eggs, fortunately. But still, he'd unwittingly trashed someone's home. It was a big one, he said, maybe having housed two or three generations.

"Amazing construction, right?" I said.

He nodded. "And the stuff you find in there," he added, shaking his head. "Pet collars."

"No."

"Oh yeah," he said gravely. "There's *always* pet collars."

I'm taking a break from the water today, though it's still very much on my mind. I'm sitting at my computer to visit with Cedar Swan, CEO of Adventure Canada, for her unique take on our walkable shores. Cedar's company runs small-ship expeditions globally, which include research, education, and a focus on the environment along with adventure-based travel. *Canadian Geographic*, for example, is a frequent collaborator on many of their sailings.

An adventurer and outdoor enthusiast, recipient of the Citation of Merit from the Explorers Club, and founding member of Canadian Women for Nature, Cedar's an active participant in preservation, stewardship, and environmental activities. She explains that her career and her passion centre on living and working near water, and she sees her role as facilitative in nature, creating opportunities for people to visit coastal communities. Ironically, she explains, there's a grounding in being near water.

"Many of the communities we travel to are small, often isolated," she says. "There's a common attraction to these places. Not so much a simplicity, but a going with the pulse of the natural world. It's incredibly grounding. A throwback to earlier times. The largest destination we visit on our excursions is a village of four thousand people in Greenland, which there feels like a metropolis. I find these smaller places refreshing.

It's reinvigorating and renewing. That ebb and flow feels like a more natural way, a more connected way of living. Places like that, I find, are more community focused. That's what I see. Resilience as well, and resourcefulness. Family groups in small coastal communities tend to run deep. It's really special."

Which I hear as an echo of my time at the MOA, descriptions of lineage going "all the way back." The depth of connection, engagement. *Deep* was a word used there too. And I think of things I've read about "deep time," when connection surpasses epochs, beyond calendar time, the time frame of planets and stars.

I mention some of this to Cedar. She nods. And I think of her using the term *grounding*, a noun and a verb. Not only a state of attainment, realization, but ongoing as well, progressive. In a way, aspirational.

We talk a bit about travel in general, then the specifics of being near water. "Tell me, how does water, a shoreline, influence people and place?" I ask.

Cedar glances at a window, which I imagine might have a view of the water. "Well, I live just a few doors from a lake. Which is quite different from, say, a real coastal town. I didn't grow up on an ocean. But travelling there, I find that ebb and flow so natural when I take people there—travellers, guests. I think that's often one of the biggest takeaways. I don't know that it's the reason people come on these journeys. People join us, are booking with us, to experience not only the polar world but coastal communities. And I think it's a pleasant surprise, these takeaways. That and a reminder of just how resilient, how resourceful we can be."

She ponders a moment more. "I also find it's a function of the size of the places we're visiting, where there's a very real connection to the past and to heritage. Because it does tend to be family groups who inhabit many of these remote coastal places. I don't know a lot of city dwellers who have that same attachment to place. Which, as I say, runs deep and resonates with visitors. It's not something that a lot of urban people still have in their lives."

I smile and nod. It's well summed up. Not a separation as such, but a kind of detachment, bordering on having forgotten a part of our past.

That lineage connection to place I saw carved in house posts and totems. This isn't just where we are, where we're from, but who we are too. The whaling pole, for example. Drawing lines like a blade down the grain of the timber, when one's avocation, vocation, is the same as their being, when who we are is what we are. What I think of as being *on purpose*, when focused activity dissolves time.

I see some of this in what Cedar does and how she does it as well, connecting, melding lives into nature, individually and collectively. All of it happening next to or on top of the water. Reminiscent of exceptional teachers who make learning fun, Cedar engages, entertains, and educates people while connecting small groups to each other, along with the land. Fostering that connection is an important element, a facet, she explains, critical to the longevity of all conservation work: cultivating relationships to strengthen natural ties.

Thanking Cedar, I sign off, giving me a chance to reflect on my feeling, at the moment, of having whisked more of that water with a froth of culture and land. What started out as a few simple walks near my home has expanded like a rising tide, gathering pebbles of people and place like insights of flotsam and jetsam. Only these bobbing bits hold connection and sensory learning. I'd say pearls, but that's overused. And with that, I switch off my screen, grab an apple, and head to the beach.

A swirl of walking and talking ensues, as though navigating between Charybdis and Scylla—not the monsters, as such, but a dervish whirl of oceanic activity—as I take part in a writers festival, where I spend time with author James Bradley.

While I've been strolling these shores, excavating cusps of water and land, James has departed from his bestselling novels with his work *Deep Water*, an award-winning plunge into non-fiction. He's exploring the same water I'm searching, as his home is the seaside of Sydney, making his research not only the whole ocean, but drawn from the Pacific's alternate side, an antipodean look at what I'm now tracing. As though he too hitched a ride on a *Nautilus* imagined, plumbing and plotting these depths.

Rather adeptly, James articulates what I feel with each leap into the sea, that sensation experienced at the edge of the world on Rose Spit. *Boundlessness* is a word often used in his writing, quoting scientists, surfers, even Freud's correspondences. Along with that inherent lack of bounds, this near-euphoric state is described as "an intimation of something larger, a sense of time's depth." He references surf, that "inkling of infinity experienced in the face of the ocean's immensity," along with a "primal at oneness." The Freud reference, by the way, is taken from a letter written to him by his friend Romain Rolland, which again cites the infinite and a "sense of oneness with the universe."[53] And I like knowing these feelings are universally shared, generations of swimmers and dreamers grasping descriptors like flotation aids.

Now James is off to watch whales on a tour leaving from False Creek. I wish him well as he heads out to sea. (Later, he shares snaps of three transient orcas hunting for seals.)

From Granville Island I return to the Vancouver Maritime Museum, scan for eagles and coyotes, but nothing today. A harbour seal bobs under Burrard Bridge, and that's about it, apart from seagulls and crows.

At the museum I meet Zoe George, local artist and expert on canoes and design work derived from the water. Today she'll deliver a presentation on Salish paddles and canoe culture. Hailing from the Tsleil-Waututh and Squamish Nations in North Van, Zoe comes from a very long line of paddlers and paddling tradition.

"These are our ancestral highways," she explains. "As a Khatsahlano relative said to me, 'Why walk when we can paddle?'"

An audience gathers on shared padded benches as if seated side-saddle in umiaks. Around us are vintage photos of Zoe's family, Elders, and paddlers. Along with this are actual paddles and vessels, the same leather craft I saw at the *St. Roch* event, as well as a slender six-and-a-half-metre painted dugout canoe of red cedar. With four slender thwarts it's a craft built for hunting and speed, a southerly version of that thinly framed kayak hung near the ceiling.

The dugout cedar canoe is called *Salmon*, with a chinook painted on its stern, an eagle on its bow, depictions of motion and lineage. Clean-painted lines sweep the hull, what looks like an orca piercing a wave, described as a show of traditional and contemporary design, family, and culture. There's a plaque to describe the eagle emblem, indicating knowledge and peace, while a human motif emanates from the image's centre, representing a family tree with the ancestral link between carving and kin.

A wall mural next to this shows a simple canoe outline from above, a dark oblong, much like the stylized display at the MOA. Only here the boat's component parts are shown with their Salishan names. For easier note-taking I translate terms to the shared Halkomelem language: *q'lhól* and *iláq*, the bow and the stern; *sth'íkwe'í:lwelh* and *s'eyí:wsí:lwelh*, port and starboard; as well as *íxel*, to paddle; and *sq'émél*, the paddle itself.

Next is a series of sepia photos of canoeing the səlilwətał or Tsleil-Waututh waters of Burrard Inlet. From left to right, the photos gain colour, a timeline in snapshots with contemporary carvers and carving. More pictures of canoe racing, and with it, a video shot from a drone. The brief film follows eleven-paddler racing canoes as they jostle by Cates Park or Whey-ah-Wichen, where Burrard Inlet veers into Indian Arm. The pace looks frenetic but is tightly contained and controlled while fierce and remarkably fast.

"The training," Zoe says, "is intense. Even in the past. Look at these old shots." She points to family photos from the 1950s, '60s, and '70s of shirtless paddlers with well-defined muscles. "See here, strong and fit. They're all buff!" she laughs. "Eggs and mush, that's what they'd eat. Big breakfasts, then nothing. A supper of soup and lean protein. Just paddle and train, every day."

The group moves to a hanging display of wood paddles—canoe tradition and family—and I feel I could be back at the MOA. Then I learn that Zoe also works there, for Damara, as part of the anthropological team. Fellow paddlers joining forces, a new form of blend, lift, and glide.

Next to a wall, eight paddles are hung, dangling from ropes like wooden chimes. The styles all vary: light wood and dark, grains in amber and black-coffee tones. One blade comes to a point, a true carving paddle, something to serve as a weapon as well. Others flare like balalaikas or long ukuleles. Two more are two-toned, with strips of mocha and blond wood spliced into stripes. And I think of the cedar-bark hat Rebecca Duncan wore as she welcomed the group to the Maritime Museum. Functional, wearable art.

The assemblage now heads farther in for more exhibits explained, reimagined. I see layers of meaning being added, removed, strengthening clarity. Maybe a new form of midden as well. Not accumulated shells, but a buildup of shared knowledge and truth, a fortified cultural concrete.

Today I'm inside, and it's cold. My heating (and cooling) system won't work, and I'm waiting for a tech to come by and determine what needs repairing. Finally a friendly ginger-haired man named Dennis arrives, kicks off his boots, and surgically removes the wall-mounted unit.

"Hmm, Italian," he says. Which probably explains why I couldn't decipher the manual.

I ask him about his work and learn, remarkably, that much of it's done on the water. He laughs when he sees my expression, my jaw no doubt slack.

"Fishing boats," he explains, "the big ones. They all have industrial freezers. I repair them. All around Vancouver and Vancouver Island."

"Huh, of course," is all I can think to say. "What's that like? That part of the job, on the water. All those shoreline perspectives."

Another laugh and a shake of the head. "Well, quite honestly, crazy. Those guys, don't get me wrong, they're all great, really nice. But fishermen, they're wild. Wild men going for tuna."

"Deep, open water?"

"Oh yeah. Four, five hundred kilometres offshore. Out there for weeks at a time." He shakes his head again as though to emphasize the lunacy of such a career, and I decide to never take my tinned tuna for granted.

But I think of the points that he's stressed—"They're all great. Really nice."—and liken what he's said to my experience at the Harbour

Authority and Fisherman's Wharf. Not of being crazy, but nice and welcoming. And I feel certain I've gained insight into life on the water.

With a bit more effort and just one mild curse, Dennis affixes the vent plates back in place, twists a dial, then jiggles a plug.

"There you go. Should be good. Any issues, let me know."

Simple as that, I have heat and a user manual too. In English. And as Dennis heads out, I wonder what I should eat with my tuna.

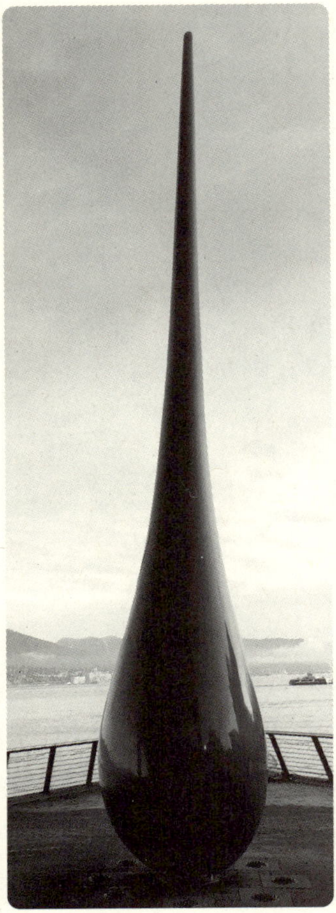

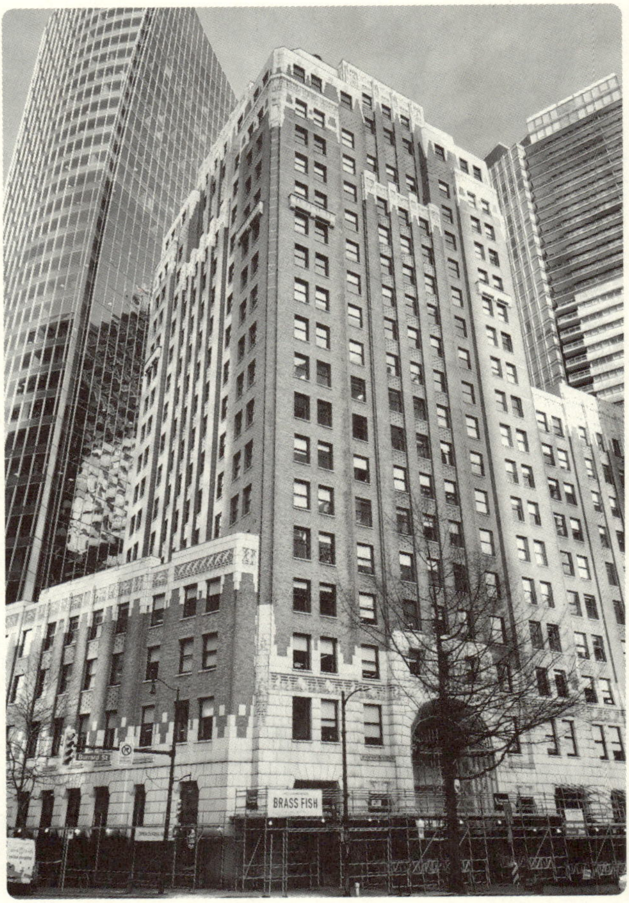

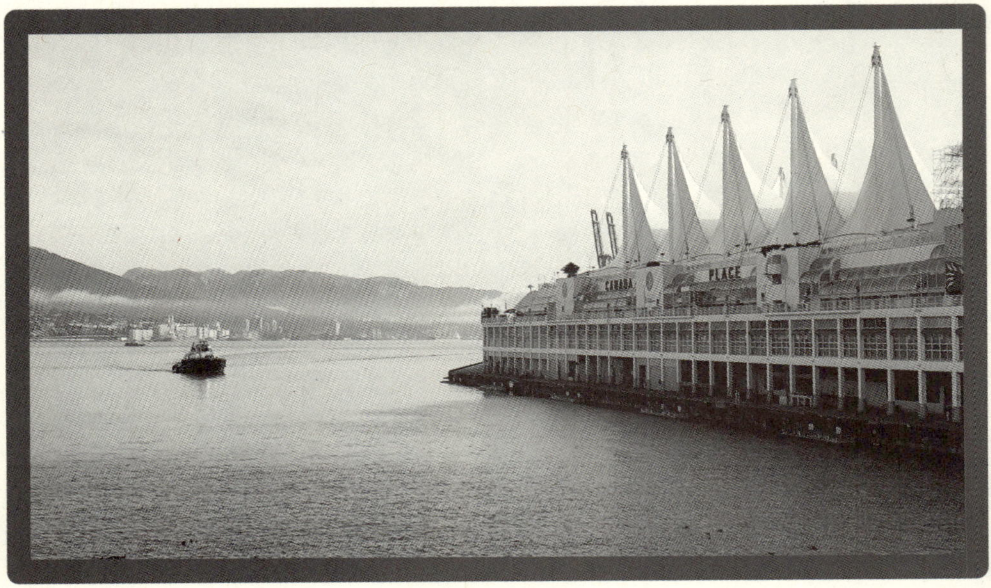

CLOCKWISE FROM TOP LEFT: *The Drop* by Inges Idee, with Burrard Inlet beyond, looking northeast; the Marine Building; a tugboat approaching the Canada Place sails.

Downtown's North Edge

LINKING SEA, LAND, AND AIR

BACK TO THE STREETS FOR A STINT, taking me once more to the water. I start with a beeline north from False Creek to the Marine Building, architectural linkage of ocean and land. This iconic structure, old by Vancouver standards, has been here for roughly a century. Behind me, to the south, the current Hotel Vancouver pokes a low-clouded sky with its copper-peaked roof, the chateau line of railway hotels. I take in the ornate Marine Building again, its facade looking as though an ocean traveller hauled their steamer trunk ashore, dumped its contents out here, then stuck it all together in this stoic yet fussy construction. I can imagine the racket, like an upended box of Lego, an aural assault of unleashed potential.

Moving on, I pass beneath hornbeams and sweet gums with bright leafy maples, the curbs covered in leaves. City workers are putting diverters around low drainage points. The next heavy rain will bring flooding for sure, more than street sweepers or budgets can handle.

A few steps north and I'm on fully reclaimed (reinvented?) shoreline, where the Vancouver Convention Centres, East and West, elbow

Burrard Inlet. To my right, the iconic white sails are catching a breeze and getting nowhere. Today a cruise ship is berthed, its outline not unlike the Marine Building block, but with less flash and more function. It's a pleasant day for passengers, lightly overcast with patchy blue promise. This time of year, I doubt the ship is heading north. Likely a repositioning cruise bound for waters near Baja from which whalers might summon their kin.

Turning west, I watch the Canada Place globe slowly spin behind glass. A good visual, with our planet mostly a deep ocean blue. There's a static white cloud over Africa and Asia, blending with ice at the poles. I can't help but think of Cedar Swan's modest ships picking their way through that mist of blue-white. An astronaut's view of the argonauts, finding those coastal communities.

Following the Seawall in a quadrangle of walkways and historical plaques, I reread text that guided me previously, though now with a view to the water. One bit of signage revisits Chief Joe Capilano, his work with longshoremen and his journey to visit the king.

Another plaque refers to the multicultural makeup of not only the Local 526 longshoremen's union but of this whole stretch of seaside as well: Indigenous locals, Europeans, South Americans, Native Hawaiians. Reminiscent of Navvy Jack's family tree and the blended marriage of Mary See-em-ia. Building on this is a reference to vigilante groups, hired gangs used to quash protests under the guise of fighting a Communist threat. No doubt the same sort of thugs who chased Mary from her Kanaka land at Coal Harbour.

The next informative installation offers a radically alternate view of how this portside was transformed; it describes the devastating explosion of the *Greenhill Park*.

> March 6, 1945, 11:15 a.m. The *Greenhill Park*, a 10,000 ton merchant freighter, was taking on cargo which included 7½ tons of signal flares, 94 tons of sodium chlorate (for bleaching wood pulp), and barrels of over proof whiskey—all in the same hold. 3 volatile ingredients, waiting for a spark ... In an instant, 4 explosions tore apart the vessel, killing 2 seamen, 6 longshoremen and injuring 26 more, including

7 firemen. Downtown, the shock wave shattered thousands of windows. Glass and cargo rained on the streets for 15 minutes.

Another iteration, in its way, of the city's Great Fire, more salvage of sorts. Only here, rather than paddles and song, it was those undersung tugs to the rescue, as well as the horrid task of recovery. Later, when I shared this story with my mother-in-law, Donna, she remembered the event from her childhood. Her father had worked on that boat. The only time he ever took a day off was that very day when the boat exploded. It's one of those stories, like those of the passengers who chose not to board the *Titanic*—nearly impossible odds. Donna also recalled finding bits of fabric, charred swatches they gathered and reused to make quilts, part of the wreckage that rained on the city. Shreds of blankets, she believed, from the *Greenhill Park* lifeboats.

As though taking a break from devastation, the next plaque in the sequence tells the story of the carefully planned detonation of Ripple Rock, a seamount in the Seymour Narrows. Another shoreline legend of reinvention, but rather than a tale of creation, one of progressive destruction, clearing the Salish Sea to the north to make way for safe transport and cruise lines.

In 1955, work began on an unprecedented feat of engineering: to shatter Ripple Rock with the biggest non-nuclear, man-made explosion in history.

The story continues with details of the explosives, of drilling and planting detonators, then triggering it all. A filming studio bunker was even constructed for the CBC to broadcast it live on the air, a postwar version of watching Oppenheimer's blast in the desert. The trepidation, intensity, and fear must've been overwhelming.

Ripple Rock blew on April 5, 1958, at 9:31 a.m.—a time chosen to avoid a major fish run. Some 700,000 tons erupted in a blast 300 metres high. It was over in 10 seconds. Porpoises and orcas, spotted before the explosion, reappeared, unharmed. And Ripple Rock was gone.

Now I angle toward rising sun and enjoy a fine view. Despite the clouds, the sky's bright, and I find myself squinting as a Helijet roars to its passenger pad by the port. I get a good look at one side of the cruise ship now moored by the sails. The aft of its hull is in primary hues, giving it the look of a cartoonish mural. I imagine nods of approval from OSGEMEOS.

A few more steps, and I pass art depicting a huge water droplet known as *The Drop*, a nod to the weather here and to this place in particular, where water, it seems, remains ever present above and below.

With a swivel northwest I can see Deadman's Island, images of John Morton gauging board feet. The North Shore is brooding, with fog in a low, heavy brow and an overcast, flickering sun. The overall weather undecided. Maybe more imminent drops, or the inlet unstitching its water-cloud quilt.

Neatly enough, the next plaque speaks of living with precipitation, acknowledging this wet coastal climate. The plaque is titled "The Rain People," which refers to the coast north of here, toward Bella Bella, roughly midway between the top of Vancouver Island and Haida Gwaii, with its beach where humanity started. Much the same path as those vessels that now traverse the inside passage over Ripple Rock's undersea shards.

Walking west around the exterior of the Convention Centre, gulls luff the water, and cormorants have commandeered a jetty, perching in a slick-feathered line. More plaques catch my eye like a slow-moving storybook.

One tells the story of Mattie Gunterman, who explored the province with her husband and son in the late 1800s armed with a Kodak camera and a tripod. Fifteen years after her passing, quite by accident, a Vancouver librarian discovered two hundred negatives of photos Mattie had taken. A remarkable archive from when pictorial records were rare.

Next are the stories of lumber workers who branched, trimmed, and cleared spars of "Doug fir." In its way, another bridging of forest and water, as lumberjacks partnered with land, using inclines and hills to guide timber to beaches for lashing in booms for mill transport.

I stop and then listen. The drone of a Helijet. Next, a float plane. As cloud thickens, the sun finds some cracks. The sunlight's reflection, refraction, makes the hills of West Van appear to be dusted in snow, which they aren't at the moment, their appearance a meteorological shrug.

Now a plaque tells the story of the SS *Komagata Maru*, a vessel that sailed from India in 1914 on the cusp of the First World War, transporting would-be immigrants to Canada, their destination the Port of Vancouver. Those aboard, like those who'd come here since 1903, considered the relocation an uncomplicated emigration, "citizens of the British Empire" moving between colonial countries. But the shipload of South Asian passengers were turned away, disallowed to dock in Vancouver, reinforcing a Eurocentric stand within Canada: non-white immigrants were no longer welcome. The ship had no choice but to leave, taking families back to a violent and deadly state police reception in Kolkata. Government records indicate that as passengers disembarked, left with no other option, twenty-six people were killed. Witnesses counted seventy-five.

Next, a leap from exclusion to a gradual mixing of cultures, with a plaque describing Pacific diversity by way of boat craft and design—specifically, Japanese boatbuilders working in Steveston. By employing new keel construction with innovative moulding, hull ribs, and the use of Japanese push saws, plank fittings were created with advanced and much finer precision, making heavy caulking (and subsequent bailing) almost unheard of. A quantum leap in marine engineering, credited not only to an opening of borders but also to an openness toward learning and change.

At the northwest corner of the seawalk, set apart from the info boards, I arrive at a metal art installation, an outsize sculpted weather vane with a Seuss-like appearance, as though a cluster of penny farthings are collectively dragging a scoop. Everything pivots and spins with the wind to create an anemometer that turns with the breeze. Considered a bookend to *The Drop* at the walkway's east corner, this piece, called the *Wind Wheel Mobile*, is part of a memorial honouring victims of asbestos.

Beneath the sculpture are photos of activists from the 1970s drawing attention to the "magic" mineral's dangers. Suddenly the movement of air feels like a threat. This piece, or rather these pieces, were officially unveiled through a joint dedication by the provincial government, the BC Labour Heritage Centre, the BC Federation of Labour, and WorkSafeBC.[54]

Moving west, three more stories link the city with water. First, the commemoration of female riveters working in shipyards during the Second World War. Beside this, a plaque tells of Lucille Johnstone, former president of the Rivtow Group of tugboat companies. And to round out the water-linked stories, one final plaque memorializes Métis inventor and carver Phil Nuytten, also known by his Kwakwa̱ka̱'wakw name, Tlaxan. Working with NASA, Nuytten explored deep BC lakes thought to replicate planetary development on Earth and on Mars. He also carved Kwakiutl Nation totems and canoes. On the plaque is a photo of him in his bright-yellow Newtsuit—the deep-sea diving suit he invented—his grinning face peering through its thick glass helmet, as though he's just ambled ashore from his own Jules Verne expedition.

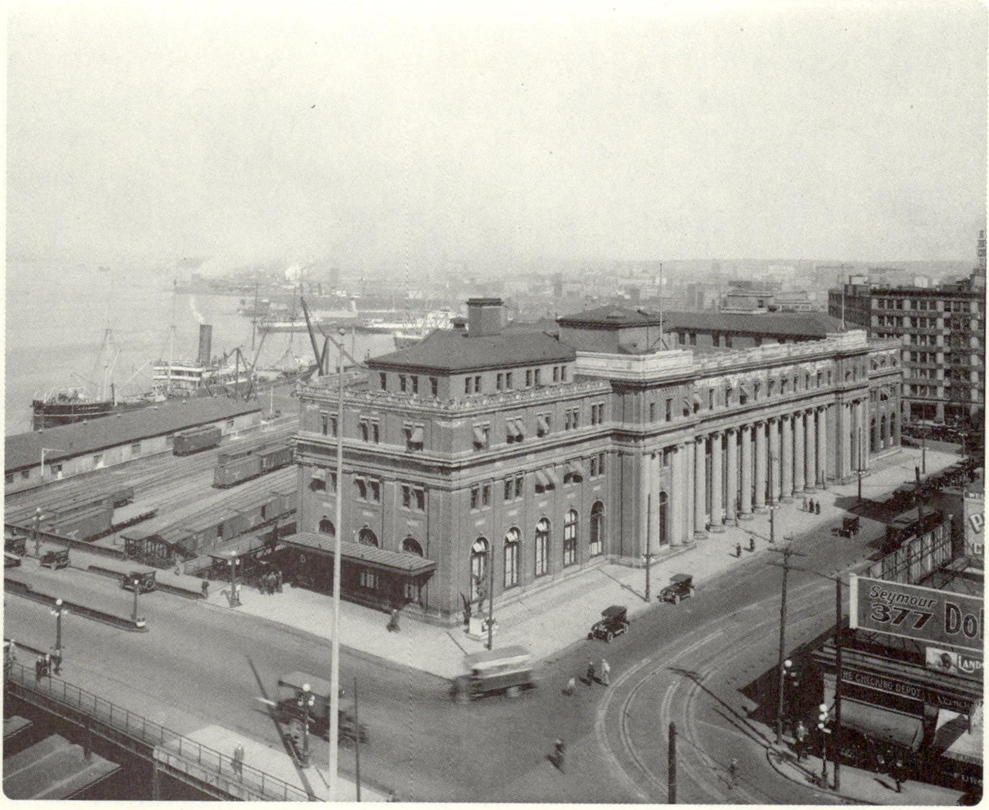

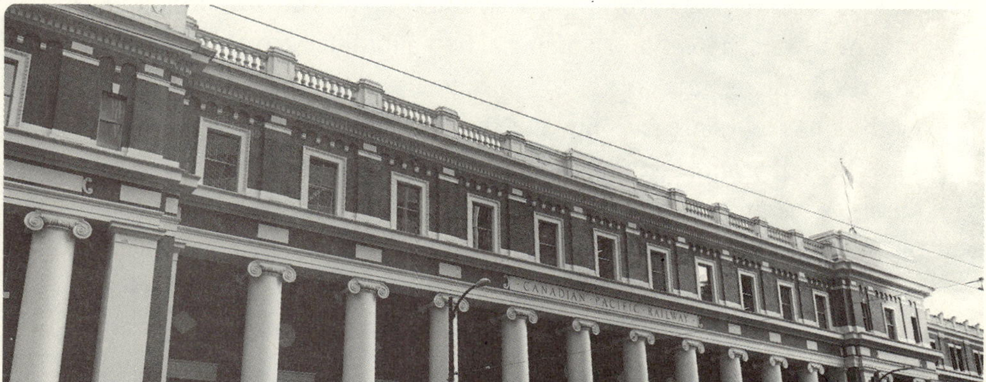

TOP: Waterfront Station, 1923.
BOTTOM: Waterfront Station, present day.

Gastown and the Port of Vancouver

VANCOUVER'S GREAT FIRE

LEAVING COAL HARBOUR, I spin east and cross downtown through porcupine towers, hotels, and a financial hub. Buildings shorten somewhat as I reach the red brick of Gastown, angled streets to accommodate rail, with tight real estate gaps plugged by flatiron construction. On a map, this sliver of original city centre is a blunt-ended wedge: Hastings Street kinks the south, railway tracks form a northerly lip, and the west and east edges are Richards and Main Streets.

Passing Canada Place and Waterfront Station, you'll likely see a SeaBus arriving or departing, the old Navvy Jack link now a commuter exchange. I spot the *Chinook* in rotation, a SeaBus custom-wrapped in the art of three Indigenous artists—Kelly Cannell, Siobhan Joseph, and Angela George—as though a mural selection and cultural tags found a spot on this vessel. The craft's artwork effectively captures rebirth with jagged stripes in blue, yellow, and red. It's playful and proud, sharing water's circularity with an essence of stewardship too. That symbol, the life of a salmon, captures it all. Akin to Celtic knot whirls, with no beginning or end, simply ongoing.

Eastbound on the red brick are a few vintage street lamps, porticoes, and glass overhangs. Some leafy black pine, basswood, and brush box, their roots cracking brickwork and concrete. Past the steam clock, huffing away like a vaper, a wedding photoshoot's happening: a bride in a long dress, her train fanned into place. There's a groom in a tux chewing gum, standing well out of the frame and trying not to be noticed.

Immediately north are the rails. A few cars sit idle, some for produce and goods (CPR and CNR), others for people (the West Coast Express). Passenger cars are painted in sleek purple-gold lines, an illusion of movement even when still.

Dumpsters in side alleys are painted as well, the work of street artists. Less refinement than Vancouver Biennale exhibits, though equally skilled in design. Phone poles too have been tagged, with symbols I don't understand. Maybe a new-generation Banksy.

Buildings here show their age. More brick made of sandstone from the early to mid-1900s. If I'm not mistaken, bits of Portland stone can be found in the corners as well. There's an oval sign fixed to a wall, a Vancouver centennial plaque marked "1886–1986," with additional text: "Reading of the Riot Act. April 23, 1935. From the steps of the Cenotaph, Mayor Gerald McGeer read the Riot Act to disperse a crowd protesting conditions in the relief camps." Which dovetailed from unemployed trades and rail employees looking for work as the world hobbled through the Depression. Many involved came from the shanty communities and cooperage yards lining False Creek. Now, high-end retail, fashion, and art are set here, moving east in dichotomous gentrification. There's even a record shop; vinyl that only recently sat dusty, ignored, now fills a window in prime real estate.

I pass Maple Tree Square, once a birthmark, now a slow-healing scar where a statue of "Gassy Jack" Deighton once stood but has since been removed, as his atrocities against Indigenous people became publicly known. My last time through, an art installation dangled from branches, letters hung like tree ornaments, spelling words in a delicate script: "Engage," "Peace," "Love." Sentiments that are determined yet cautious as well, a tentative coaxing toward healing.

Now to an obtuse intersection, an off-kilter half roundabout where roads sidestep rail boundaries. More turn-of-the-century street lamps, another flatiron building. A guy in red shoes plays a song I don't know on a beat-up guitar, maybe something he's written. His vocals are good—there's confidence there. Behind him, a graffito of a heart made of wings taking flight, a dream symbol. All of this a few steps from the shop with the record display.

Suddenly the red bricks underfoot aren't rounded and worn but impeccably new, crisp ochre blocks almost perfectly square. Every few strides, a lone brick is stencilled with a symbol or words, black on red. The languages vary. "Para conectar," Spanish for "to connect." "Att ansluta," Swedish for "to connect." (Ah, I get it.) Then a Chinese symbol. One in Korean. Another in what I believe to be Hindi. All, I presume, relaying the infinitive "to connect." Not merely a masonry link but encouragement and hope, single-word media fused onto brick.

I take a refuelling stop in the neighbourhood of what was Japantown, now relabelled Railtown. It's the east side of Gastown, the north edge of the Downtown Eastside. A swinging glass door opens onto a diner, an old building somewhat refurbed. Vintage but with bracket-creep pricing. Not quite the affordability I can find a bit south, farther east in the neighbourhood, where only last week I had breakfast and coffee and got change from a ten-dollar bill. But the food and the service are good, and I loiter in a booth with a view. The place fills with city police, friendly and vocal and *not* having coffee and donuts. Until a few in the group finally cave, change their orders and live the cliché.

A few black-and-white photos hang from the walls: an aerial shot of the port, one near the corner of Maple Tree Square, one of a now defunct bank along Hastings that has the look of a Monopoly hotel. There's a fabulous shot, heavy with sepia, taken from behind Deadman's Island looking back at the city, the camera angled southeast. The scene is Coal Harbour, the north side of downtown with the port to the east. Though in the distance, the Marine Building commands the skyline. At the south edge, the right side of the frame, the Hotel Vancouver is the other towering landmark. Two bookends to rival *The Drop* and the *Wind Wheel Mobile*, but with more function than message or art. The picture must be from around 1950. A few wooden boats sit at the Vancouver Rowing Club, a vista that would make a fine jigsaw to reassemble an instant in time: "Historic Vancouver, a City of Water."

Two more shots grab my eye. One is of Gastown in which everything looks rather new. A car in the frame indicates it must be post–Second World War. The other captures a Thunderbird totem on a rise over Stanley Park's Brockton Point, its view the city's downtown.

From the diner, a turn south brings me to the heart of the Downtown Eastside. I could spend months simply walking through the grit and life stories here. Optimism, despair, camaraderie, hope. With a market, always open, for everything. What resonates are the mosaics that pepper the sidewalks, single-pane stories. The website Mosaic Art Source best describes it.

> Artists were hired to direct the conceptual development and production of mosaic and banner markers and a guide book that together capture historic events, natural history and cultural stories from the rich history of the Downtown Eastside. Artists worked with participants from the Carnegie Street Program in a storefront studio over a six week period to research, design and produce 31 mosaic markers and 100 banners that mark the Old Vancouver Townsite.[55]

One of these images is the Carnegie building, a neighbourhood community centre and library. In the words of the City of Vancouver online, "Carnegie Community Centre— often referred to as the living room of the Downtown Eastside—provides social, educational, cultural, and recreational activities on-site and nearby at Oppenheimer Park. The programs serve low income adults with the goal of nurturing mind, body, and spirit in a safe and welcoming environment."[56]

Safe and welcoming: an accurate summation, and it's a place of nourishment too. Essentially what Carnegie had in mind when he financed the build at the start of the twentieth century, in part, it's been said, to assuage his guilt regarding his vast fortune. A Scrooge-like turn of emotion, this being one of 2,500 such libraries that now dot the planet.

To the south is another settler-based city birthplace, Chinatown, home to the Chinese Cultural Centre Museum and the Dr. Sun Yat-Sen Classical Chinese Garden. Even here I can still feel departure, conversation in arrays of language that match those sidewalk bricks with their various terms for connection.

What ties this city locale, now landlocked, with my watery walks is the fact that this neighbourhood, False Creek—a geographic oblong running west to east from Homer to Gore, and north to south from Hastings to Georgia—previously reached into here, lapping eastward and northward like a flexed arm, almost giving a lewd gesture to the rest of downtown.

Being in the Classical Chinese Garden, which was largely transplanted from China, creates its own wrinkle in time. A rustle of bamboo, gentle paths with undulation and curve, a reflecting pool too. The result: a contemplative glint to keep the bustle of elsewhere at bay.

That bent arm of False Creek, however, was eventually "reclaimed." Filled to allow for a railway terminus, hotels, and subsequent services. Now, St. Paul's Hospital is being built here, moving from Burrard, to occupy this neighbourhood extension of False Creek Flats.

Pivoting north, I follow Main to cross Alexander Street at Wendy Poole Park, an unassuming green space with patched grass and a short path where a roughly round piece of granite sits like a headstone or cairn. On the stone, etched in black, is a flower encircled with feathers. Under this, a dedication: "Wendy Poole Park. Tsay Keh Dene. Like water, truth embraces both stone and starlight." A bronze plaque set on concrete adds more.

> In September 2000, the Vancouver Park Board dedicated this park to Wendy Poole (1968–1989), a First Nations woman from the Tsay Keh Dene (People of the Mountains) Nation in the northwest of the province. Wendy was known as a kind, trusting person. She was one of a number of British Columbia aboriginal women who lived and lost their lives in the Downtown Eastside.

Though excessively softened in wording, Wendy's story is one of too many: an Indigenous woman murdered, the murder unsolved. Or, rather, unsentenced. A grisly reminder of violence in these narrative streetscapes that follow the water.

Across the road to the east, a faded sign for Burrard Iron Works hangs from a vintage facade. Unsure of what I'm looking at, I search Canada's Historic Places and learn this was part of the Terminal City Iron Works, a structure completed in 1913. The business made winches and parts and conducted repairs for marine operations. Later, it became an Army & Navy retail store. Its early twentieth-century design was considered fire resistant—heavy timber around millwork flooring, with plenty of brick. What's left has been landscaped into a courtyard and garden as part of a housing co-operative developed by the Downtown Eastside Residents Association.[57] More layers than I might have imagined, caught in chipped paint on a wall.

From here it's a bit farther north to the Burrard Inlet shore. A shared walkway for pedestrians and traffic curls over the railway tracks, giving a brief lofty view. Two ornamental dragons in concrete frame the street, poised at either side of the throughway. Bewilderingly, someone's placed a turd in one dragon's mouth. Not from a pet, I suspect.

Past the shit-eating dragon, the footpath deviates from the road to open onto CRAB Park. Beyond that is the spiked false horizon of the Canada Place sails. An agreeable tartan of trees frame the view: maples in assorted Life Savers candy hues, hemlock, and cedar, with blackberry shrubs shedding their leaves. Farther on, descending while curving back west, I pick up another planned walk, Footprints Community Art Project, where a vertical plaque on a pole introduces the inlet and some of its recent history. There's a reference to crossing Burrard Inlet via bridges and SeaBus with a quote stating that in the past, "the trip across the inlet was more of an excursion."

An excursion for sure, as a SeaBus picks up its cue to rumble this way, like Navvy Jack's ferry and the *Hollyburn* too. Not to mention Damara Jacobs-Petersen's recounting of pulling through the inlet. "A tough paddle. Really tough."

By the port, I pass the former City Hall site. One of them, anyway. As a Places That Matter plaque and its website explain,

> Since 1886 Vancouver City Hall has had four locations around the city after moving out of the tent erected after the Great Fire. 125 Powell Street, 425 Main Street, 16 East Hastings Street were all home to civic officials until the construction of City Hall at 12th and Cambie after the amalgamation of South Vancouver, Point Grey and Vancouver in 1929.[58]

That City Hall tent, this location, brings us—or, rather, returns us—to the story of Vancouver's Great Fire. The blaze that destroyed the new township was actually two separate fires, both intentionally lit to clear the downtown peninsula. This took place on June 13, 1886, shortly after the city's first survey stake was hammered into place by what's now the Victory Square Cenotaph. The town had just changed its name from Granville to Vancouver, and the surrounding forest was still thick in the area. While big trees were cut, hauled, and boomed to the mills, burning the small growth and scrub was simpler (and cheaper) than removing it.

One of the two fires was started in what's now the West End, the other in Yaletown, to clear land for the CPR Roundhouse. But immediately after both controlled burns were lit, a gale surged from the southwest, fanning the flames with increasing gusts. Embers leapt between buildings to engulf the area almost instantly. The resulting inferno was intensified by the unusually dry season. Plus, most buildings were made of fresh lumber, much of it sticky with resin. No doubt the new build aroma was lovely, but the city was effectively tinder and fuel.

Within a half-hour, the whole town was gone. The Old Hastings Mill Store was one of only three buildings left standing. The total damage can only be estimated. A thousand buildings were destroyed, with two dozen lives lost, although many suspect it was more.

As the fire grew, residents fled to False Creek, where the Classical Chinese Garden is now, or to here on Burrard Inlet. Still, the heat from the blaze was too much, making the air a great scalding wall. People swam farther from shore, fighting currents, clutching belongings, some hanging from boats, others clinging to anything that might float. Then, from across the inlet, members of Damara Jacobs-Petersen's and Zoe George's families and other Squamish and Coast Salish Peoples responded, carving through waves to cross the səlilwətaɬ, the Tsleil-Waututh water of Burrard Inlet.

Imagine the flotilla of mass rescue, canoes not fleeing but pulling toward the blaze, the chorus of paddle songs being chanted. Survivors being grabbed, hauled aboard. One of the paddle songs that was sung through that ordeal is still shared at Squamish celebrations of life. The heartbeat of paddle and beater on drum in this instance not only oral history but a lifesaving transfer as well, another form of mouth-to-mouth rescue.

Which brings us to a street mosaic I find particularly poignant, that of the Coast Salish phoenix, a round graphic depicting that rescue, the salvage and the city's rebirth silently scored with a soundtrack of paddle and song. *Phoenix* is the name of the mosaic, the mythic bird rising from a waver of flame in Salish design. Within a week of the fire, Vancouver was largely rebuilt, with tents for essential services and new trade finding its footing in ash.

I spend a long while by the shore where much of this happened. That next iteration of city came about because of that rescue, and with it a resoundingly evident reliance on the region's First Peoples.

I'm now in CRAB Park. My view north and east is mostly of the port. Berthed under the swinging orange cranes is what looks like a sheer wall of blocks. Until I realize it's a ship loaded with containers, and I'm only seeing one end of it! Maybe it's one of those three-hundred-metre-long beasts, the largest that enter the inlet, although many around the globe are now up to four hundred metres in length.

Closer to me and the shore is a network of piers and boathouses. A compact Boston Whaler is heading this way, its wake a sharp curve. Crows are combing the sand between driftwood. One has an acorn clutched in its beak, what I imagine will make a good feed. The occasional gull kites my view.

To my left, to the west, is the cut of the Canada Place sails. A Helijet purrs, leaves the ground heading north by northeast. More plaques by the path share their history snippets. The next one is titled "Camping for CRAB Park."

> CRAB Park would not exist if not for the work of the Create a Real Available Beach Committee (CRAB) and activists like Don Larson. They started with the dream of a Downtown Eastside waterfront park on a vacant site owned by the federal government. In 1982, CRAB organized a community music event on the site with the band Industrial Waste and singer Ian Tiles while Ports Canada Police circled the event in their patrol cars.
>
> Two years later, campers in 60 tents occupied the site for 75 days. Members of Parliament Pat Carney and Margaret Mitchell kept their promises to pressure the federal government and the occupation led to the creation of the present park—CRAB Park at Portside. The victory is celebrated every July 1 with live, local, free music.

A few steps away is another plaque, titled "Not Welcome," describing the fate of the SS *Komagata Maru*, a continuation of the story I read by the Convention Centre's blue globe. Behind this, on a slope of clover and grass sits a pyramidal hunk of grey granite. On the stone is a bronze sign with the words "Portside Park." At the moment a crow's standing on the rock, scrutinizing the sign as though reading the words, and for all I know, that's exactly what it's doing.

I look around for more plaques put here to create a brief history walk. But the numbered signage comes to a needle-scratch stop. I find a sign numbered "three," the next "four," and that's it. Whether they've been removed by design, taken down for repair, or simply destroyed, I don't know. In its way, the absence creates new narrative, stories patchy and fading, almost leaving the park and the shore as mementoes, memories that may or may not remain.

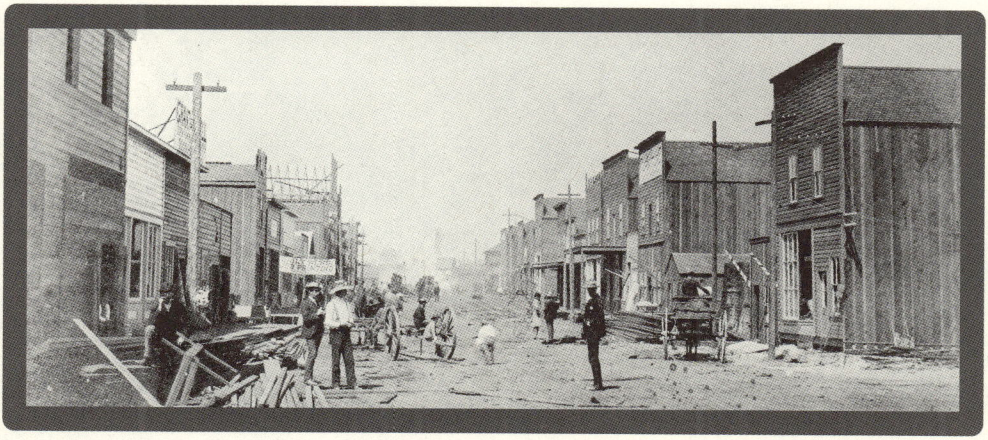

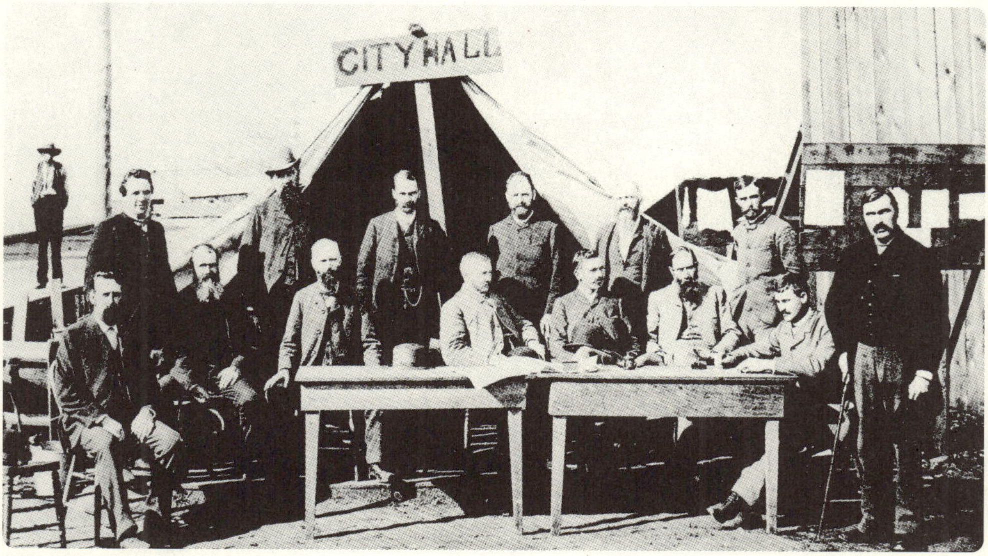

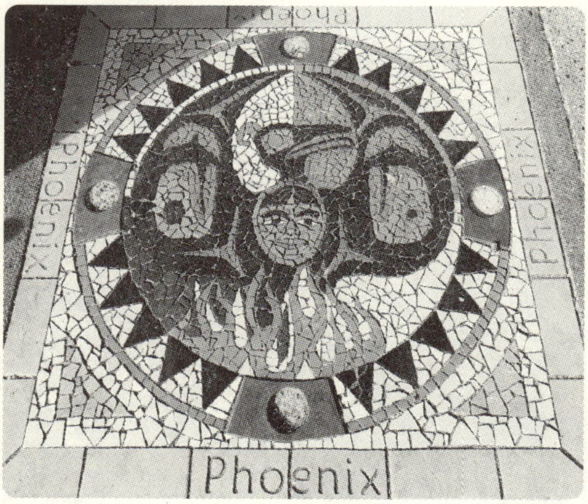

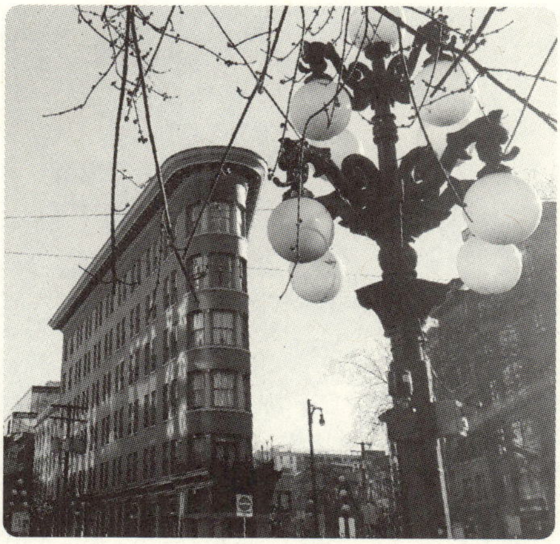

CLOCKWISE FROM TOP: Gastown after the Great Fire, 1886; City Hall at Gastown, after the Great Fire, 1886; a vintage street lamp and the Flatiron Building in Gastown; *Phoenix*, a street mosaic in Gastown depicting the Great Fire and rescue by the Coast Salish.

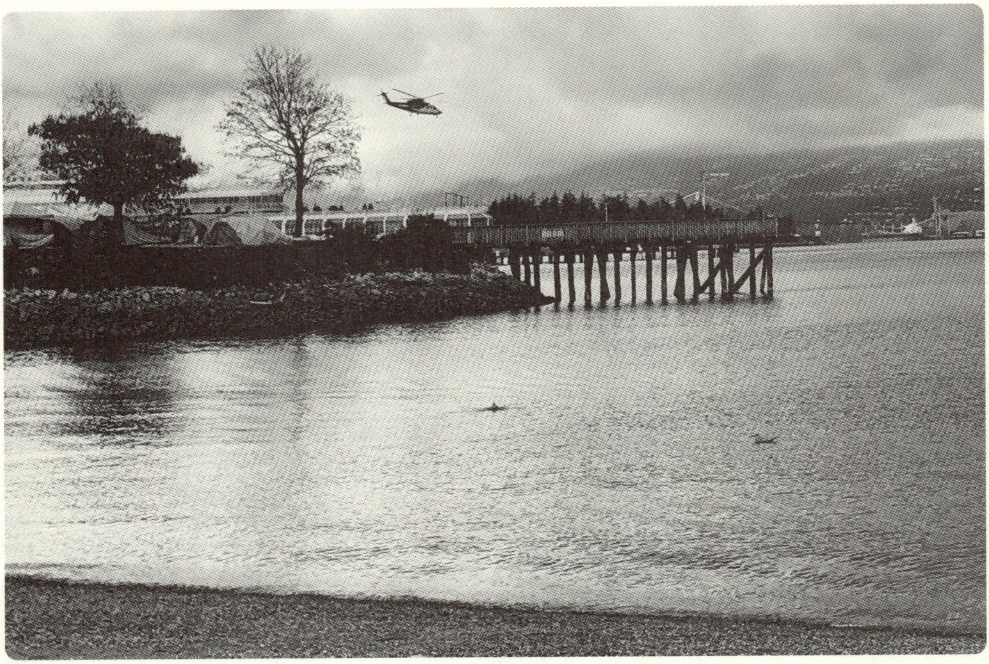

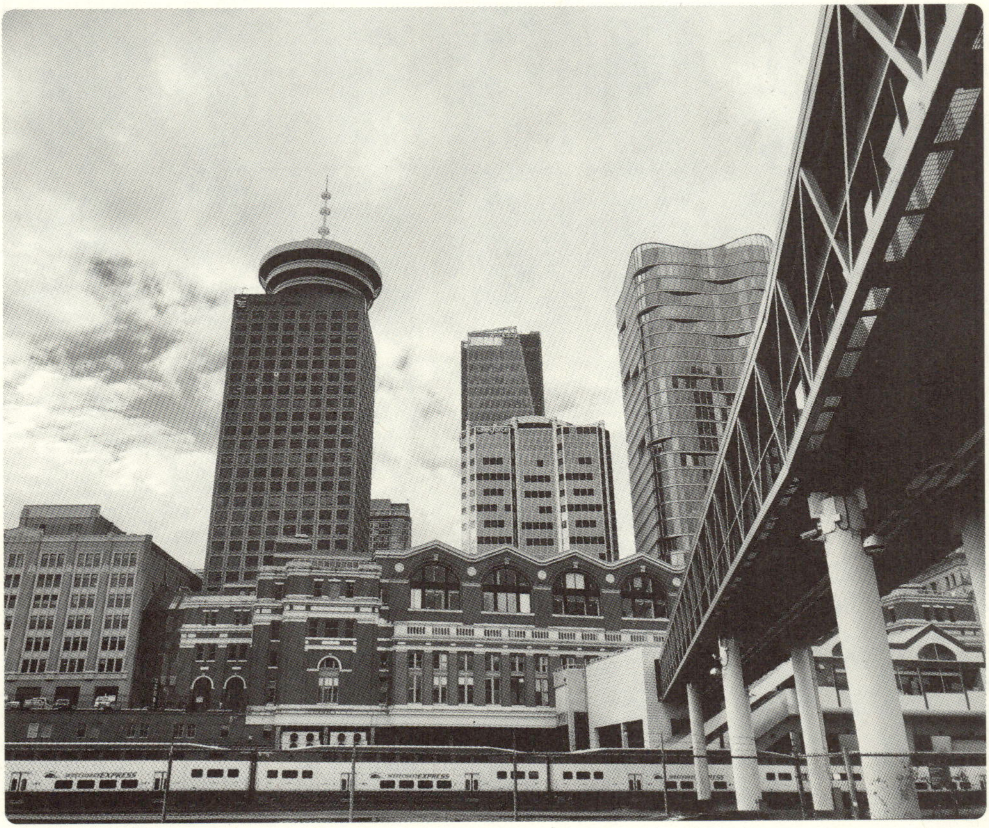

TOP: a Helijet flying over a tent city, from CRAB Park.
BOTTOM: the SeaBus accessway downtown, with the West Coast Express and Harbour Centre beyond.

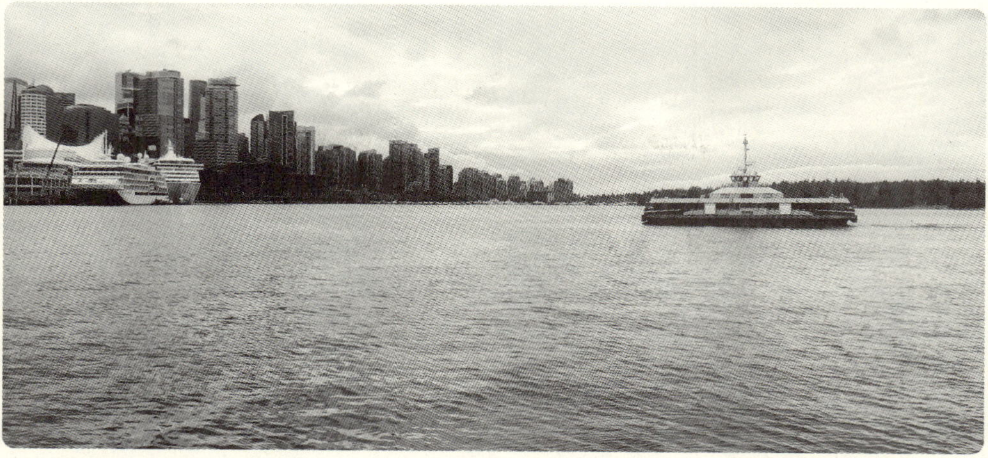

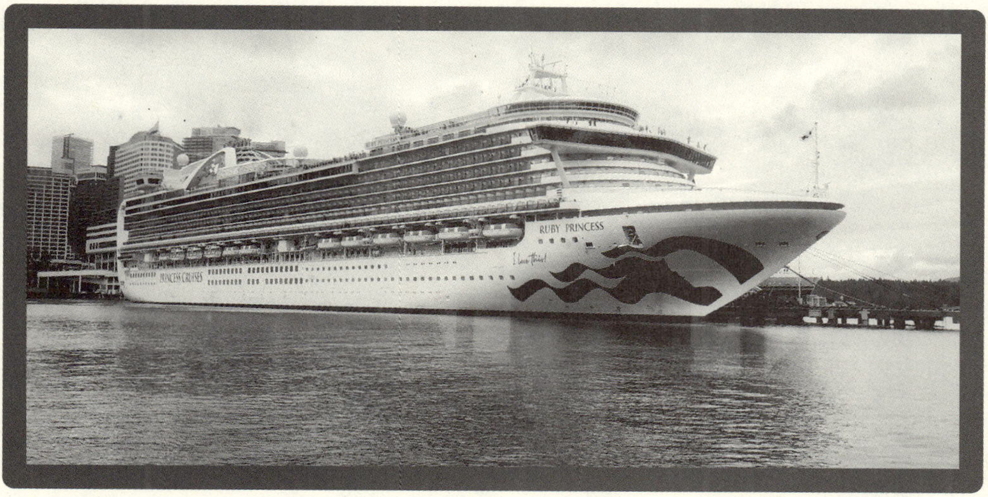

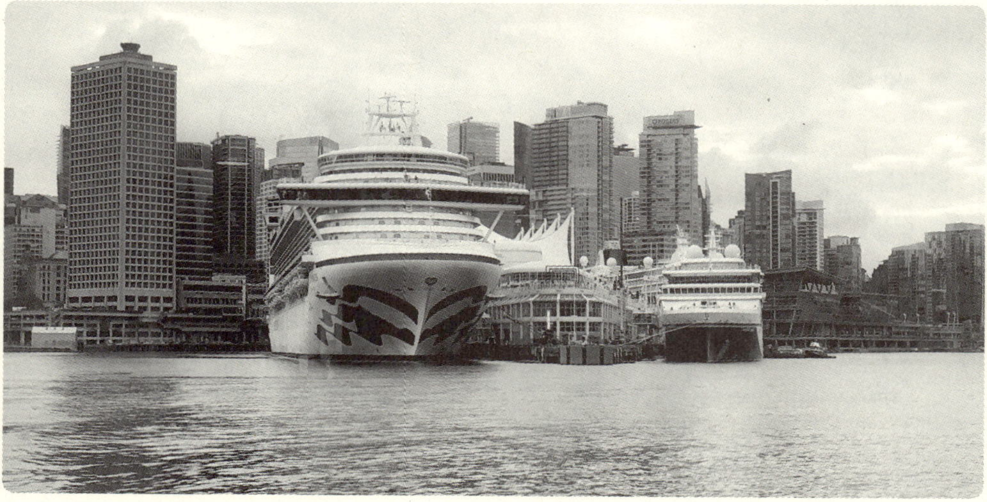

TOP TO BOTTOM: a SeaBus southbound, approaching downtown; a cruise ship at Canada Place from a SeaBus; moored cruise ships from a SeaBus, with downtown beyond.

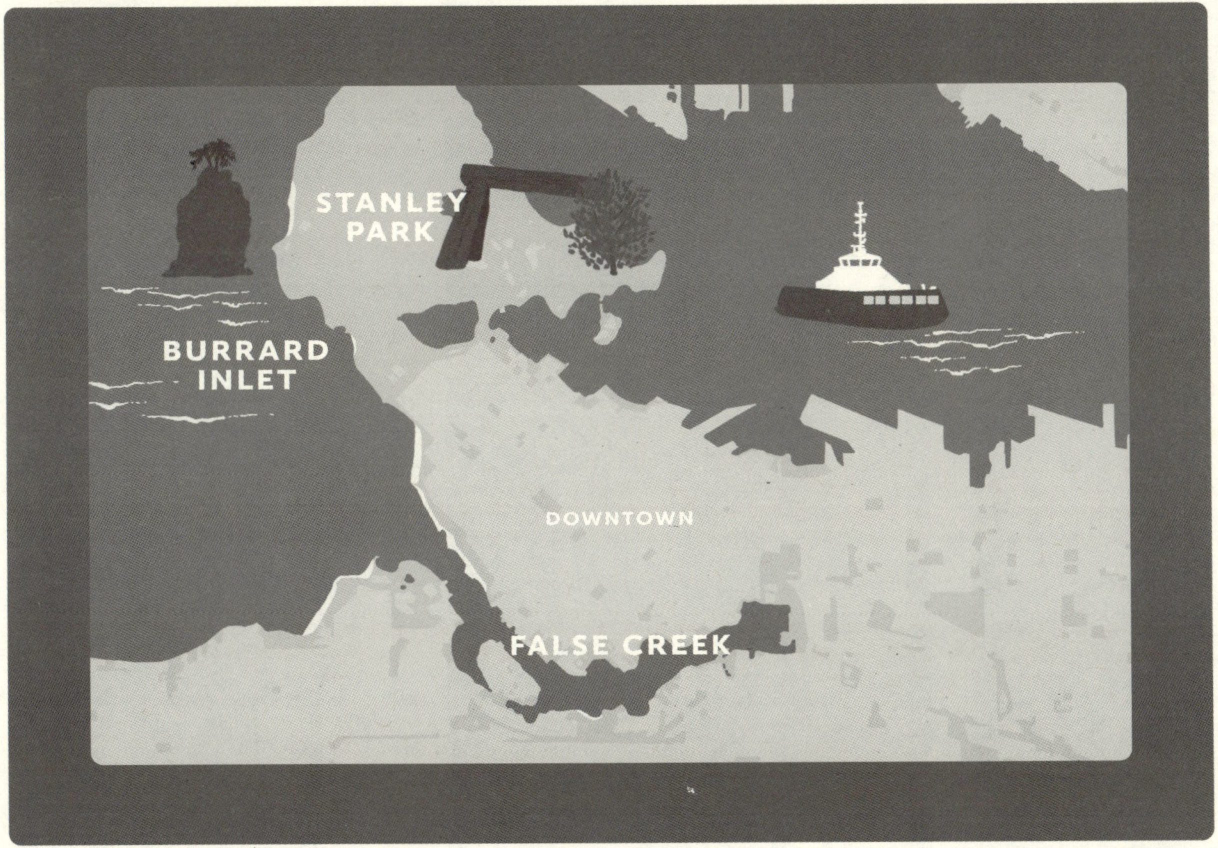
STANLEY PARK
BURRARD INLET
DOWNTOWN
FALSE CREEK

STANLEY PARK

to

DOWNTOWN

and

FALSE CREEK

Aboard the Chinook

IN THE WAKE OF THE *PHOENIX*

THE HELIJET I'D BEEN WATCHING has disappeared in the mist, the fog almost thick enough to dampen the roar of the engine. I keep moving west, my route the same bend as that boat with its long trailing wake. On a jut of headland, a tent city stands between the port and the Canada Place sails. Tarps, flysheets, umbrellas, anything rain resistant and tieable has been lashed into covers and canopies, even walkways and passthroughs. There are a few shopping carts, some transactions, but it's mostly quiet and peaceful.

With a one-eighty turn comes a fresh view. On the road, cyclists in a loud-talking line, what looks like a tour on wheels. There's a dense wall of blackberry, heavy with prickles and leaves. Geese are nibbling the grass. As I cross the soft carpet of green, I feel acorns as lumps underfoot. Maple leaves, vibrantly red, are dropping with the look of that stylized map of the Great Fire at the Old Hastings Mill Store.

To shorten my shortcut, I bushwhack through cedar, then find a gap in the blackberry shrub. Partway through, it's too tight—I don't fit and get stuck. I keep pushing, hear a rip as my jacket gives way, the nylon no match for the thorns. Barbs draw blood from my hands, and I'm beyond relieved (and embarrassed) when I finally break free. Final score: blackberry 1, walker 0.

Past the heliport is a perimeter fence of barbed wire. The tents and park slowly shrink while Canada Place starts to loom. Behind a glass door, unlocked with a transit pass tap, stairs lead to the SeaBus, but I want to see what's straight ahead. By continuing at street level under the Convention Centre, I'll keep close to the shoreline and water.

Trucks are turning, unloading at dim portals in concrete, the comings and goings of loading bays. If I had X-ray specs and looked north, I'd see through the Canada Place bowels, its basement supporting the hotel, conference halls, and cruise ship terminal. I'd see a broad shelf of concrete supported by pilings in rock on the shore. Land reimagined, reclaimed. What now is a reef cross-pollinating the rock and cement where mussels and barnacles live with molluscs and urchins, anemones, small fish. Which in turn draw the gulls and the cormorants. There are flounder and salmon as well, bringing seals, and deeper, the occasional whale. Development hasn't exactly created this, but in the vein of Habitat Island, building in this manner has helped alleviate, somewhat, the infringement of city on sea.

Finally I emerge, spat from the troglodyte world to the wharf of the seaplane terminal. One vintage plane in bright crimson is set to take flight, aiming east and then west. A bright sign in red with white lights spells "VANCOUVER." Behind it, the east edge of Stanley Park, a slice of Deadman's Island, and beyond that, the North Shore. A few frigid gusts, snow inching down mountains. From left to right, Cypress, Grouse, and Seymour are prodding the sky as though seeing which one can reach highest. The vista: blue, green, and white, with a collar of fog at the water.

Despite the cold, the onset of snow, it feels like a day between seasons here by the water—misty, chilly, and damp. Now I'm trekking the last of downtown. Above the reef of poured concrete, I've been "called to the bridge," so to speak, to join a ship's captain, not at their table for dinner (whew, I have nothing to wear), but to ride shotgun on the *Chinook* SeaBus in the wake of those Coast Salish heroes.

Back to the brick of the CPR building, now Waterfront Station, the east side of what was Kanaka. The angel statue *Winged Victory* is just taking flight, memorializing rail workers lost in the First World War. Into the echoey foyer, a tap of a card, then a stroll above tracks, this time on flooring, in glass. Then through a turnstile to wait with other commuters for the next northbound vessel.

My ride's on its way. A digital clock on the wall counts down, a few minutes to go. And I watch the *Chinook* approach from North Van in another gentle, smooth curve, bold colours in profile as it slides to its berth, the painted likeness of salmon gliding forward. Passengers disembark and then load. I'm ushered in past the seats to a door and tight steps leading up, in the same upward curl as a jumbo jet stairwell, to access the bubble. Another architectural-style reveal as I reach the bridge: the cabin is spacious, surrounded in perfectly clear glass, as though the whole helm is outside.

This is the newest craft in the fleet; everything slick and refined, high-tech in mirror image: two captain's chairs, two control panels, two radar screens. The skipper simply switches seats, facing north, facing south, given the vessel's direction.

First Mate Leon offers a handshake and a smile, welcomes me in. His hair is closely cropped, his eyes a warm brown. He indicates my seat, a padded office-style chair, making it clear that I have free run of the space. Bundled in a navy-blue fleece, he looks cozy, and a heater warms the cabin as well.

Now I meet the captain, or skipper, named Hark. He has a long ponytail, snow with pepper, and a uniform shirt with gold epaulettes. With his handshake and smile comes a proper Pallursi-eye crinkle, and I know we're in excellent hands.

Hark's been doing this for eighteen years, while Leon is in his fourth year. Hark points out technical features, bringing me up to speed with the vessel. Four engines, four throttles. He revs one, a deep diesel *vroom-vroom*. My smile, I'm certain, touches my ears. Now I know what I want to be when I grow up: forget Viking or race-car driver, I want to make a big boat go *vroom*!

"So," Hark says, "are you writing an article? Or a book?"

I describe my *Perfect Day* walks in the city and on the coast.

He nods. "Good. Okay, you want to know about this water? Our shores?" He gestures through the glass that surrounds us—impeccably clean, cantilevered, and tinted—his hand sweeping across the harbour. "One of the things that makes Vancouver such a great livable city is that a whole range of craft, all craft really, are able to explore BC through the water."

Leon's nodding as well. "Living here, it's more exciting, more adventurous being surrounded by water. The ocean, it regulates our temperature, makes our weather the very best. That and our transit, like SeaBus here, and our buses and trains. You couldn't ask for anything more."

Sun breaks through, glinting on the water we'll cross, a shimmering yellow brick road. On a wall, a polished barometer indicates the weather is now "FAIR." A matching steel analog clock states it's time to depart.

Hark takes the helm, and Leon scans the screens, makes a quick radio exchange. All fine with the harbour master, the transit teams either side of the inlet. Hark studies the radar, blip depictions of each vessel out there, their specifics as well: weight, length, and speed. And with a gentle shift of the two forward engine toggles, we leave precisely on schedule.

"The older boat, the *Burrard Beaver*—one chair at the helm. You have to turn it around when you change direction." Hark indicates the control panel with his chin and a tilt of the head. "We're monitoring, watching for harbour traffic and air traffic. Victoria Marine Traffic Services is the proper name. Then there's SeaBus internal communications and our north-south comms."

On our starboard side, a huge crane at the port loads containers onto a ship.

"Always watching for ships," Hark explains. "The shipping ships, 'deep seas,' we call them, they get right of way, west to east."

A tug toddles by, dragging a barge. "Now," Hark adds, "that one there, with a load, has limited mobility, so we'll let it through. But see that one there?" He points at another tug with no load. "We're arriving at a point the same time. We have right of way; yield to starboard."

The tug and the barge carry on as the untethered tug zips from view.

"Cruise ships too," Leon adds.

An "mm-hmm" from Hark. "April to October, they're running. Even though they can *really* maneuver. Just their size, they get right of way. Pilots bring them in. Both ways, in and out."

A smaller craft angles in our direction, its path from the east, past the port.

"Ah, there!" says Hark. "That's a Tymac, a pilot transfer. Must've just come from that deep sea over there. Now, see the edge of the port there, with the extra big crane?"

I nod.

"The container terminal added fifty or sixty metres in size, farther into the inlet. It's tougher to navigate, a tighter turn. Now when a big ship comes in, it's a bit more challenging, and with fog, it's much more challenging." He chuckles, underplaying it all.

Calm expertise fills the space. Same as I've felt in the cockpits of jets, and what I imagine it's like during surgeries. A few dozen monitors show camera angles covering the vessel: the engines, the interior, exterior. Passengers too. And I study the bustling views.

"We need to keep an eye on our passengers," Hark says. "People are unpredictable. Maybe fall, maybe fight. Never know. But 95 percent of the time, it's okay." The radio crackles to life: A commuter is hurt at the terminal. "You see? There, someone just fell from their wheelchair at the other terminal. A team member will help them, see if they need EMTS. If there's a fight, there's just four of us here, two up and two down. We do our best to handle it, or if we need to, we call the police."

Hark points to the west, to the east. "There, seaplanes coming through. Over there, Helijets." We skirt a hunk of driftwood with branches, a big upended tree floating by. "There's another Tymac, another pilot. Ah, look at that." A muscular craft drags a sailboat. "That's city police. The sailboat's probably stolen. That, or adrift. We have Port of Vancouver police, and fire, plus RCMP boats as well. Things we see every day. See back there?" Hark points to the sails. "The Port of Vancouver has their office at the top of Canada Place. That includes the harbour master, controlling the deep seas and others."

I shake my head at the complexity, the busyness of it all.

Hark smiles at my reaction. "Writing must be hard too."

"Well, yeah, but no one's life's in my hands!"

A laugh from Hark. "I guess so."

The police vessel with the sailboat in tow beelines by.

"The police, they also escort big ships under Lions Gate Bridge. Have a presence. People do stupid things sometimes."

We're nearing Lonsdale Quay, where a large, blanched, and unbranded vessel is moored.

I point to it. "What's that?"

"*Spirit of the Nation*," Hark says. "An old, stripped-down ferry. It serves as a breakwater now. The marina there, Mosquito Creek, I believe it's Indigenous owned." Rows of blue-roofed boathouses and docks front the inlet. "There's a lot of downsizing of those boathouses around the marina. And there?" He points to the east section of the quay. "That's Seaspan. It's huge."

Leon nods. "Huge! That's Burrard Dry Dock right there."

Hark point to the west at what looks like new build apartments overhanging the shore. There's a crane too, working at what could be any high-rise getting built.

"That's a navy vessel being constructed," Hark explains. "Looks like a building, doesn't it? Enormous. We don't have many big ships being built here anymore. It's good to see it happening again."

A swarm of pigeons flutter ahead as we slow and ease into the terminal. The birds seem to take right of way. There's a small vertical stripe on the outer wall of the berth, a short red line.

"See that red line?" Hark says. I nod as we stop right beside it. "That's our high-tech alignment," he chuckles. "Line it up and we're there." And with that, we cut engines, neatly and snugly in place.

The monitors are a bustle once more as passengers disembark and reload. Now a switch at the helm: Leon takes the bridge, facing the way we just came, for our southbound return. Together we watch the screens, and I feel like a high-tech security guard. Or the computer whiz in every heist movie, the one who changes the traffic lights for the gang's getaway.

Hark scans every image, each screen. "We have to call police and ambulance fairly often. Just a safety thing. We can have up to 395 passengers, and as you saw, there's just four of us. Two on the bridge and two crew. And the engine room there." He points to a monitor. "Always watching for smoke or for fire. Here, check this out."

He taps one of the two radar screens, which clicks on a ship in the inlet, a yellow image on black. The ship's details emerge. "This allows us to triangulate any vessel. Its name, stats, speed, everything. It's a great system. Critical in the fog."

Looking back at the whole inlet before us, we have a moment to take it all in.

"We're time sensitive, as you can imagine," Hark says. "Only two minutes either side, and we need to weave around traffic, usually eleven to twelve knots. But these boats are fast. We can make up time if we need it."

Leon eases the other two engine throttles forward, guiding us south to downtown. Hark sips a coffee, and I exit the bridge on a narrow railed walkway that wraps around the bridge's exterior. It's a sensation much like walking around a ferry, but compact, with just room for one. Both skippers have assured me I'm not in the way, so I linger in front of the wheelhouse, enduring an ice-slap of wind. A quick Kate Winslet pose, and I hustle back to the cozy interior, where the heater now works overtime.

"Watch here," Hark says. A large tug motors by with nothing in tow; its thick wake heads our way. I steady myself and we rock, a great port–starboard lurch, more noticeable up here than for the passengers. "Big tugs, high speeds, big wakes. Plus wind makes for really big wakes and big waves. Passengers get jostled, but there's not much we can do about it. Sometimes breakers wash all the way over. Not up here, but over the bow, just below us."

"What about the high-speed passenger ferry from Vancouver Island?" I ask.

Hark nods. "Yeah, they really move. Well, until they get to the harbour."

"So, how do you spend your time off?" I ask him. "Do you still want to be on the water?"

"Oh, we like the water, obviously. And being a passenger too, ferries and cruises. A colleague took three cruises this year! Some are avid anglers, love fishing. We even have retired pilots leading fishing tours off the west of Vancouver Island."

I can see the appeal. In a similar vein to my realization that ghosts can be much more than spectres, maybe Pallursi is more than just eyes. A persona, perhaps. Passion for being on, in, and next to the water. The same pull that started this quest. A shaman's call to a whale, radar and echolocation. And I can't help but wonder if this has been planned, lived before, many times. All that's left is to step into faint footprints, waymarks that fade with the tide.

"One more round?" asks Hark, as a new wave of passengers board.

"Yes, please!"

The three of us shift across the wheelhouse to launch *Chinook* once again. The crew below do their check, the passengers sit, and there's a safety announcement. Then a rev as we enter the inlet again, alongside the port with its pinnacle cranes. To the west is Stanley Park, with Deadman's Island photobombing the view. Another SeaBus heads to where we just left. We scoot past a freighter, its containers like tightly packed bricks. Away to the northeast, a hint of Moodyville wraiths where the Spirit Trail sutures the shore.

I consider the path that we're on, transit linking the city—buses, SkyTrain, the vessel we're on. All of which came to be in part because cars arrived to Vancouver later than they did to most major cities. A function of early, reliable transit—trams and trolleys and buses—until, gradually, cars were the norm. With that came more bridges, then fewer passenger ferries. And for the past half century or so, transit here looked much like it does now, with more buses and trains but an increasing reliance on cars. One major feature being the absence of a major highway piercing downtown. I've heard activists say this is the result of protests and effort, keeping neighbourhoods intact, freeways elsewhere, while city employees have explained the situation to me differently. They say it simply didn't make financial sense to have a highway cut through downtown; highways bypass the city centre solely for expediency and cost management. Regardless, for those of us choosing to walk, the lack of a central motorway remains one of this town's finest features.

Another on-time arrival. More smiles and pics, a shaking of hands, and I disembark, thanking Leon and Hark. It's about halfway through their ten-hour day, which they'll repeat all week long (seven days on, seven off). Then have some free time, maybe back on this water they love.

Leaving the SeaBus on the north side of Burrard Inlet, I consider this throughway, the same one that was pulled by canoe. ("Why walk when we can paddle?") Which now seems glaringly evident to me, even having just left my perch on a rumble of diesel, as though I can feel, truly feel that connection of city and ocean, the thread of our beaches and shore.

I spend time around Lonsdale Quay, looking south to downtown. That deep sea we passed, the one with rainbow containers, centres the frame. The city skyline from here is not as shapely as what I admired from the west; it's more snaggle-toothed, crooked and gapped. Downtown has a definite look from a distance. Each new build, it seems, like the mountains, is stretching upward to outdo its rivals. Kids on tiptoes, pencilled lines on a wall by the fridge. Ironically, many of the highest-value units, those topping hotels, often find themselves hidden in cloud, left to imagine their unending views.

Encircling the shore walk, the pier, and a Spirit Trail branch, the quay's a tight cluster of shops, restaurants, and galleries. Seaspan sprawls to the east, while a yellow crane watches it all, this past part of Burrard Dry Dock, a more recent version of what lined False Creek on the south side, where shipping construction rivalled the logging and tinworks that fuelled Industrial Island a century ago. Another iteration of Salish hunting and gathering grounds rebuilt by settlers—dredging, construction, the manipulation of natural cycles.

Overhead, a few crows do a lap of the rotating "Q" market sign. On a previous visit here, the water pulsated with jellies. Fist-sized jellyfish, some pearly, some white, gave this side of the shore the look of a snowglobe, the greenish water an aquatic dance floor. Against long odds, a UK vintage steamer was moored at the dock, here from Penzance, a boat that I knew from having been there with strangers who turned into friends. This strip of water, with a few polished planks and some sails, shrank the world in a way I'd not felt on that level before.

Now, with North Shore mountains rising behind me downtown to the south, and the səlilwətaɬ waters of Burrard Inlet spreading left to right, I find a pair of historical plaques to sum up this section of coast. The first is printed in nautical tones, white letters on blue, almost the look of those jellies that surrounded the quay. There are images of Victory ships, grey cargo vessels that could pass for destroyers, used for transport in the Second World War. As German submarines patrolled the Atlantic and sank Allied craft, ship supply could barely keep up with demand.

> During the Second World War, Burrard Dry Dock launched 109 Victory ships. Part of a North America-wide shipbuilding program, they made possible the movement of men, supplies and equipment across the Atlantic and Pacific Oceans to undertake the successful allied invasions of Europe and Asia, 1944–45.
>
> Canadian "Victory" and American "Liberty" ships were based on the same design. Production line construction methods and thousands of standardized parts encouraged speed and economy. Burrard employed up to 14,000 workers at one time, contributing over 30% of the Canadian total of 354 such ships; the United States shipyards built 2,710.

The next sign shows an image of three extravagantly dressed women in ribboned hats, heeled boots, and long fur coats, all holding bouquets. There's a footnote. One of the women is Eliza Wallace, another is Mabel Stevens, while the third woman is unnamed, her identity a mystery. Eliza owned and ran Wallace Shipyards with her husband, Alfred, while Mabel's spouse was Henry Herbert Stevens, Vancouver city councillor and federal cabinet minister. This was indeed a power ensemble, exemplifying the tightly woven relations between shipping, coastlines, and government. Beside the women is a photo of a compartmented wooden box called a launching kit. These little transport containers were purpose-built, "made at Burrard Dry Dock to hold 2 bottles of champagne for the launching ceremonies." One for bashing the boat with a blessing, the other, I presume, to get tipsy.

The heading of the plaque reads, "During 86 Years of Operation, 320 Vessels Were Launched at This Shipyard." It goes on to explain that from 1942 to 1946, to meet the demands of the war effort, a South Yard was added, with more shipbuilding taking place near the present-day port and the ill-tempered blackberry bush.

I almost see this side of Burrard Inlet as an evergreen, its growth rings increasing, expanding by way of new restaurants, condos, event space. Nice energy too. Not as perennially busy as, say, Granville Island, but with a similar feel, that presence of water with commerce and nature harbouring, quite literally, the seaway.

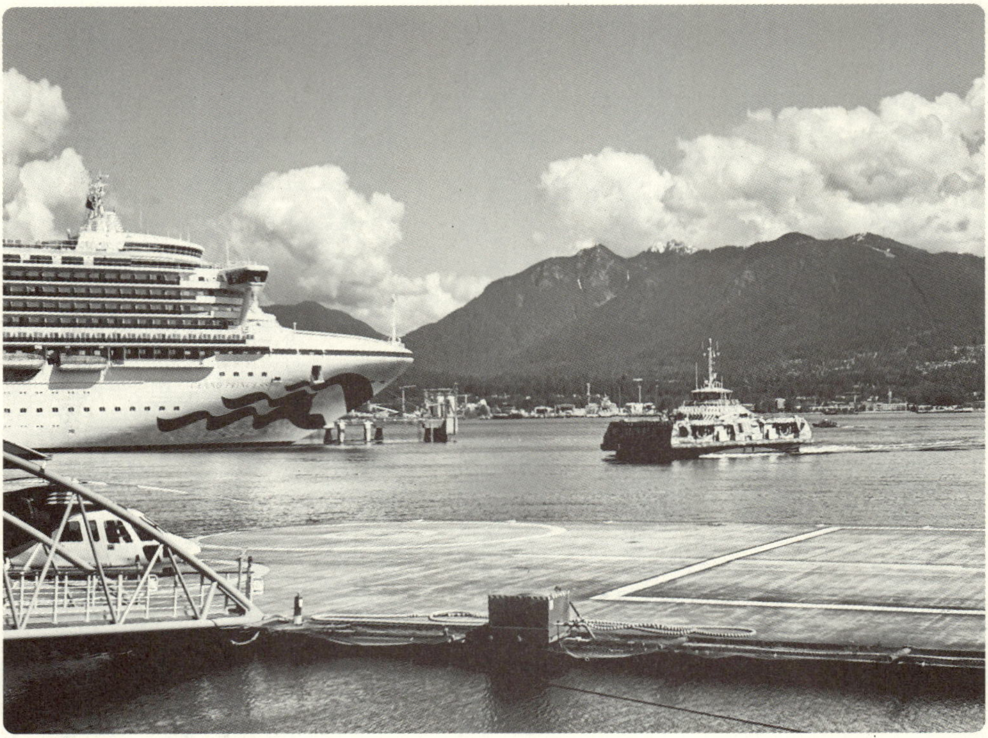

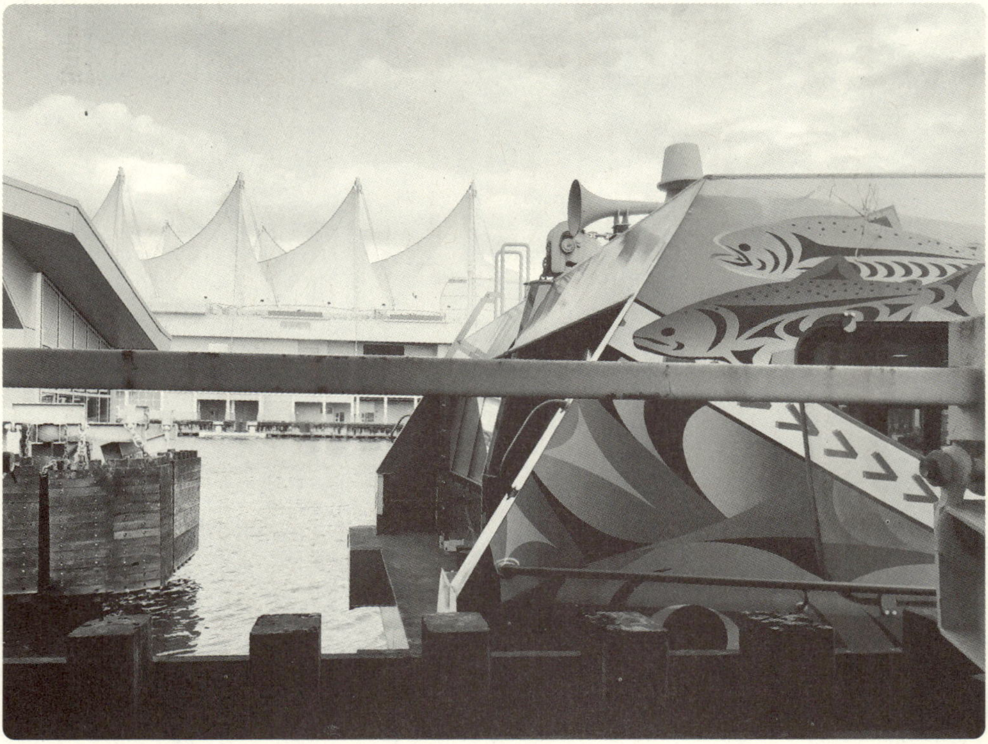

TOP: the *Chinook* SeaBus approaching Waterfront Station.
BOTTOM: the *Chinook* SeaBus arriving at Waterfront Station downtown.

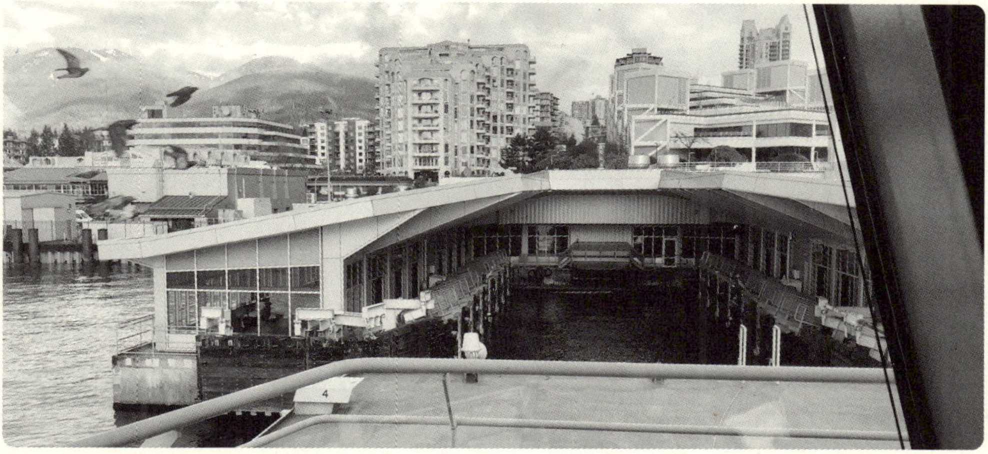

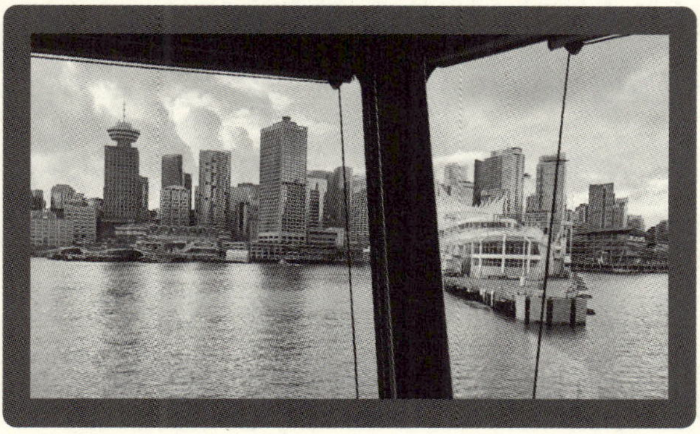

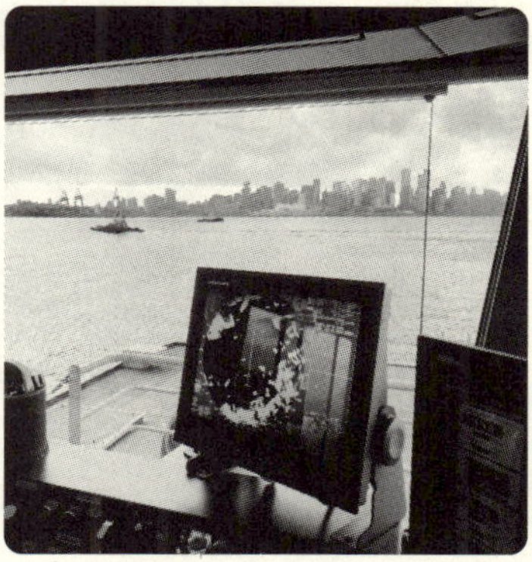

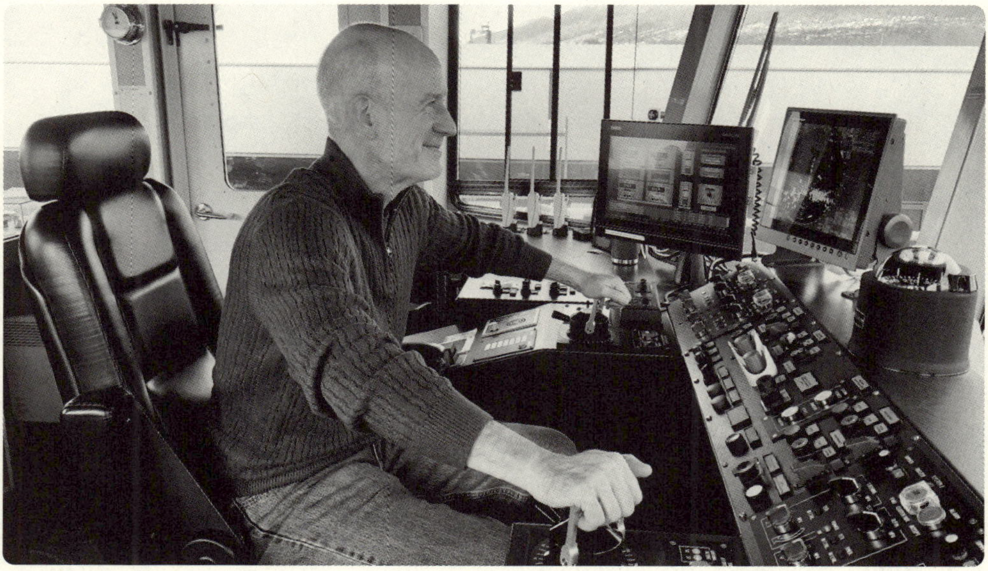

CLOCKWISE FROM TOP: easing into Lonsdale Quay, viewed from the captain's bridge of the *Chinook* SeaBus; navigating Burrard Inlet, southbound, viewed from the captain's bridge of the *Chinook* SeaBus; the *Chinook* SeaBus, with Bill at the helm; nearing Canada Place and downtown, viewed from the captain's bridge of the *Chinook* SeaBus.

South Side of Downtown

WATERSCAPE ART

THE SEASON HAS CHANGED. No new solstice or equinox, just the feel of the water and sky. Long gone is the Halloween decor, apart from a brick building on Pacific Street where an exterior south wall is still covered in life-sized skeletons clambering up an old-fashioned fire escape. One huge specimen must be the skeletons' leader. It's two storeys tall and peers into a top-floor window. (How did *that* strata meeting play out?)

Today I'm walking the south section of downtown, what borders False Creek, the north side of the water meshing with Yaletown around Science World and BC Place. To the south: Olympic Village, Granville Island, Fairview, and Kits. A return to a facet of previous *Perfect Day* walks, as I'm following artwork, this time searching for pieces that draw from the water.

A pass through downtown and a library visit to start. Into the curved glass and concrete of the Vancouver Public Library's Central Branch, which looks like something built with ancient Romans in mind. I pass ground-level displays of various things on offer for borrowing. Musical instruments, for example, to equip a whole orchestra, with percussion and strings from all parts of the globe. Upstairs to the Inspiration Lab, where budding musicians and voice-over artists are recording soundtracks and videos. Upward again toward Travel, where long rolling shelves slide into place with futuristic mechanization. Past the *clickety-clack* of term papers and novels being typed. In the stacks, I smile at titles written by friends, take photos to share. (Everyone loves seeing their work on display.)

Then a little mental exercise, my version of finding thin space in bookish terrain. I ponder a project I plan to start soon that'll involve research into the winter of 1953. I haven't yet looked this up, don't know what I might find. I let my mind drift in that same relaxed manner as when floating in water. Granted, I'm standing, not swimming, and I'm predominantly dry at the moment. But without really looking, I reach for a shelf, letting my subconscious guide me. My hand finds a slim hardback book, the spine font too small to read. I slide out the volume. Jan Morris, *City to City*. Flip to the introduction and read this: "I was taking part in a trans-Canada lecture tour in the winter of 1953, and the one image of the venture that remains overwhelmingly in my mind ..."[59]

Remarkable. A book from the moment in time I wanted to find. Needle in a haystack doesn't come close. Leaving me certain I've no clue as to how the world works.

With the Jan Morris slung in a bag, I traipse across Yaletown, home to the CPR Roundhouse and Engine 374, the locomotive that hauled passengers on that "first final leg" of the transnational train to Kanaka and the end-of-the-line depot that preceded Waterfront Station. Past a casino lies BC Place with its spiky white crown, a carving workspace, and the replica voyageur canoes. Looking at the water I only recently paddled creates a fresh visual inversion. Like seeing charts you've just mapped displayed on a wall, a shift in time-space perspective.

Two passenger ferries—one False Creek, one Aquabus—approach, meet, and pass, melding their wakes under Cambie Street Bridge. Both skippers nod as they pass. I turn west to follow the shared walkway hugging False Creek's north side. Bridge stanchions are blue striped with the artwork *A False Creek*. I wonder how much the sea level's risen since the paint was applied.

Now through Coopers' Park, home to many of those unemployed tradespeople who protested work conditions through the Depression. Where shanty villages lined this stretch of shoreline, it's now walkway and grass, with a dog park as well. The footpath is raised from the beach, the water's edge gravel and shingle. There are a few meaty rocks that've likely been here for a very long time. Erratics, perhaps, from a glacier or seismic activity where a concrete wall now lines the shore.

There's a patchy-cloud sky splotched aqua and grey, with a pocket of sun in its midst. The light on the dark is intense, focusing rays like a laser. A simple but effective historical art installation sits next to the path. No signage, just intuitive to this part of the city. It's a likeness of a barrel, what a cooper would build, in this case fashioned into a square. Four-by-fours have been planted in soil, five to a side, to create a roughly shaped block of wood with steel bands to imitate the barrel's loops and its staves.

I'm reminded of another passage from James Bradley's *Deep Water*, a reference to how shipping containers revolutionized transport and commerce. Barrels like these, the round ones, that is, accomplished the same thing, the technological precursor to those giant blocks stacked at the port. Bradley says it's places like these, where enterprise meshes with sea, that are truly without boundaries. Goods in containers, in transit, are in fact global commerce creating its own liminal space.

Tacking west, the shelf of beach rock cuts a timeless expanse. I consider the shoreline, its eons of harvest—"When tide's out, table's set"—and recall unique wildlife encounters. Unique to me, anyway. A beaver nibbling young alder just over there. (Where was its home? Is there a dam around here?) All those seals, the birdlife, the fish we see as they leap, and the less lucky ones that become meals. The otters, the mud shark. Even a grey whale that came through in the spring of 2010. A juvie, they believed, but still over ten metres long. It fluked its way through in the morning, returned in the evening, bypassing the pier. One scratchy video showed a kayaker bobbing along, unaware of the whale in their wake.

No sign of cetaceans today, but a couple of paddlers pull through, both in single-person outriggers. The tide must be out; the water is shallow, and I can see the seabed right under their craft. The weirdly lit sky creates a soft mirrored effect, as though the boats have inverted twins. Water amplifies the paddlers' voices as they share about their day, their stupid co-workers, the usual.

Ahead stands one of Arthur Erickson's last projects before dementia took its toll, a high-rise of condos named for him. Blue-green glass rises in a squiggle design with the look of a wave set on end. The path too, at this point, deviates from true lines. Much like the Erickson build, the walkway takes on a weave, the same shape a slalom skier might carve on the water.

Which brings us to what I've come here to find, more waterside art. Not Vancouver Biennale exhibits, but pieces with a similar open-air accessibility. A brochure by the City of Vancouver Public Art Program gives context, referring to "contemporary art in public spaces throughout the city. The program features emerging and established artists working in new and traditional media through stand-alone commissions and artist collaborations."[60]

By following the Public Art Program's Yaletown–False Creek map, a dozen exhibits can be found in a small area. This time through, I'll pass half the pieces, those specifically linked to the inlet. First up, a copper-green lump that resembles an alien craft that's just landed. Called *Time Top*, it was created by Jerry Pethick in 2006. The piece "looks like a 1940s-style space ship and represents fantasies of time travel. Its position on the shoreline encourages the idea that it has washed up from the depths of history."[61] Sure enough, the art has that look of a retro graphic novel, a precursor to *Star Trek*, and could even serve as a probe to be launched from an undersea vessel.

Now I'm at the marina, with high-rises that resemble the yachts, the same white with aquamarine. Along the path is an array of groomed plants and trees: burning bush the same colour as late maples, Japanese snowball, beautyberries, spurge, and madronas spaced between ash trees and cedar.

Next, a piece called *Lookout* by Christos Dikeakos and Noel Best, placed here in 1999. This is along Coopers Mews, the present toeing the past. The piece of stainless steel, glass, and bronze resembles a bus shelter with words in block letters embossed on its sides. But the whole carries on, spilling from the shelter onto chairs on three balconies overlooking the shoreline to trace the site's natural and industrial history. Which creates an innovative new bridge, not so much physically spanning as tying together the area's natural past with citified urban development.

Here a traffic roundabout mimics the CPR Roundhouse, with historical chunks from the railyard on display. Between the circular road and the water is what looks like an unfinished building, another skeleton of sorts, this one resembling construction framing gone wrong, lopsided and lacking floors. What it is, however, is an elevated history book, its pages large single-pane panels, each depicting a moment in time around here: rail workers, marina vistas, residents smiling for the camera, all in period black and white. The piece, called *Street Light*, was created by Alan Tregebov and Bernie Miller in 1997. The images, from city archives, are perforated metal, not only letting sea breeze pass through but also adding an ethereal presence. Another hinting of waterside spectres.

Now, the sweeping installation *Welcome to the Land of Light* by Henry Tsang. Aluminum lettering spells out phrases in English and Chinook, pidgin used for a few generations in the Pacific Northwest. The jargon blends Indigenous Chinook with French, English, and First Nations Nuu-Chah-Nulth into language created for trade. Like pidgin in ports, Chinook not only spanned language and race but kept commerce well oiled as well. The city's Public Art Registry describes more:

> *Welcome to the Land of Light* is a contemporary monument to the relationship between those who have lived on the False Creek waterfront and those who will arrive in the future to call this area their home. For the artist, this public art project is about the concept of home, the building of community ... the juxtaposition of English and Chinook Jargon functions as a metaphor for the ongoing development of intercultural communications in this region.[62]

This intercultural mosaic could just as easily represent the interdependence of water and land, the meshings of people with place, construction, and natural growth.

Having a sense of what's up ahead, I find a game plan taking shape, a mental wayfaring map, as three more pieces of art form a stepping-stone path to my stroll.

First, *Brush with Illumination* by Buster Simpson. Approaching this high piece, which sits in the water, I scribble notes, trying to describe it. The best I come up with is that it looks like one of those decorative birds that repeatedly tips up and down to simulate sipping water. But what the piece actually depicts is more complex; it represents a calligraphy pen charting environmental narrative. The city's Public Art Registry describes it as "an illuminated environmentally interactive 'brush' [that] responds to wind, tide, and wave action, and rests on a steel piling balanced by two large spun steel buoys. The brush moves with the currents and originally transmitted weather data and tide changes to an artist website ... but is no longer functioning."[63]

The piece does indeed glide, in a manner, like the penwork of an ancient yet modern cartographer. Highly sophisticated, yet timeless as wind in a sail. The artist adds to the overview, hinting at his motivation.

> *Brush with Illumination* is the evolutionary successor of an ancient communication tool: the calligraphy brush. The piece is fitted with an array of sensors that glean environmental data from the air and water as the sculpture responds to environmental conditions, and transmit it both visually, through the laser-lighted pulsations of the cursor at the tip of the brush, and electronically to a land based computer. Mathematical functions translate these elemental events in a series of characters that are continually on display.[64]

It's ironic that the high-tech part no longer works but the power of sun, wind, and water keeps it moving and gathering data, despite no one recording or storing that info. Mind you, the blue stripes at the base of the Cambie Street Bridge convey all those facts, that the water is rising and warming.

I stand by the piece, that notion of quilling new maps, contemplate it for a while, unsure whether I see any movement. Maybe it's the same as that boat on its side, sunken in blue-green, vaguely shifting with a longing to sail.

On to the second of the three pieces I want to explore: *Marking High Tide and Waiting for Low Tide*, at the beachside of David Lam Park. Placed at the edge of the green space, it's a half-step between parkland and water, with the installation's round concrete extending into the inlet, the cusp of low and high tides. Curved pillars rise to the sky, inscribed with a prose poem by Don Vaughan created in 1996: "The moon circles the earth, and the ocean responds with the rhythm of the tides." To read the whole poem, you're forced to move in a circle, as though plotting the path of a planet. At the moment the tide is still low, and with a few stretching steps I can walk on the art's descending, ascending stairs to curve out and then back from the water. Were the tide any higher, I'd be sloshing through sea. It's a truly interactive, time-bounded exhibit, pulling the elements into its daily reveal.

You can locate this piece on numerous city maps, walking routes, and cultural guides. It creates its own little headland and has even earned a spot on a site dedicated to Vancouver's fountains, another means of wayfinding.[65] The fact that it's a water feature comprised of the tides makes it unique, a classical structure within the False Creek tidal zone. With another phone search, I find details about tides, planets and gravity, solar and lunar phases, coastal shapes, and watery amplitudes, all of which is somewhat interesting but mostly just dull.

The last piece I want to examine today is a clever mingle of story and sea called *Khenko*, created by Doug Taylor in 2006, which sits in the water fronting George Wainborn Park. The walkway approaching it curves out from the shore for a spell, over the inlet, the same bend as a gunnel on the side of a vessel, a stout one for carrying cargo. Along the curved wall is some graffiti. More politics. A snippet of hate, yet with the hope of more positive things taking precedent, as though taggers are determined to blot out the bad with the good. Maybe it's just as effective as the data that's no longer gathered by the giant calligraphy pen. Optimism, kindness, and healing. And I like that it's all a few strides from Tsang's *Welcome to the Land of Light*, especially on an overcast day, a display of mixed culture and linguistics designed to bridge multiple tongues.

Back to *Khenko*. Its styling is not unlike the *Wind Wheel Mobile*, scoops grabbing at wind, a mixed media of sea breeze and air. But rather than warning of toxic asbestos, this piece celebrates nature's triumph in the midst of the city, exemplified by the return of herons to these waters.

Ingeniously, as wind moves the steel sails on the sculpture, they flap the great metal wings of a heron as though the bird's flying east. It could almost pass for a giant marionette, with its mesmerizing up-and-down movement of wings. The City of Vancouver's website offers further description from the sculptor:

> During the industrial era, many fish and wildlife left the area. This piece celebrates the heron's return to False Creek as a symbol of hope and restoration. The main focus of my practice, as a sculptor, has been to build kinetic assemblages which are in some way moved by the wind or water. The presence of a whimsical element is signature to my work and in part accounts for its popularity with children.[66]

Sure enough, two children are admiring the steely bird gently flapping in the wind. The sun, meanwhile, wrestles with cloud overhead and looks like it's losing. The result is a bright greyish swirl that the photographer in me finds appealing. I click a pic of False Creek with a sliver of Granville Street Bridge. To make the picture bookworthy, I'll tweak it to black and white. But, to my fascination, the photo, snapped in overcast light, already looks black and white. Fiddling with colour, brightness, and tint makes no difference. Making me think that maybe *this*, more than tides or the calendar, indicates a change in the season.

Done for the day, I bear north toward a bridge deck to make my way home. Turning at the west edge of George Wainborn Park, I pass a burbling fountain, which takes me through a stand of redwoods, their alternate names the poetic "water fir" and "dawn cypress." Then along the base of the Charleson apartment tower, its south side a high mural in pink, yellow, and blue, with a deep navy slash like a tree branch in profile.

The splash of colour on mute steel and glass is a welcome contrast, a jolt on a monochrome day. I wonder if the residents on this side of the building can get a glimpse of the art they're a part of. The mural has been described as fingerpaint canvas, ragged and playful. The navy-blue line that both zigs and zags could absolutely have been put there by fingers. Monstrous fingers, but fingers just the same.

One more turn through downtown, where another water feature grabs my eye, one I've passed many times, but like directional signs that appear when we're ready, this one leaps out in this moment. It's a multi-stepped fountain that resembles a fish ladder or stairs. Atop this, a granite boulder rests in a pond, the same kind of rock you might find in installations around town. I understand now that it's local bedrock, likely blasted when roads were put through. Much of that rubble found its way into making concrete, crumbled and blended with sand, while some of the largest chunks were repurposed into art—simply a change in perspective, earth upside down, inside out, on display rather than buried. Almost like tumuli, where the interred aren't merely put underground, but the earth around them is raised to make knolls and daises.

Beneath this nearly round granite, concrete walls house the pond. Next to that, shallow stairs match the ones underwater. And on the wall facing north, an engraving, a quote from Leonardo da Vinci: "In rivers the water you touch is the last of what has passed and the first of that which comes; so with present time." Nice phrasing, caught in the midst of those past-present-future continua. Analogy and metaphor in a continuous flow.

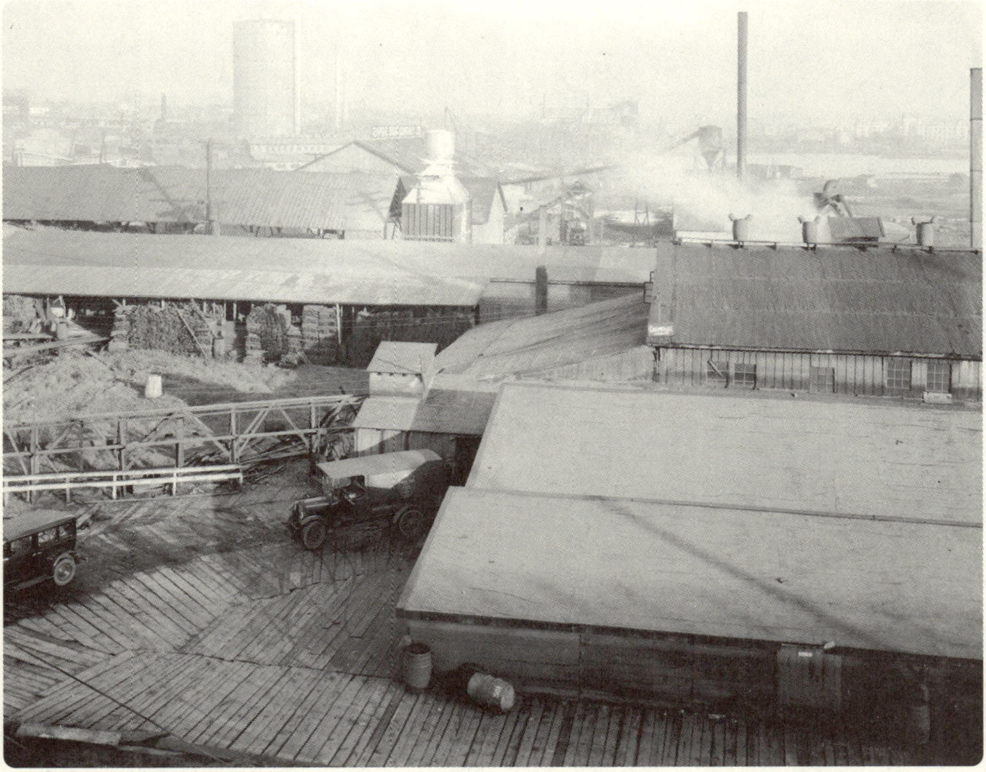

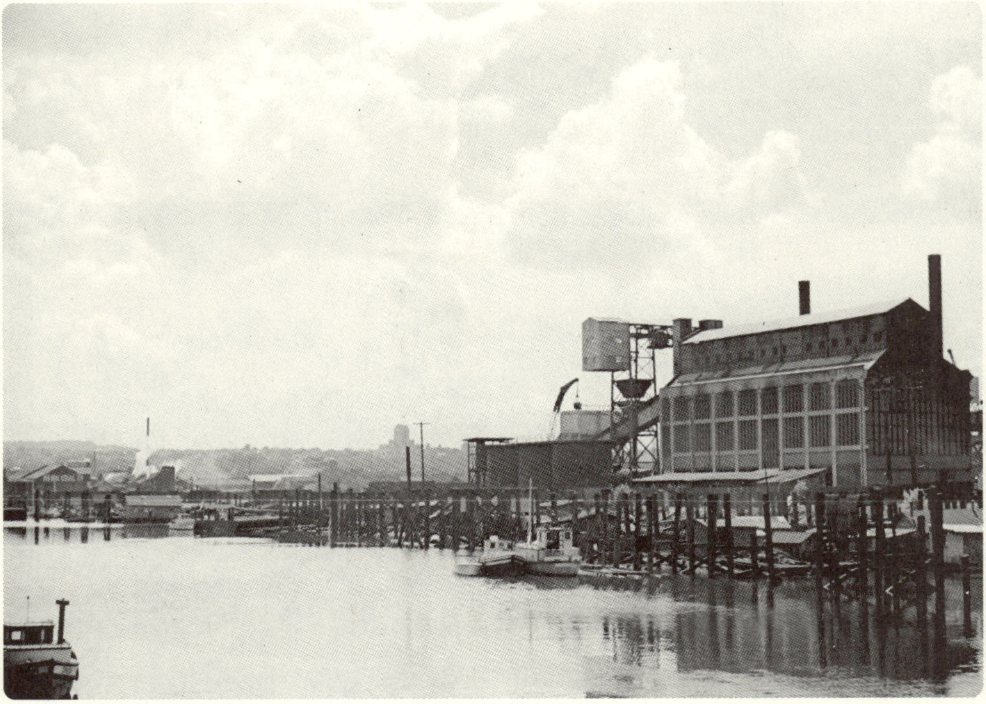

TOP: Canadian Western Cooperage, False Creek, 1933.
BOTTOM: coal and gas works on the north side of False Creek, 1939.

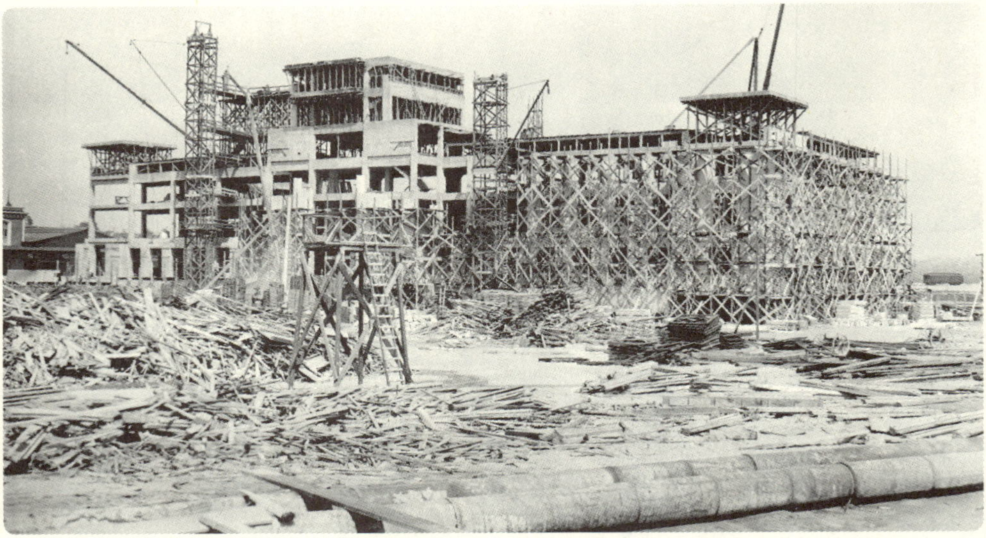

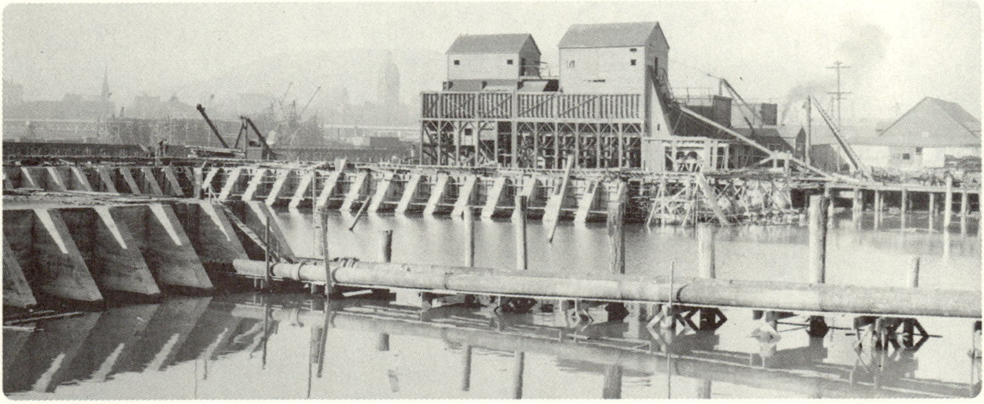

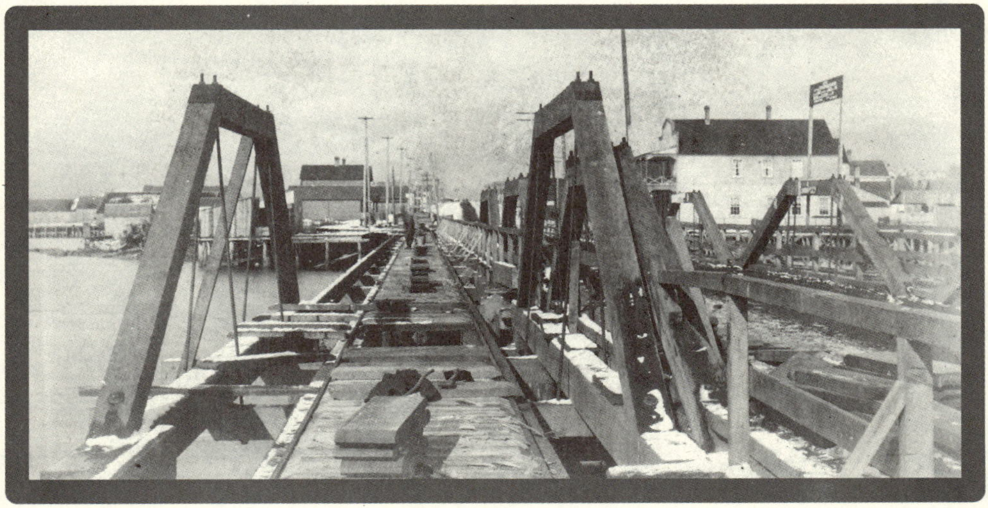

TOP TO BOTTOM: construction of the CNR depot, False Creek, 1917; construction of the False Creek Seawall, 1917; construction of the False Creek Trestle Bridge, 1889.

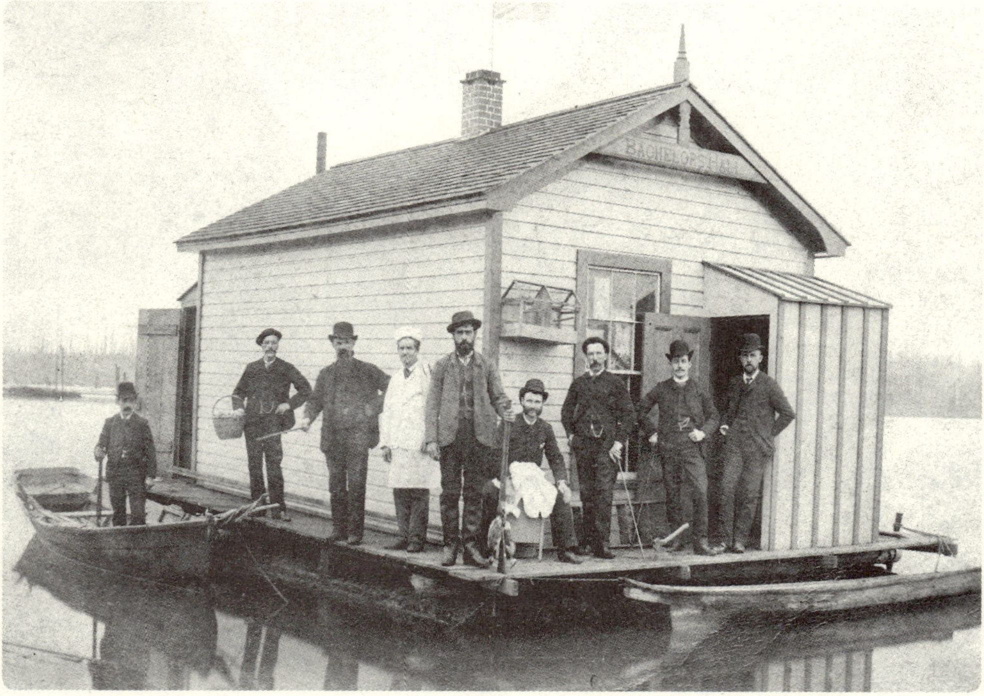

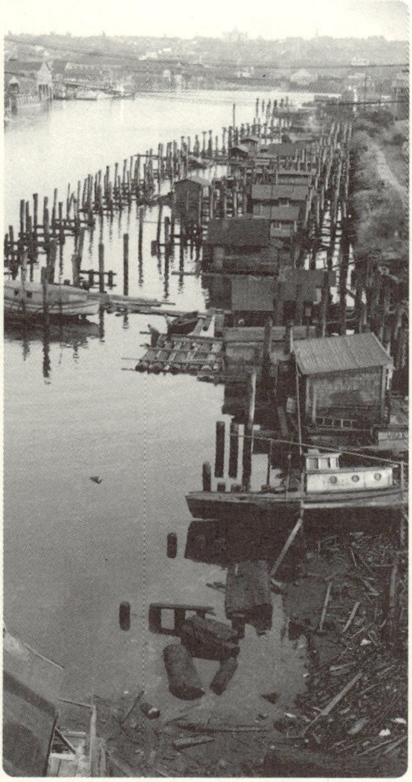

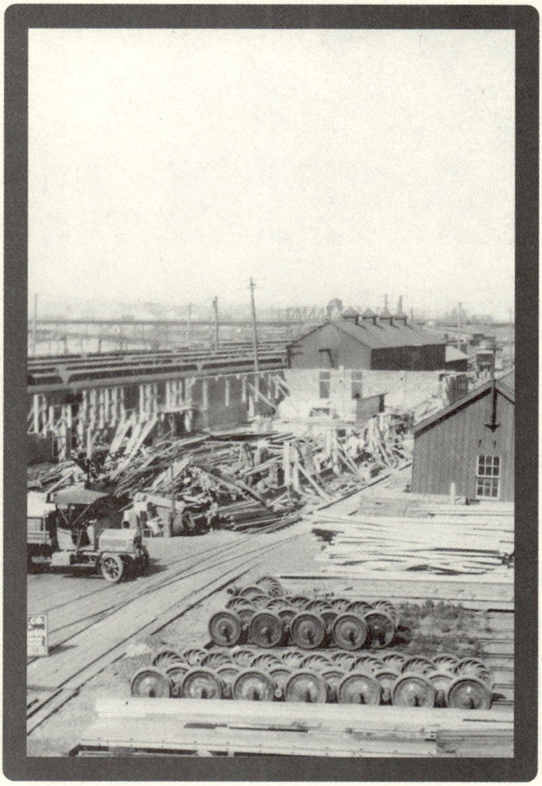

CLOCKWISE FROM TOP: CPR floating hall, False Creek, 1887;
CPR storage depots, False Creek, 1913; False Creek at Quebec Street, circa 1940s.

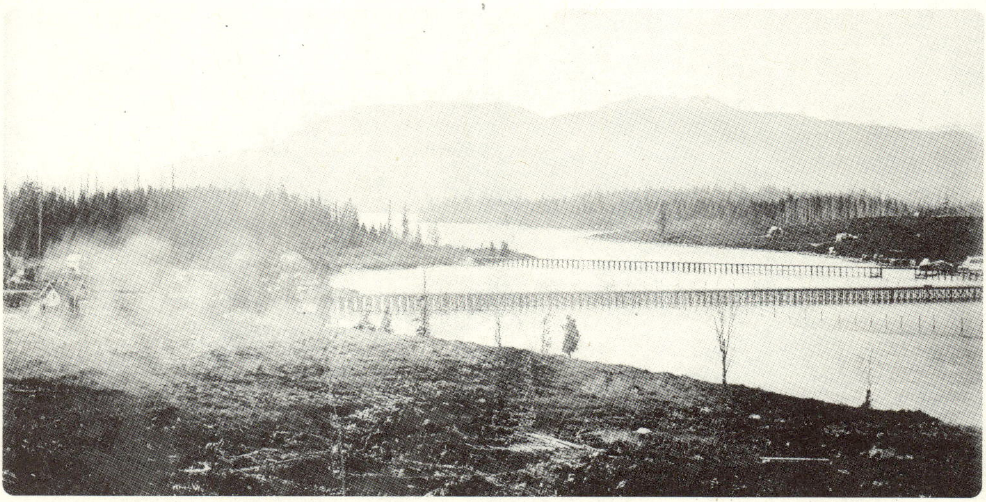

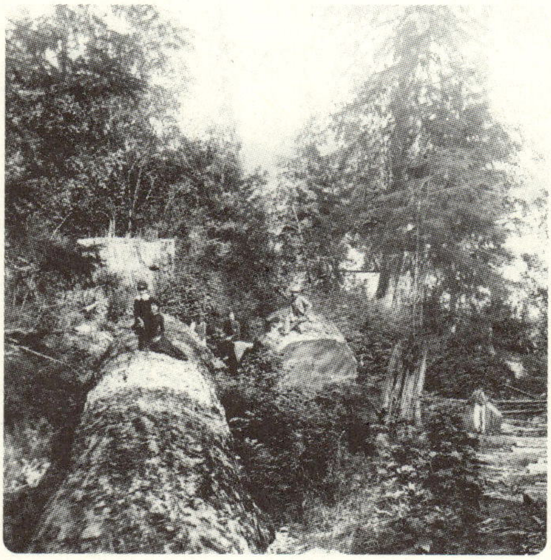

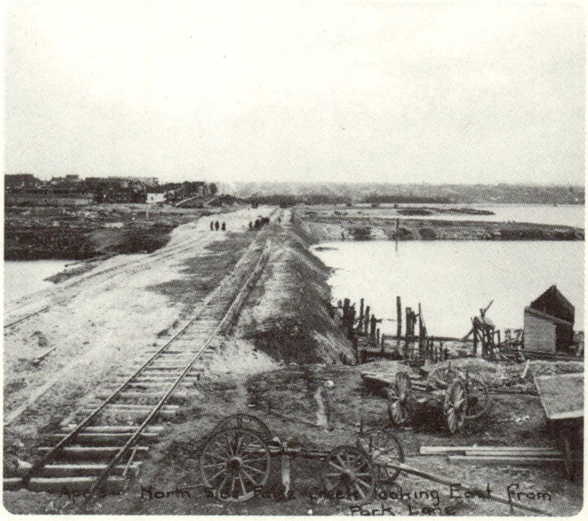

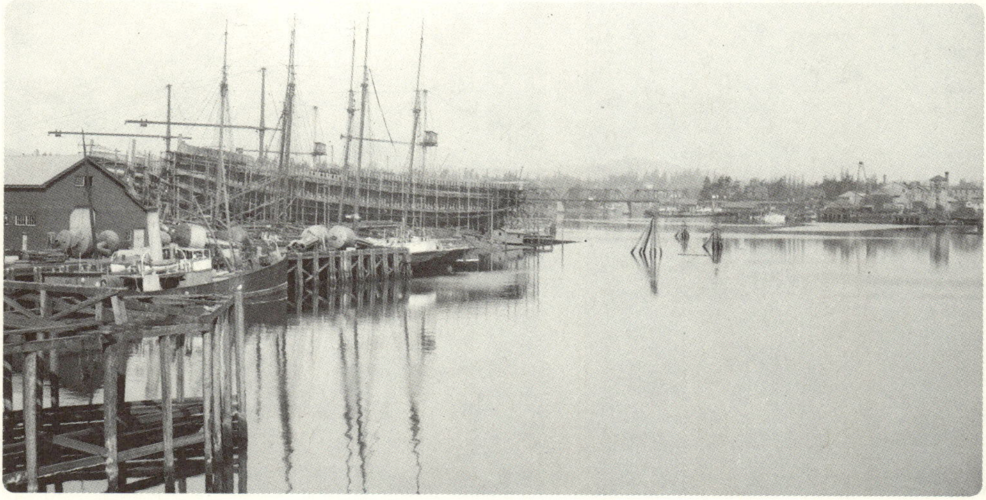

CLOCKWISE FROM TOP: looking west along False Creek, 1890; north side of False Creek, looking east, 1913; False Creek shipyards, circa 1910s; logging at False Creek, 1886.

Stanley Park

TIMBER AND TOTEMS

TODAY'S PLAN: A saunter toward Stanley Park, then to follow its meandering shore with a fresh eye from my last wander through. North Shore snow is creeping toward the inlet, and I wonder how much life I might see, whether the park's flora and fauna have bedded down for the winter, dropping leaves and heading south for the season.

There's the usual blend, this time of year, of bright light and grey cirrus. Blue patches, a squall in the mix. A day for layers, good shoes, and a brolly. No schedule as such, just keeping an eye on my fast-draining phone. And with that I head out, bearing north to downtown, Granville Island on my right to the east, Kits on my left to the west. Something pings on my phone, and I see it's a self-sourcing tidbit, letting me know where I am and its link to the past. References to Kitsilano's settler history, when the popular sandy crescent was known as Greer's Beach. In the Second World War many estate homes in the area were converted to rooming houses. In the 1960s more immigrants arrived, with university students filling the neighbourhood space between here and the UBC campus.

An organic thread to my exploration there, having passed countless students who make this region their home while they study nearby. The reference to the south side of False Creek, beyond what was Snauq, being heavy with rooming homes rings a bell too.

On Granville at West 10th Avenue, a plaque gives a glimpse of that world in an earlier time, with a letter written by a young working man around the time of the Second World War, making a life for himself in the city and moving to one of those boarding houses. He refers to this area being pleasantly walkable, and to the convenience of the trolleys and trams, not unlike what many experience now. The fact that the letter's handwritten brings it to life. Personality seeps from the cursive. A bit clipped with haste but thorough, with small margins, making the most of the page. There's caring in the letter, the writer wanting to let others know he was okay. Alone in a big city, but doing quite well, even thriving—no need to worry. A bit starry-eyed, getting new clothes, a new job. I imagine him in the city, or at least downtown, with its growing buildings, transit, and cafés, which must've felt promising, exotic, exciting.

For a taste of that past I detour north along Granville, past its vertical vintage neon. A cringe at the corner of Robson, where one Sunday morning a short time ago I arrived as three police cars converged, six armed officers leaped out, and a cocked shotgun was trained on a man at the corner.

"You're under arrest! Down on the ground!" The gun punctuated it all. No questions or requests for identification, just commands. Whoever the man was, he was wanted, and it was unnerving to be there, so close.

But all's peaceful today. Commuters are in transit around me, by the Vancouver Art Gallery and the Hotel Vancouver. A stop for salmon on toast, then on past the spinning blue globe, *The Drop*, and the *Wind Wheel Mobile*. Atop the Convention Centre roof, a scruff of clover and grass is home to some bees, another revitalization attempt like the reef down below.

At the water, seaplanes are berthed at their pier. Behind me, the Marine Building slides from view as I take a westerly path to the park, where a small faded sign grabs my eye—"First West Vancouver Ferry"—

along with a black-and-white photo of the boat, a smaller version of the *Hollyburn* that Margaret Gallagher described, the boat she once crewed. Under the picture, a story:

> In the area then known as West Capilano, and today as Ambleside, a former Canadian Pacific Railway conductor, John Lawson, purchased land in 1906. Lawson had big ideas for his land, which he christened Hollyburn. He subdivided the property for sale and even began the construction of a golf course, though this idea was abandoned before it was finished.
>
> To overcome the considerable problem of marketing real estate without a bridge to Vancouver, Lawson and other developers formed the West Vancouver Transportation Company in 1909 and built its first ferry, the *West Vancouver*.

The story describes that first service, a boat every two hours, running from seven in the morning until seven in the evening. Then the incorporation of West Vancouver in 1912, at which point the new municipality bought out the private ferry company, added another boat, and increased service to every half-hour.

It docked where I am, at the north end of Denman Street, now part of the Bayshore Marina. Where Devonian Harbour Park stretches west to the edge of Stanley Park, and another small inlet houses the Vancouver Rowing Club. Behind me, Georgia Street becomes Highway 99, heading northwest over Lions Gate Bridge.

A shared path bordered in dirt has a dense hedge of plants: scarlet firethorn with orange berries, dog roses in bloom, barberry, Oregon grape, ash trees, and maple, with bear's breeches or sea dock as well. It feels like a botany book, its pages left open.

"Would you look at that. Roses in bloom!" a woman says just beside me.

"Not bad, this time of year," I reply.

"I'll say!"

"I got some in bloom, I'm sure of it," the man with her mumbles. Her husband, I presume. She rolls her eyes.

"Where are you visiting from?" I ask.

"Toronto," she says, and he nods.

"And where are you going while you're here?"

"Oh, just staying here in Vancouver," she says.

"Here for a birthday," he adds. "Love it here. Any time of the year. How 'bout you?"

"I'm local. Behaving like a traveller today."

They smile and nod. Eager to walk a brisk pace, they wave and move on while I linger with the plants. A few moments pass, and a side trail of mud draws me to where a granite lump holds a commemorative plaque titled "First Known AIDS Memorial." A photo of fifteen men in a casual group, all wearing warm jackets. The weather, the season, much like today. The photo's not posed, just an impromptu pic. A few smiles, familiarity and comfort in the faces. The look of friendship, strength, and support.

> This grove of cherry trees is a living monument planted in loving memory of those we lost in the very early days of the AIDS epidemic here in Vancouver. The first fallen pink petals were followed by too many others. Gone, but never forgotten.

Only now do I realize the trees in this patch are all cherries. Not obvious from their bare branches, but now I can tell by the bark in their trunks and remember walking here in the spring. This whole stretch becomes a bright-pink explosion, with shutterbugs snapping their Instagram shots.

I contemplate that seasonal turn, the memorial. Then hear the whirr of a hummingbird as it centres in my sightline, between me and rock and the inlet. It almost looks big. I've read that juvies can appear larger than adults, their feathers plumped or something like that, and I wonder how old this one is. It hovers for a moment at eye height, then zooms up like a drone, as though on a puppeteer's string, a very long way, and then *poof*. No sign of the bird whatsoever.

From the cherry tree copse I pass the Vancouver Rowing Club. There's a centennial sign ("1886–1986") and a "Learn to Row" ad. For more rowing club info, I search the Vancouver Heritage Site Finder, which states that the club was established in 1899, a blending of the Burrard Inlet Rowing Club with the Vancouver Boating Club.

I recall public events in the clubhouse, where crests boast 1886—the same time the current city was founded—as the year the Boating Club started before merging with the Rowing Club in 1899. There's a certain feel to the building, same as the waterlogged timber in the Old Hastings Mill Store. Each step has a softly soaked squeak, so it seems, as though walking on water, or the delicate balance of standing midship in a skiff.

One night on the patio here, we had a view of the Olympic torch and its flame burning atop Jack Poole Plaza. Bringing to mind an expression I've read many times, "a place off the map"—dreamy, evocative—but that was the first time I felt that it fit. Staring at dark water, the flame burning through black. Beyond that, a blur of imaginings.

With that image in mind, I walk on. There's a chill in the light on the water. I cinch my jacket and gloves. On a hill to my left, Robbie Burns's bronze likeness is scowling. Behind him stands Lord Stanley's statue, spreading his arms with benevolence while regifting unceded land. There's a time warp with the *clip-clop* of hooves, the same sound I imagined by the hansom at the Old Hastings Mill Store. Only here, in a vaporous mist, it really could pass for the late nineteenth century, when the Boating Club was still new.

I see that my phone is near dead, but there are photos I still want to take, so I head toward the sound of those metal-shod hooves to Stanley Park's horse-drawn tours. Past a worker with a shovel who smiles and says "good morning" and on to a kiosk selling tickets and warm drinks. A coffee in hand, I visit with Krystal, who works the booth and kindly charges my phone.

"How do you like working here?" I ask. Our view is the head of Coal Harbour, the inlet beyond, muted sun on the water, with the sharp angles of the Convention Centre and sails.

"Oh, I never get tired of this view," Krystal says, waving her arm to the east. "The inlet, the harbour, downtown. Been here ten years now. Well, more, actually. Since 2013."

"How's your commute?"

"I live in Richmond, so it's no problem. Take SkyTrain. It's pretty quick, actually."

A horse whinnies behind us from under a thick-trunked sequoia.

"You like working close to the horses?" I ask.

"Oh sure. That one's Gritt." The big chestnut looks over, no doubt aware it's the topic of conversation.

"G-R-I-T?"

"Two *T*s," Krystal says. "He's a gentle giant. Super friendly with people and kids. Pets too. Good with dogs. Everyone."

A tour heads out, a carriage in tow behind Gritt, a third of the benches now full.

"Is it fairly seasonal?" I ask.

"Well, there are waves, for sure. Different parts of the world, it seems. We get lots of Brits in the summer for two months, same as their summer. Then a wave of Australians come through in the winter, *their* summer. Locals from here all year-round. Then all kinds of folks throughout the year. A real cross-section." She checks on my phone. "Thirty percent. How's that?"

"That'll do. Thanks again, very much."

"Thanks for the visit," she says, giving a big wave as I leave.

There's a rack of brochures near the booth: whale watching; the aquarium; hop-on, hop-off sightseeing buses; the Squamish gondola; and skiing. Others for galleries, culture, and art. I wonder if the Toronto couple made it this far and imagine cruise ship passengers ambling here, wishing they had extra days. By the brochures, a plaque describes "Stanley Park Forest Management."

> Stanley Park experienced a hemlock looper insect outbreak from 2020–2023. This resulted in mortality of approximately 160,000 (30%) of the trees in the Park, most of which were western hemlock.

Accompanying the story is an aerial photo of the park with an angry red swath like a wound. At a glance it resembles maples in fall, leaves turning crimson. Only here it's the opposite, not a hint of regrowth or a seasonal change, but rather, conclusion, making me realize those hemlocks I saw on the beach as I started these walks may be lucky to still be standing.

Now I see a board with a map of the park, a green thumb to the city's West End. While I feel there are unending stories in the Downtown Eastside, here too, in the park, I could walk a very long time in narrative steps and never backtrack at all.

Setting my sights to the east and the north, a counter-clockwise direction, I pass the Royal Vancouver Yacht Club and the HMCS *Discovery* Naval Reserve. Wind picks up to a howl. Two mallards are crouched on a rock, trying to take shelter, their feet drawn up from the water. Rigging pings at the yacht club, flags snap at the naval reserve. There are few trees now on the spit of Deadman's Island. No mortuary poles, either. In fact, I can barely envision it, as though this increasing wind has blown the past clean away.

Up ahead is Hallelujah Point and a statue of sprinter Harry Jerome, forever crossing a finish line first. At the headland is the Nine O'Clock Gun. For cannon aficionados, the gun's a twelve-pounder, muzzle loaded, cast in 1816. It fires at 9 p.m. every night and has done so, more or less, for over a century.

At the northeastern point of the park are the Port of Vancouver Lookout and Brockton Point Lighthouse, landmarks with vast panoramas. Icy wind is increasing, so I trim my trek, cutting north to truncate the park. Brockton Oval is squishy with wet grass and mud, which I squelch across to the Stanley Park totems. Next to the road and a parking lot stand modern Indigenous house posts. Not taken from a village but purpose-built, a welcome to this site. On either side of the posts is a flat carving of Salish residents sharing the greeting O Siem. The decoration and trim, to my eye, border on avant-garde, the interpretive drawn from tradition.

The sun's eager to make an appearance, it seems, prodding away at the cold. Coal Harbour now gleams, and I study the view through the frame that the house posts create. Rather wonderfully, a raven soars past the posts, reminiscent of float planes splitting the Lions Gate uprights. Flying toward the sun, the bird calls a throaty *grrawwk-grrawwk*, a time-bend of visuals and sound.

As I turn to the north, totems now loom. If I let my mind follow that raven, its curve of timeline and place, I can recapture a whiff of the moment I left from Rose Spit on a Zodiac over lumpy water to Louise Island, the former Haida village of Skedans, or K̲'uuna Llnagaay. That feeling of "happening upon" a village, totems as Elders, standing and watching and waiting.

One totem here, a colossal example, is a thunderbird, set among hemlocks and cedar. And I realize it's the totem from the photo at the Railtown diner, the Rose Cole Yelton Memorial Pole of the Squamish Nation. According to an accompanying plaque,

> Raised in 2009, this pole was created to honour Rose Cole Yelton, her family and all those who lived in Stanley Park. The pole is erected in front of the house site where the Cole family lived until 1935. Until the time of her passing in 2002, Rose was the last surviving resident of the Brockton Community.

On the sign are three photos: one of Rose in her youth, one of her later in life as an Elder, and one of the team of carvers raising the pole commemorating Rose. To the right, facing east, stands a whole totem community. The volume of colour and height commands your attention, respect. I slow down. Slow down some more. A shift every ancient spot seems to demand.

Standing slightly apart from the other totems is a single squat pole, which I realize is a solitary house post. This one is topped with an open-winged thunderbird. Another plaque enlightens me.

> This pole is a replica of a house post carved by Kwakwa̱ka̱'wakw artist Charlie James in the early 1900s. Tony Hunt carved this replica in 1987 to replace the older pole now in the Vancouver Museum. James experimented with colours and techniques creating a bold new style that has

influenced generations of artists including his stepson Mungo Martin and granddaughter Ellen Neel.

A pole carved by Ellen Neel stands left of this, grouped with a particularly tall totem that has its own outcrops or wings. Called the Sky Chief Pole, it's the work of Hesquiaht artist Tim Paul and Ditidaht artist Art Thompson. Carved in 1988, it captures Nuu-chah-nulth lineage, returning me to Thompson's whaler's pole at the MOA, that echo of orcas and humpbacks and greys being summoned.

Now my eye's drawn to the right, for standing amid and yet separate from the totems is the Chief Skedans Mortuary Pole. No wonder my mind jumped to Skedans. It was here all along, in a manner. There's a plaque here as well.

> An older version of this pole was raised in the Haida village of Skidegate about 1870. It honours the Raven Chief of Skedans and depicts the chief's hereditary crests. The two tiny figures in the bear's ears are the chief's daughter and son-in-law who erected the pole and gave a potlatch for the chief's memorial. The rectangular board at the top of the original pole covered a cavity that held the chief's remains. Haida artist Bill Reid with assistant Werner True carved this new pole in 1964. Don Yeomans recurved the top moon face in 1998.

I feel a reverence here, something I'm unable to label. Not quite a cemetery, yet more than memorial. What it lacks is that ambiguous nature of temple or church burial plots, finality paired with hope, that Mirkwood of faith and belief. Here there's a certainty, a knowing, where myth and fact coexist in a carving, a painting, a raising.

A few steps east of this stands another fairly new installation, almost a bridge in design, linking not Pacific but Atlantic to this stretch of seaside. At a glance it resembles a teepee, one cast in bronze. Its name, *Shore to Shore*. At the base of the pyramid design is a round mosaic of cut stones, each in rough squares or diamonds, while set within the structure is a hunter or fisherman holding a harpoon and a fish. The piece was created by carver Ts'uts'umutlhw, Luke Marston, and with an online search I find this description:

> *Shore to Shore* ... celebrates Portuguese adventurer Joe Silvey ("Portuguese Joe") as well as his Coast Salish first wife Pkhaltinaht and second wife Kwatleemaat.[67]

Marston, the artist, is the great-great-grandson of Portuguese Joe and Kwatleemaat. And although Joe grew up in Portugal, he moved to this coast to join the earliest pioneers who settled in Gastown, compounding the area's cultural mix. The surrounding mosaic of cut rock is Portuguese stone, adding an apt stamp to the visual while creating another link to these shores, this one spanning two oceans.

> The sculpture honours the link between Portuguese and Coast Salish First Nations cultures, marks the land's rich heritage, and symbolizes unity for the Vancouver's present-day diverse inhabitants.[68]

From here I turn west and then north. Ahead lies the Stanley Park Pavilion, its railway, and the Vancouver Aquarium. Toward town sits the Rose Garden on a gentle slope, and then Lost Lagoon. Beyond that, Beaver Lake, another taste of freshwater within the surrounds of the sea.

Before leaving this east side of the park, I make one more stop by the totems where a shelter offers a panorama of plaques outlining the area's history and culture. Protected from the wind and the low-angled sun, it feels like I've crawled into a giant diorama, its peephole one side of the exhibit. Reading signs left to right becomes a time passage. I begin with an introduction, "First Nations of Stanley Park."

> The Greater Vancouver and Georgia Strait area is home to many independent First Nations who share related languages and cultures. Northwest Coast First Nations depended on salmon and the resources of the sea for much of their livelihood. This region had the most important native salmon fishery in Canada and supported a large aboriginal population. Ancestors of the Musqueam, Squamish, and

> Tsleil-Waututh First Nations are associated with the area now known as Stanley Park.

Under this are subheadings: “Centuries of Travel and Trade,” “Stanley Park Cultural History,” and “The Village of x^{w}ay'x^{w}ay.” The site of this former village is just north and west of here, at what’s now Lumbermen’s Arch. Framing the plaque are drawings of salmon and a village photo from 1867. Not the village of x^{w}ay'x^{w}ay, but a similar scene, an artist’s impression of what had been here. Plus an archival photo of a paddler passing Siwash Rock and a sketch that resembles that photo of Swanamia, Mary Anne, steering the dugout canoe at Snauq.

The next panel, “Traditional Technology,” has a quote from the Musqueam Indian Band.

> Tangible things, such as feathers to use in a ceremony, the meat of a wild duck, smoked salmon, are sometimes filled with special significance because they are used in a traditional way during the winter dances. Intangible things are equally important: the sense of community, the importance of the family, sharing, being together, hearing the old words spoken in the Longhouse as the smoke rises up through the smoke-hole. When things become difficult, we remember our ancestors, and we are proud.

There are photos of berries, cow parsnip, chocolate lily, salmon, goat, duck, and deer. Descriptions of cedar, the wonder wood used for clothing and shelter and food. And finally, what looks like collage, a curated amalgam of symbols. The pane’s title, “Our Communities Today.” A quote from Squamish Chief Joe Mathias expresses the view of First Nations.

> Throughout the period of colonization and the evolution of Canada as a nation-state, we maintained ourselves as a distinct social and political order. We retained our identity as a distinct society, as a nation. We continued to possess and exercise our right of self-government,

> a right recognized in both international and domestic law. We have never relinquished our right of self-determination.

I take time with each image in the collage. First is *Flight*, a sculpture depicting the world's largest spindle whorl carving, which sits at YVR Airport. Set by water and stone, it's a symbol of connection between land and sky. In the whirlpool design, I see people and eyes and imagine it next to a clamshell resting on sand with no footprints.

Opposite this is the two-headed serpent *Say Nuth Khaw Yum*, part of a warrior dance and a granter of supernatural powers. Looking on is the Tsleil-Waututh Nation's *Takaya*, a lone wolf drumming and singing. Facing north is a Squamish thunderbird emblem, feathers fanned, as though joining *Takaya* in dance.

There are photos as well, snapshots of stories and song and regalia, with paddles and pullers. There's the shot Zoe George shared of muscled paddlers smiling for the camera. One photo in particular makes me pause: a young drummer next to an Elder. The young drummer holds his beater and drum, holds it tight, holds it close. You can see that he wants to play, and play now! He watches the Elder with warmth. Anticipation as well. The Elder, meanwhile, has a look of contentment, relaxed. His drum sits by his feet. He will play when it's time.

One more stop to make here, like I'm dotting an *i*. Up and over the park toward Lumbermen's Arch is the old village site of x^{w}ay'x^{w}ay. I source different ways to pronounce this and settle on "kwey-kwey." Along the way are steep steps, maybe eight, leading down from the Seawall to access the beach or the water, based on the tide. The stairs are roughly blocked granite, an extension of underland brought to the surface, repurposed to lead right back down. I pass by, think better of it, return, and descend. The rock's slick. I take care. Dip the toe of my shoe in the inlet, thinking this could make for a poetic conclusion. Christening my walk like a vessel, though there are no bubbles from a custom-made box, just a pleasing and personal visual. And so I leave the image right there, shake the sea from my shoe, and carry on to the next bit of shore.

Lumbermen's Arch, the village of x^way'x^way, strikes a pose on approach. Heavy stumps bolted in place create a squared frame. On one side, two timbers are bracing a third, the crosspiece. On the opposite side, a shock of green-needled growth. When taken as a whole, it looks like a just-fallen tree, a nod to a lumberjack past. It could almost pass for a settler's take on a welcome and house posts. I imagine a faller, chainsaw in hand. *Just gimme a sec, I'll have the place cleared up in no time.*

Along with that dip of a shoe in the sea, this too links a swath of these walks with city history. For it was here that English entrepreneur Edward Stamp started what would be Hastings Mill, the business some consider the start of the city, and its store that was built by the present-day port, then survived the Great Fire before being floated and barged past the park to its new home by the Vancouver Yacht Club.

I could even pretend I'm David Thompson, get a sextant and map-making gear to triangulate the whole thing. From this forested edge of the park to the port and the fire, then north, to the home of those life-saving paddlers, along the same path as the *Chinook* and those previous ferries, and then south to right here at x^way'x^way, a ruler-straight history loop. The map might resemble that big spinning globe, in a way. Mostly blue, mostly water. And within it, a sliver of everything.

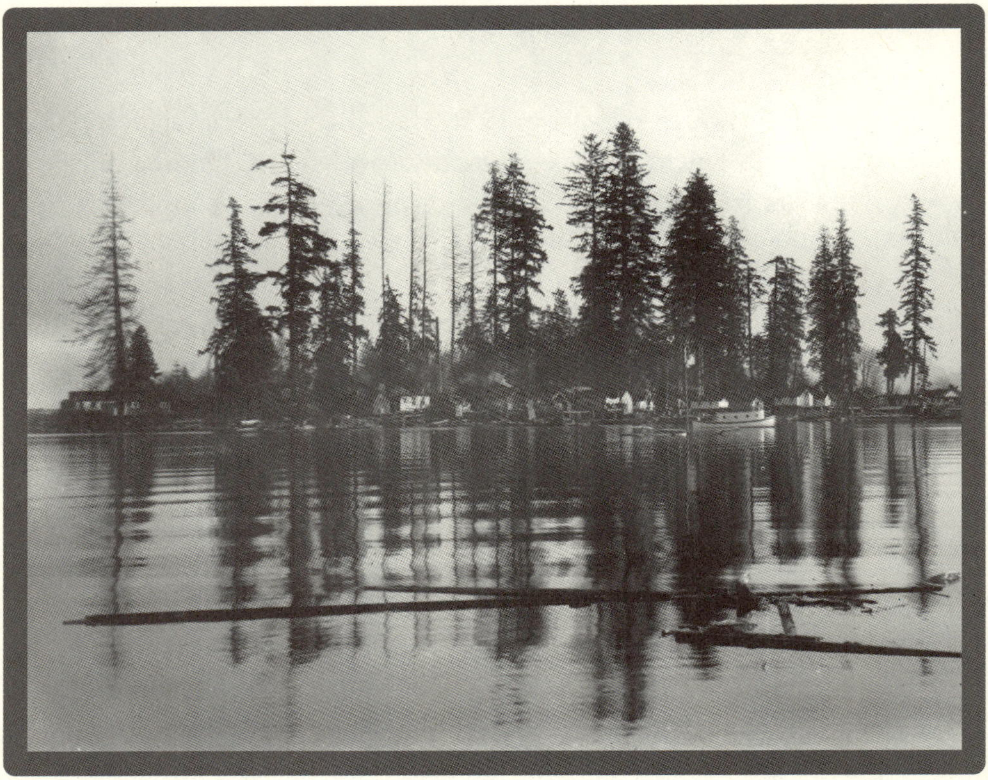

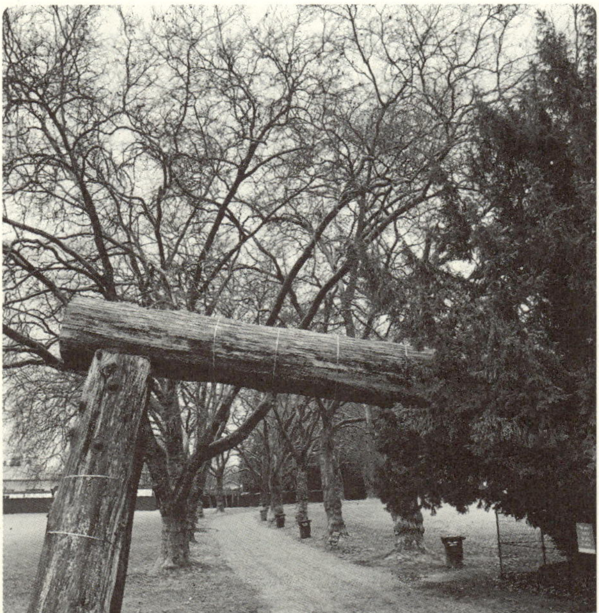

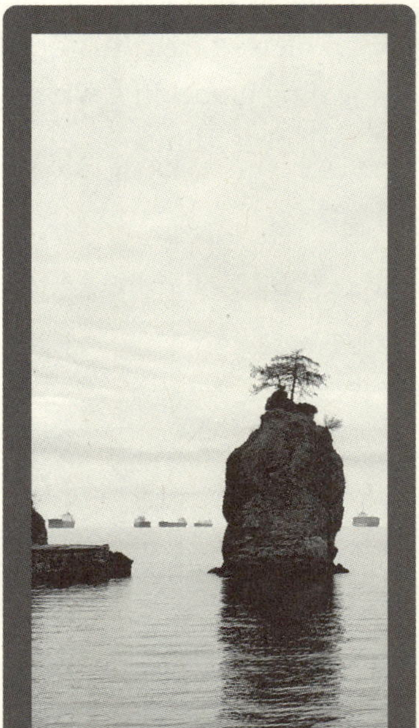

CLOCKWISE FROM TOP: Deadman's Island with Squamish homes, 1860; Siwash Rock, Stanley Park, looking west; Lumbermen's Arch, Stanley Park.

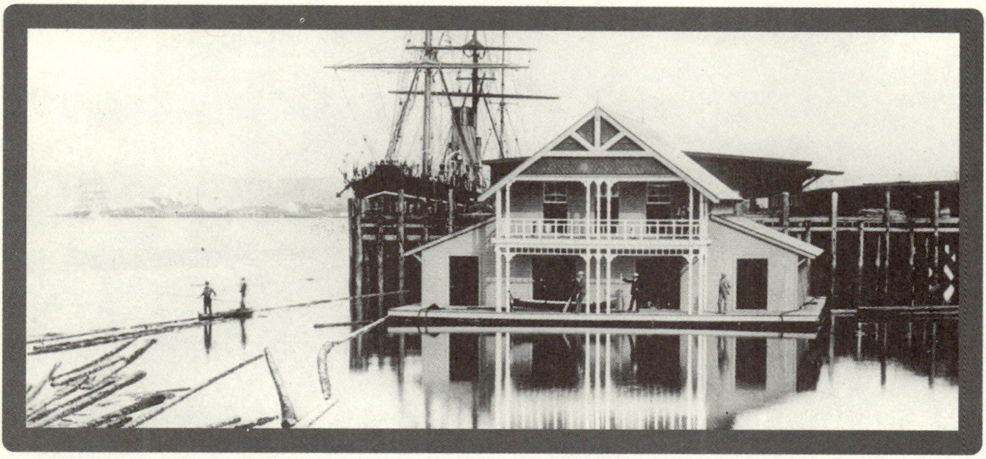

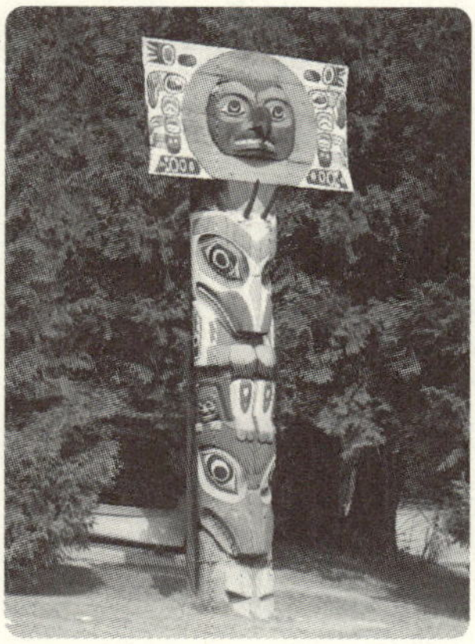

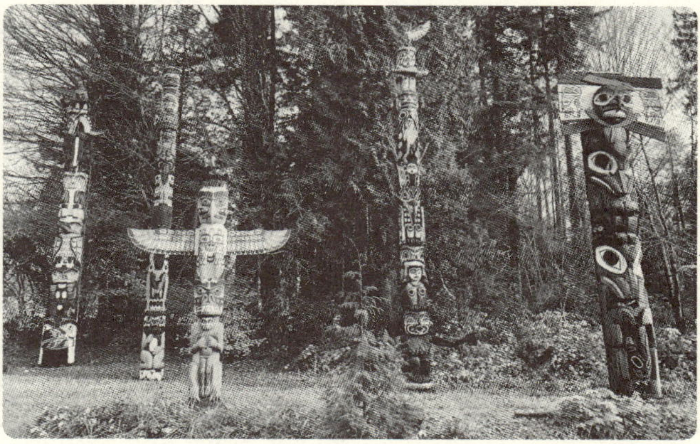

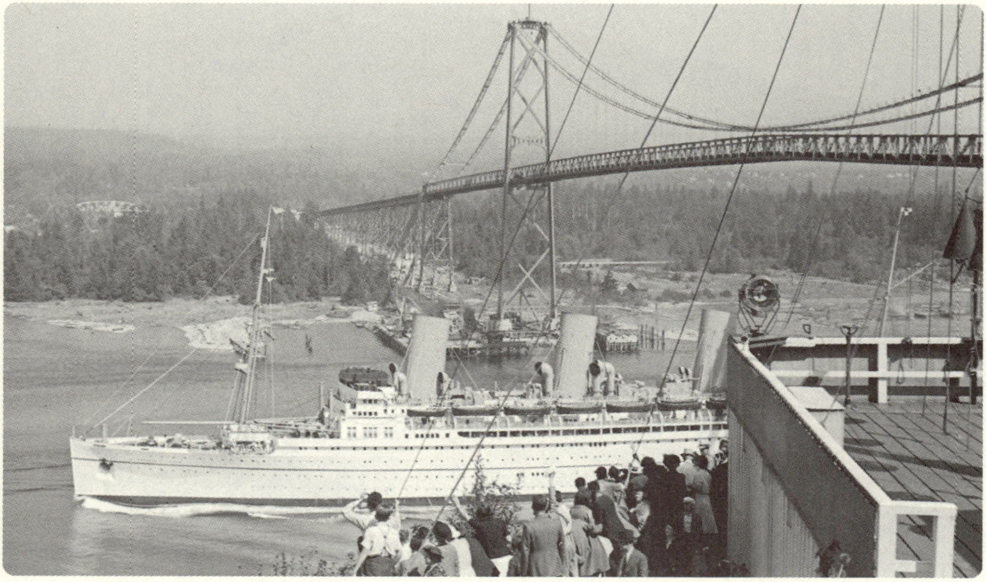

CLOCKWISE FROM TOP: Vancouver Rowing Club, 1888; Stanley Park totems; the SS *Empress of Japan* under the nearly completed Lions Gate Bridge, 1938; a mortuary totem at Stanley Park, 1946.

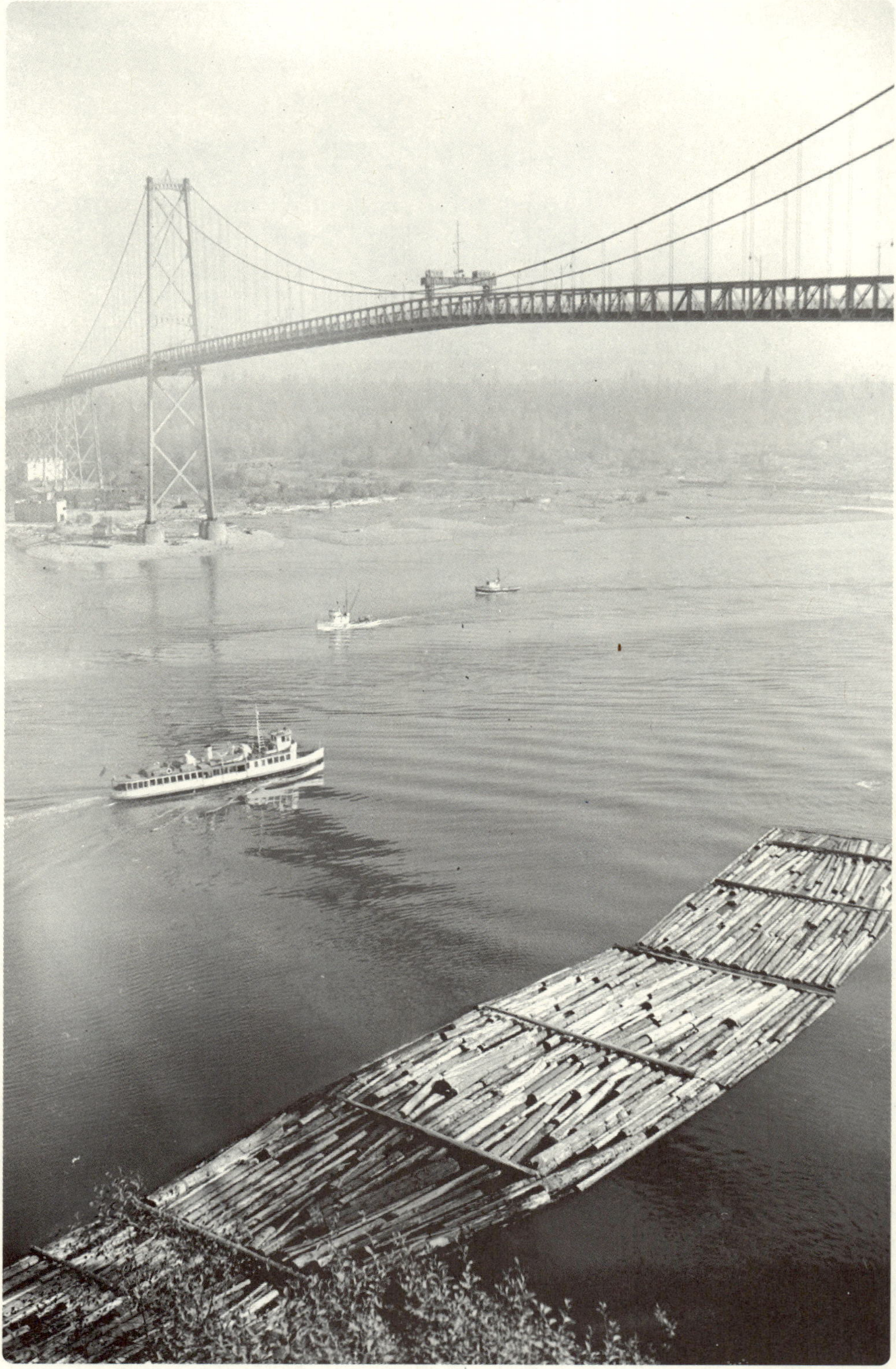

A tugboat and a log boom off Stanley Park, 1945.

Conclusion

RECEDING TIDE

I'VE BACKTRACKED TO Vancouver's west side, with shipwrecks and shorelines and reefs on my mind. I'm hoping to find one more thread, or an alternate one, to truss up my walks by the water, along with those stretches of time undersea and each stroll on a beach or beside it. Maybe another geological layer, at least one envisioned, to support the seaside bridges I've trod.

What I've arranged for today isn't an interview, as such, more a chat under branches and leaves with Monika Fischer, part of the UBC professorial team in the botany and forestry and conservation sciences departments. Monika's a mycologist (a fungal biologist) and an expert on forests and mushrooms. And yes, *fun-guy* jokes are part of the working vernacular.

We first met through previous *Perfect Day* walks, shared footsteps on parallel timelines. Interestingly, if we sketched a Venn diagram outlining our respective interests and studies, those lines would overlap like topographical cliffs, both of us being chefs with a passion for nature and science. Monika, trained under Michelin star tutelage, worked in

Seattle in a garden-to-table environment, her kitchen known as the French Laundry of the Northwest. Then, in a tangential reboot, she left that behind, got her doctorate, and returned to working with forest-bed mushrooms, but for science rather than saucepans. Even her current work straddles a culinary-esque world of forestry management and land preservation.

Next to a burbling fountain we sip coffee as campus life flows by like water. I ask Monika about the undersea mushrooms I thought that I saw by the Porteau Cove wrecks and imagined sautéing with cod.

"Hmm." She savours her drink, contemplates. "Probably not actual mushrooms down there. Likely anemones or yeastlike fungi. You might've even seen sea beans or pickleweed by the shore, what you might know as sea asparagus."

I nod, knowing there are harvesting grounds for this delicate, crispy salt-green around Tsawwassen and Ladner. One time, while travelling, I met a shepherd who grazed his flock on the shore at low tide, where the sheep nibbled similar vegetation, seasoning themselves from within. The price of that meat was double the cost of lamb raised inland. *That's* how tasty it was.

I ask Monika about her moving up the coast as she studied and worked, from San Francisco to Seattle, then Vancouver.

"It wasn't until I got here that I felt a true sense of home," she explains. "Washington to a degree, but BC for sure. This feels like home. Something about the temperate rainforest, the ocean, the air, the height of the trees. Seeing an evergreen outline on the horizon creates a sense of calm. Tree height adds a sense of protection, I suppose. Like being held. You can follow a path through the trees and stay safe and dry, mostly. Not like those Brothers Grimm tales, that Euro association with scary forests where darkness lives. It's just not the case around here."

Bringing to mind Ashley Samsone describing her wayfinding here, those paths between trees, map-making by way of desire lines, shortcuts and longcuts and trails without destinations.

"A lot of American parks that I've seen are wide open," says Monika. "I think part of it is that holdover from people being unnerved in close spaces. But I feel comfort, cozy in a more contained space. I feel I came home here. Environmentally. The ecosystem, maybe. I don't know. But there's a connection, for sure, with the shore. Forests and water have that symbiotic relationship. Water, like forests, holds you, wraps around you. My favourite forests are waterside. Water-like. Maybe the same link as your undersea woods." She smiles. "Like a kelp forest too."

Symbiosis. What I feel when I dive, float, or paddle as well. Boundlessness too. That interdependence of water and land, same as culture and people and place. A dissolving of present and past, time eclipsed with the passing of tides.

We finish our coffee and stroll, swap kitchen stories, how best to serve mushrooms, what works and what doesn't. Which all seems to fit rather well. And with smiles and a bumping of knuckles, just like we'd do after a good meal service, we part ways. Both returning to shared space where forest and shoreline commingle, these neighbourhood places that keep us alive.

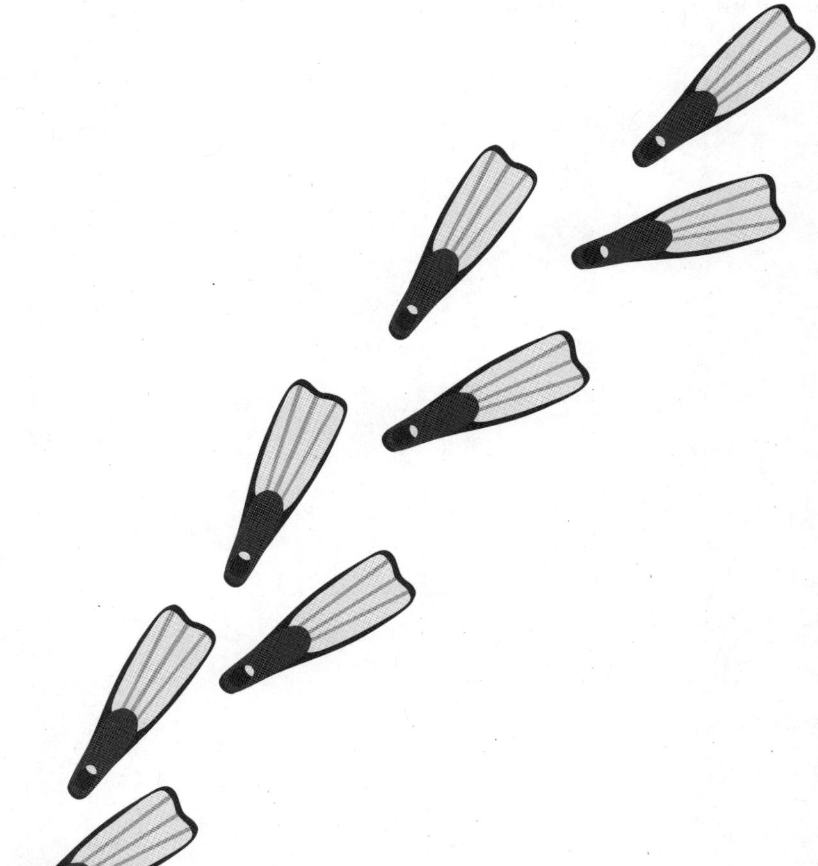

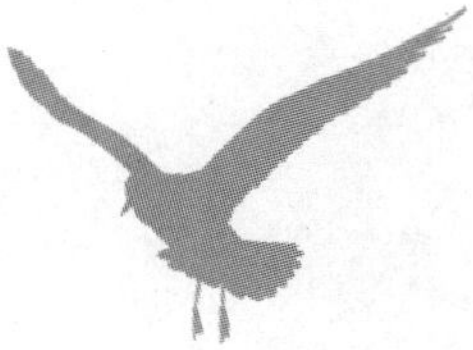

Sunset horizon
Softly sparkles as journeys
Return to the sea

ACKNOWLEDGMENTS

WRITING REMAINS A solitary endeavour, but creating a book takes a team. And I'm incredibly privileged and grateful to work with the exemplary team at Arsenal Pulp Press, consummate professionals who are a pleasure to work with, generous, kind, and fun: publishers Brian Lam and Robert Ballantyne, editors Catharine Chen and JC Cham, marketers Cynara Geissler and Erin Chan. The publicists at Serif. And Jazmin Welch, with thanks for designing another beautiful book capturing what I envisioned.

Everyone I've met with as well, on these walks, has contributed to my ongoing learning and appreciation of this city and its shores. My sincere thanks go to Ashley Samsone at UBC; the gang at Vancouver Diving Locker; my instructors and classmates; Craig and Mr. Mann; Michael "Turk" Turkington and Nicole at Fisherman's Wharf Harbour Office; Carolyn, Alden, and Archie aboard *Argo Navis*; Lesley at False Creek Racing Canoe Club; CBC's Margaret Gallagher for great conversation and company; Devian at Creekside Paddling Centre; Colin and Dan at the shipwreck; Rebecca Duncan, Maarta Kyak, Deborah Kigjugalik Webster and Zoe George by way of the Vancouver Maritime Museum; Frank Wolf for the stories and beers; Anita at the Old Hastings Mill Store Museum; Dana Gee and Tom Sandborn at the *Vancouver Sun* and *The Province*; Damara Jacobs-Petersen and Karen Duffek at UBC Museum of Anthropology; Jon for the fishing excursion; Grant the arborist; Cedar Swan of Adventure Canada for her insights; author James Bradley; Dennis the HVAC technician; Donna for her visceral share; Hark and Leon aboard *Chinook* SeaBus and Jag Gill and Steve Vanagas for setting it up; Krystal at Stanley Park Horse-Drawn Tours; and Monika Fischer for culinary tips and mycorrhizal explanations. With thanks again to City of Vancouver Archives for helping to source historical photos, and the ongoing efforts of the Vancouver Heritage Foundation and their inspiring Places That Matter project.

My gratitude also goes to every supportive reader and friend. If you've picked up this volume from a bookseller, library, or online, whether borrowing, buying, or sharing as a gift, you're contributing to the well-being of a great many people, their households and families, by reading and forwarding books. Thank you. It makes a huge difference.

And from my heart, thanks to Deb, who makes things worthwhile and the spaces we live rather perfect.

ENDNOTES

1 "Symbols of the City of Vancouver," City of Vancouver, accessed April 24, 2025, https://vancouver.ca/news-calendar/city-symbols.aspx.

2 Squamish Atlas, Sníchim Foundation, accessed April 24, 2025, https://squamish atlas.com/.

3 Squamish Atlas, Sníchim Foundation, accessed April 24, 2025, https://squamish atlas.com/.

4 Squamish Atlas, Sníchim Foundation, accessed April 24, 2025, https://squamish atlas.com/.

5 "West Point Grey," About Vancouver, City of Vancouver, accessed April 24, 2025, https://vancouver.ca/news-calendar/point-grey.aspx.

6 "Vancouver's Jericho Beach," Vancouver's Best Places, accessed June 27, 2025, https://vancouversbestplaces.com/top-attractions/vancouvers-best-beaches/jericho-beach/

7 Detailed accounts of these adventures appear in my *Gone Viking* travelogues (Rocky Mountain Books).

8 Roy L. Carlson, "Charles E. Borden," Canadian Archaeological Association, accessed April 24, 2025, https://canadianarchaeology.com/caa/about/awards/recipients/smith-wintemberg-award/charles-e-borden.

9 "The Raven and the First Men: From Conception to Completion," Museum of Anthropology at UBC, January 9, 2020, https://moa.ubc.ca/2020/01/the-raven-and-the-first-men-from-conception-to-completion/.

10 "The Raven and the First Men: From Conception to Completion," Museum of Anthropology at UBC, January 9, 2020, https://moa.ubc.ca/2020/01/the-raven-and-the-first-men-from-conception-to-completion/.

11 "Lighthouse Park," Parks and Recreation, West Vancouver, accessed April 24, 2025, https://westvancouver.ca/parks-recreation/parks-trails/lighthouse-park.

12 Rick Crosby, "A Railway Runs Through It," *The Squamish Chief*, March 24, 2019, https://squamishchief.com/local-news/a-railway-runs-through-it-3349645.

13 "Squamish, British Columbia," Wikipedia, accessed April 24, 2025, https://en.wikipedia.org/wiki/Squamish,_British_Columbia.

14 "Jack, August," Squamish History Archives, accessed April 24, 2025, https://squamishlibrary.digitalcollections.ca/chief-august-jack.

15 "Sen̓áḵw," Sḵwx̱wú7mesh Úxwumixw Squamish Nation, accessed April 24, 2025, https://www.squamish.net/partnerships-entities/partnerships/senakw/.

16 "FAQ," Seńáḵw, accessed April 15, 2025, https://senakw.com/faq.

17 "səńaʔq^{w}," Places That Matter, Vancouver Heritage Foundation, accessed April 24, 2025, https://placesthatmatter.ca/location/musqueam-səńaʔq^{w}/.

18 Squamish Atlas, Sníchim Foundation, accessed April 24, 2025, https://squamish atlas.com/.

19 Tom Zoellner, *Rim to River: Looking into the Heart of Arizona* (University of Arizona Press, 2023).

20 "Chief Joe Capilano," *The Canadian Encyclopedia*, October 26, 2021, https://www.thecanadianencyclopedia.ca/en/article/chief-joe-capilano.

21 See https://commons.wikimedia.org/wiki/File:Postcard,_photographic_print_(BM_Am,B59.60).jpg.

22 "Moodyville: Legend and Legacy," MONOVA: Museum & Archives of North Vancouver, accessed April 24, 2025, https://monova.ca/moodyville-introduction-2/.

23 "1958 – BC Infrastructure Disaster – Ironworkers Memorial Bridge – Vancouver 1958," BCcampus, accessed April 24, 2025, https://pressbooks.bccampus.ca/engineeringinsociety/chapter/infrastructure-disaster-ironworkers-memorial-bridge-vancouver-1958.

24 Brent Richter, "North Shore Bridge Traffic Returns to Near Pre-COVID Levels," *North Shore News*, August 26, 2020, https://www.nsnews.com/local-news/north-shore-bridge-traffic-returns-to-near-pre-covid-levels-3126765.

25 "səĺilẃət," The Bill Reid Centre, Simon Fraser University, accessed April 24, 2025, https://www.sfu.ca/brc/our-work/imesh-mobile-app/coast-salish-place-names/tsleil-waututh/sleilwaut.html.

26 "səĺilẃət," The Bill Reid Centre, Simon Fraser University, accessed April 24, 2025, https://www.sfu.ca/brc/our-work/imesh-mobile-app/coast-salish-place-names/tsleil-waututh/sleilwaut.html.

27 "Kitsilano," About Vancouver, City of Vancouver, accessed April 24, 2025, https://vancouver.ca/news-calendar/kitsilano.aspx.

28 Sonja Koene, "Deadman's Island Vancouver," The Little House of Horrors, accessed April 24, 2025, https://thelittlehouseofhorrors.com/deadmans-island-vancouver.

29 "Seraphim 'Joe' Fortes," Places That Matter, Vancouver Heritage Foundation, accessed April 24, 2025, https://placesthatmatter.ca/location/joe-fortes/.

30 Robin Cody, *Voyage of a Summer Sun: Canoeing the Columbia River* (Oregon State University Press, 2012).

31 "Coho Festival," Coho Society of the North Shore, accessed April 24, 2025, https://cohosociety.com/coho-festival.

32 "Habitat Island," ParkFinder, Vancouver Board of Parks and Recreation, accessed April 24, 2025, https://covapp.vancouver.ca/parkfinder/parkdetail.aspx?inparkid=241.

33 Robert Macfarlane, *The Old Ways: A Journey on Foot* (Penguin Books, 2013).

34 "St. Roch National Historic Site of Canada," Parks Canada Directory of Federal Historic Designations, Government of Canada, accessed April 24, 2025, https://www.pc.gc.ca/apps/dfhd/page_nhs_eng.aspx?id=83.

35 Kenn Harper, "Joe Panipakuttuk on the St. Roch: Through the Northwest Passage," *Nunatsiaq News*, August 7, 2020, https://nunatsiaq.com/stories/article/taissumani-aug-7.

36 Kenn Harper, "Joe Panipakuttuk on the St. Roch: Through the Northwest Passage," *Nunatsiaq News*, August 7, 2020, https://nunatsiaq.com/stories/article/taissumani-aug-7.

37 Kenn Harper, "Joe Panipakuttuk on the St. Roch: Through the Northwest Passage," *Nunatsiaq News*, August 7, 2020, https://nunatsiaq.com/stories/article/taissumani-aug-7.

38 Kenn Harper, "Joe Panipakuttuk on the St. Roch: Through the Northwest Passage," *Nunatsiaq News*, August 7, 2020, https://nunatsiaq.com/stories/article/taissumani-aug-7.

39 Kenn Harper, "Joe Panipakuttuk on the St. Roch: Through the Northwest Passage," *Nunatsiaq News*, August 7, 2020, https://nunatsiaq.com/stories/article/taissumani-aug-7.

40 Squamish Atlas, Sníchim Foundation, accessed April 24, 2025, https://squamishatlas.com/.

41 Squamish Atlas, Sníchim Foundation, accessed April 24, 2025, https://squamishatlas.com/.

42 Squamish Atlas, Sníchim Foundation, accessed April 24, 2025, https://squamishatlas.com/.

43 "Tatlow and Volunteer Park Stream Restoration," Parks, Recreation, and Culture, City of Vancouver, accessed April 24, 2025, https://vancouver.ca/parks-recreation-culture/tatlow-and-volunteer-park-stream.aspx.

44 "Tatlow and Volunteer Park Stream Restoration," Parks, Recreation, and Culture, City of Vancouver, accessed April 24, 2025, https://vancouver.ca/parks-recreation-culture/tatlow-and-volunteer-park-stream.aspx.

45 Jack Kerouac, *On the Road* (Viking Press, 1957; repr. Penguin Books, 1976).

46 Don Gilmore, "David Thompson," *The Canadian Encyclopedia*, last edited March 14, 2025, https://thecanadianencyclopedia.ca/en/article/david-thompson.

47 "David Thompson (Explorer)," Wikipedia, accessed April 24, 2025, https://wikipedia.org/wiki/David_Thompson_(explorer).

48 Don Gilmore, "David Thompson," *The Canadian Encyclopedia*, last edited March 14, 2025, https://thecanadianencyclopedia.ca/en/article/david-thompson.

49 Don Gilmore, "David Thompson," *The Canadian Encyclopedia*, last edited March 14, 2025, https://thecanadianencyclopedia.ca/en/article/david-thompson.

50 "A-Maze-ing Laughter," Vancouver Biennale, accessed April 24, 2025, https://www.vancouverbiennale.com/artworks/a-maze-ing-laughter/.

51 Dana Gee, "5 Great Places to Go for a Walk in Vancouver," *Vancouver Sun*, September 18, 2024, https://vancouversun.com/entertainment/books/five-favourite-vancouver-city-walks.

52 Vicki Duong, "'Keepers of the Salish Sea' Explores Addiction Recovery, Land Stewardship, and Coast Salish Teachings," *Georgia Straight*, September 5, 2024, https://www.straight.com/arts/keepers-of-salish-sea-explores-addiction-recovery-land-stewardship-and-coast-salish-teachings.

53 James Bradley, *Deep Water: The World in the Ocean* (HarperCollins, 2024).

54 Kenneth Chan, "Giant Kinetic Weathervane Installed at Vancouver Convention Centre Seawall," *Daily Hive*, September 19, 2022, https://dailyhive.com/vancouver/wind-wheel-mobile-weathervane-vancouver-convention-centre.

55 Donna and Aurlie Young, "Vancouver BC Canada—Sidewalk Mosaics," Mosaic Art Source, accessed April 24, 2025, https://mosaicartsource.wordpress.com/2006/12/15/vancouver-sidewalk-mosaics/.

56 "Carnegie Community Centre," Parks, Recreation, and Culture, City of Vancouver, accessed April 24, 2025, https://vancouver.ca/parks-recreation-culture/carnegie-community-centre.aspx.

57 "144-146 Alexander Street," Canada's Historic Places, accessed April 24, 2025, https://historicplaces.ca/en/rep-reg/place-lieu.aspx?id=7950.

58 "Original City Hall Sites," Places That Matter, Vancouver Heritage Foundation, accessed April 24, 2025, https://placesthatmatter.ca/location/original-city-hall-sites/.

59 Jan Morris, *City to City* (Macfarlane Walter & Ross, 1990).

60 "Explore Public Art Yaletown–False Creek," Public Art Vancouver, City of Vancouver, accessed April 24, 2025, https://vancouver.ca/files/cov/public-art-brochure-yaletown.pdf.

61 "Explore Public Art Yaletown–False Creek," Public Art Vancouver, City of Vancouver, accessed April 24, 2025, https://vancouver.ca/files/cov/public-art-brochure-yaletown.pdf.

62 "Welcome to the Land of Light," Public Art Registry, City of Vancouver, accessed April 24, 2025, https://covapp.vancouver.ca/PublicArtRegistry/ArtworkDetail.aspx?ArtworkId=213.

63 "Brush with Illumination," Public Art Registry, City of Vancouver, accessed April 24, 2025, https://covapp.vancouver.ca/PublicArtRegistry/ArtworkDetail.aspx?ArtworkId=214.

64 "Brush with Illumination," Public Art Registry, City of Vancouver, accessed April 24, 2025, https://covapp.vancouver.ca/PublicArtRegistry/ArtworkDetail.aspx?ArtworkId=214.

65 Vancouver Fountains, https://vancouverfountains.com/.

66 "Yaletown Art Walking Tour," Parks, Recreation, and Culture, City of Vancouver, accessed April 24, 2025, https://vancouver.ca/parks-recreation-culture/yaletown-art-walk.aspx.

67 Luke Marston, "The Sculpture in Stanley Park," Shore to Shore, accessed April 24, 2025, https://shoretoshore.ca.

68 Luke Marston, "The Sculpture in Stanley Park," Shore to Shore, accessed April 24, 2025, https://shoretoshore.ca.

BIBLIOGRAPHY

Bradley, James. *Deep Water: The World in the Ocean*. HarperCollins, 2024.

Cody, Robin. *Voyage of a Summer Sun*. Oregon State University Press, 2012.

Harper, Kenn. "Joe Panipakuttuk on the St. Roch: Through the Northwest Passage."

Nunatsiaq News. August 7, 2020. https://nunatsiaq.com/stories/article/taissumani-aug-7.

Kerouac, Jack. *On the Road*. Viking Press, 1957. Repr. Penguin Books, 1976.

Macfarlane, Robert. *The Old Ways: A Journey on Foot*. Penguin Books, 2013.

Morris, Jan. *City to City*. Macfarlane Walter & Ross, 1990.

Zoellner, Tom. *Rim to River: Looking into the Heart of Arizona*. University of Arizona Press, 2023.

WEB SOURCES

Canada's Historic Places, https://historicplaces.ca/.

Places That Matter, Vancouver Heritage Foundation, https://placesthatmatter.ca/.

Public Art Registry, City of Vancouver, https://covapp.vancouver.ca/PublicArtRegistry/.

Squamish Atlas, Sníchim Foundation, https://squamishatlas.com/.

Vancouver Biennale, https://www.vancouverbiennale.com/.

IMAGE CREDITS

VANCOUVER'S WEST SIDE

Spanish Banks
26 All photos courtesy of City of Vancouver Archives

Point Grey, Locarno, and Jericho
30 Top left: City of Vancouver Archives; all other photos by Bill Arnott

Around UBC
37 All photos by Bill Arnott

TOWARD HOWE SOUND

West Side to West Van
46 Top: City of Vancouver Archives; all other photos by Bill Arnott
47 City of Vancouver Archives

Howe Sound
52 Second row: Bill Arnott; all other photos courtesy of City of Vancouver Archives

Toward Squamish
57 All photos courtesy of City of Vancouver Archives

BURRARD INLET AND NORTH SHORE

The North Shore
68 From top: City of Vancouver Archives; Museum and Archives of North Vancouver
69 All photos courtesy of City of Vancouver Archives

Burrard Inlet to Indian Arm
74 From top: Bill Arnott; City of Vancouver Archives
75 All photos courtesy of City of Vancouver Archives

Waterside Healing
78 All photos courtesy of City of Vancouver Archives
79 City of Vancouver Archives

COAL HARBOUR AND GRANVILLE ISLAND

Kits to Coal Harbour
88 Bottom: Bill Arnott; all other photos courtesy of City of Vancouver Archives
89 All photos by Bill Arnott

Fisherman's Wharf
97 From top: Bill Arnott; City of Vancouver Archives
98 All photos by Bill Arnott

Granville Island
104 All photos by Bill Arnott
105 All photos by Bill Arnott

CONNECTING CITY SHORELINES

Who's Navvy Jack?
113 Bill Arnott
114 Bill Arnott

Paddling False Creek
122 All photos by Bill Arnott
123 All photos by Bill Arnott

St. Roch *and O Siem*
133 All photos by Bill Arnott
134 Top row: *Nunatsiaq News* (Kenn Harper collection); all other photos courtesy of City of Vancouver Archives
135 All photos courtesy of City of Vancouver Archives

ENGLISH BAY BOUNDARIES

Tributaries
148 All photos courtesy of City of Vancouver Archives

The Floating Museum
155 All photos courtesy of City of Vancouver Archives

Around English Bay
160 Clockwise from top: Bill Arnott; Bill Arnott; City of Vancouver Archives; Bill Arnott
161 Bottom: City of Vancouver Archives; all other photos by Bill Arnott

AROUND THE PORT OF VANCOUVER

Headline News
170 All photos by Bill Arnott
171 All photos by Bill Arnott

Water Views
192 All photos by Bill Arnott

Downtown's North Edge
199 From top: City of Vancouver Archives; Bill Arnott

Gastown and the Port of Vancouver
209 First and second rows: City of Vancouver Archives; bottom row: Bill Arnott
210 All photos by Bill Arnott
211 All photos by Bill Arnott

STANLEY PARK TO DOWNTOWN AND FALSE CREEK

Aboard the Chinook
226 All photos by Bill Arnott
227 All photos by Bill Arnott

South Side of Downtown
237 All photos courtesy of City of Vancouver Archives
238 All photos courtesy of City of Vancouver Archives
239 All photos courtesy of City of Vancouver Archives
240 All photos courtesy of City of Vancouver Archives

Stanley Park
254 Bottom left: Bill Arnott; all other photos courtesy of City of Vancouver Archives
255 Second row, right: Bill Arnott; all other photos courtesy of City of Vancouver Archives
256 City of Vancouver Archives

All maps illustrated by Jazmin Welch

INDEX

Page numbers in italics refer to maps and photographs.

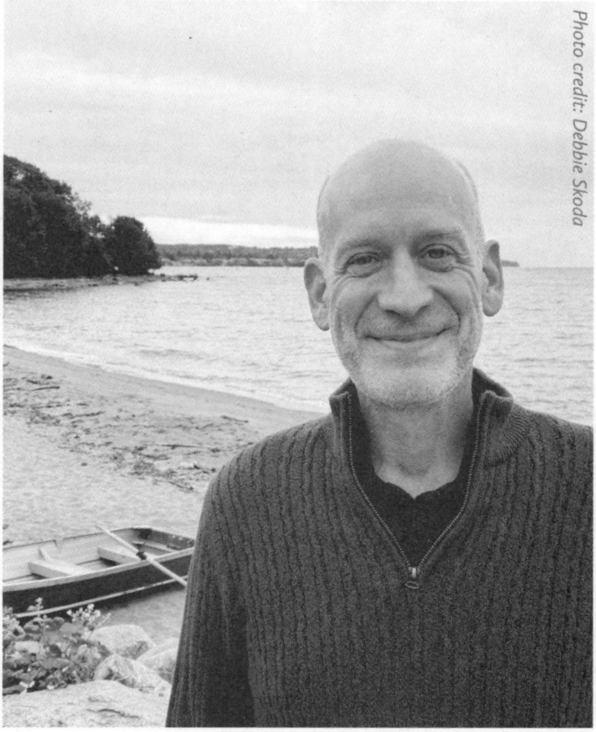

Photo credit: *Debbie Skoda*

BILL ARNOTT is the bestselling author of the *Gone Viking* travelogues (Rocky Mountain Books), the *Season* memoirs (Rocky Mountain Books), and *A Perfect Day for a Walk: The History, Cultures, and Communities of Vancouver, on Foot* (Arsenal Pulp Press), award-winning titles that are among British Columbia's top-selling books. A recipient of fellowships at London's Royal Geographical Society and the Royal Canadian Geographical Society for his expeditions, Bill is a frequent presenter and contributor to universities, podcasts, magazines, TV, and radio. When not trekking with a small pack and a journal, Bill can be found on Canada's West Coast, where he lives near the sea on Musqueam, Squamish, and Tsleil-Waututh land.

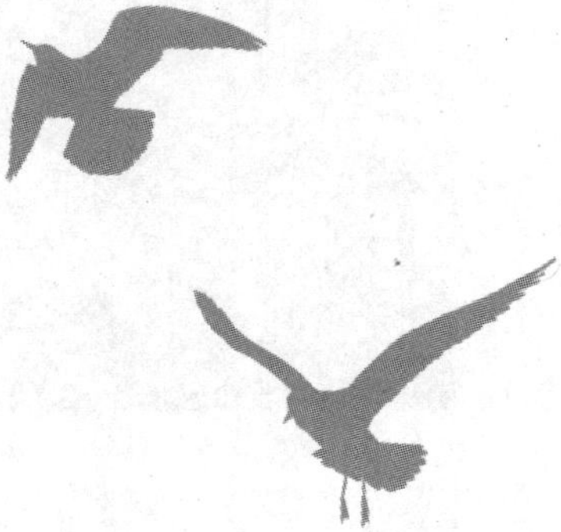